PAKISTAN
LEFT REVIEW
THEN AND NOW

PAKISTAN
LEFT REVIEW
THEN AND NOW

Edited by

NADIR CHEEMA AND STEPHEN M. LYON

OXFORD
UNIVERSITY PRESS

OXFORD
UNIVERSITY PRESS

Oxford University Press is a department of the University of Oxford.
It furthers the University's objective of excellence in research, scholarship,
and education by publishing worldwide. Oxford is a registered trade mark of
Oxford University Press in the UK and in certain other countries

Published in Pakistan by
Oxford University Press
No. 38, Sector 15, Korangi Industrial Area,
PO Box 8214, Karachi-74900, Pakistan

ISBN 978-969-7341-53-5

Typeset in Minion Pro
Printed on 68gsm Offset Paper

Printed by Mas Printers, Karachi

Acknowledgements
Cover art © Salima Hashmi, *The Dark Weight of Night II* (2020)
Cover design © Maryam Saeed

This book is dedicated to

Aziz Kurtha and Iqbal Khan, the *PLR* editors,

and

in honour of the lifelong struggle of Amin Mughal and I. A. Rehman

for a progressive Pakistan

Contents

Preface

There are moments in history that seem to accelerate. The pace of change seems noticeably faster and more disruptive than people and societies can cope with. Revolutions can happen in these moments, and perhaps revolutions may even cause these moments, but regardless of causes, what matters is that sometimes it is challenging to make sense of what's going on around us. We are living in one of those moments in history when the pace and volatility of change are making life 'as normal' decidedly more difficult to maintain. It is at moments like this when we believe it behoves us to reflect on the past. Mark Twain's oft quoted point about history not repeating, but rhyming, with itself, is a useful point of departure for understanding not only how we got into our current situation, but where we might go from wherever we are.

Looking back within living memory to the 1960s, we see another time of rapid change. The 1960s were perhaps more optimistic and certainly hoped for more utopian trajectories than would be tenable at the beginning of the third decade of the twenty-first century, but there is much we can learn from the rhetoric and arguments of those heady days of change. This volume is an homage to an earlier generation of giants upon whose shoulders we like to think we might stand (or at least rest a while as we plough on with surviving our own turbulent times).

The contributors to the *Pakistan Left Review* (*PLR*) sought to foreground workers and those who had been marginalised and ignored. Coming from an unabashedly Marxist, leftist intellectual starting point, they confronted their parents' traditions, histories, and assumptions about what was virtuous and what was desirable in life. In a very real sense, they punched way above their proverbial weight as early career scholars and many of them went on to continue to do so throughout their careers.

Bringing some of the important contributions from this short-lived, but inspirational, journal was a labour of love, but it involved a lot of sweat. This would not have been possible without the support of a great many people. The contributors to *PLR* themselves, of course, must be thanked first and foremost. Without them, we would not have this priceless snapshot of critical debates and arguments from a unique moment in time. Among those contributors, we owe a very special debt of gratitude to Salima Hashmi, who provided moral support, encouragement, and reminders that what we were trying to do was important and needed to be done. We are even more indebted to Salima for generously providing the stunning cover art for this volume and to Naiza Khan for her support. We would also like to acknowledge the creative design of Maryam Saeed, who took Salima Hashmi's incredible artwork and integrated it into the cover of this volume. Transforming the delightfully hand typeset, multilingual documents from an earlier era into the digital age was no small feat, and we are extremely grateful for the unfailing support of Nilanjan Sarkar, Mohammad Altaf, and Ammar Loan for help in preparing the manuscript. Narayani Gupta and Niharika Gupta were critical for helping prepare the Bangla text. For the new text that we felt was vital for situating the journal in its rightful contemporary context, we are indebted to Ayyaz Mallick, Anushay Malik, and Kamran Asdar Ali for their sage and insightful feedback. The heart of the volume is, of course, the original *PLR* texts, and we are especially grateful for the comments provided by I. A. Rehman, Mahir Ali, Adeel Malik, Tayyab Safdar, Zubair Abbasi, Zulfiqar Khimani, and Adeel Khan that helped us better understand how to curate this selection from the whole.

We must also thank the tireless proofreading of Mahnoor Cheema and Umber Khairi. David Taylor has a knack for providing just the right support at just the right time, and as on so many other occasions, he did so with this volume through his timely and astute editing of various aspects of the new text. And we would be remiss if we did not include our 'partner in crime' Tariq Suleman. While Tariq was not directly involved in preparing the volume, he was one of our principle cheerleaders behind the scenes encouraging us not to give up or deviate from our original aim of bringing this important history to the attention of contemporary audiences. We would like to acknowledge the friendship and mentorship of Amin Mughal, who has inspired generations of London-based scholars with an interest in Pakistan, social justice, and people power. Finally, this volume would not have been possible without the intellectual infrastructure and community that has emerged from Bloomsbury Pakistan (*https://bloomsburypakistan.org*).

Lastly, it goes without saying that while we owe a debt to people that can never be repaid, any failings in the curation or twenty-first century text are our responsibility alone and none of our incredible supporters are to be blamed for mistakes, confusion, or omissions.

Nadir Cheema and Stephen M. Lyon

Introduction: A Leftist Intellectual Journal

Stephen M. Lyon and Nadir Cheema

There are moments in history when societies undergo profound change. The late 1960s were arguably one of these moments. Protests erupted around the globe and shook comfortable political and economic establishments. In the United States, five decades before Black Lives Matter, riots broke out across multiple urban centres. The assassination of Martin Luther King in 1968 attests to the extent to which civil rights movements were understood as a threat to those with unfair historical privilege. In Latin America, the Marxist revolutionary, Che Guevara, had himself been executed a year earlier, indicating just how disruptive leftist movements had become. The riots that overshadowed the Democratic Party convention in Chicago in 1968 not only provide a powerful example of the widespread dissatisfaction with US government policies, but also the reality that discontent could not be contained in the usual ways. In France, the *soixante-huitards* (68ers) were literally tearing up the streets of Paris to break the institutions of power in their demands for radical change. In Western Europe and the United States, the usual tactics of state violence exercised through the institutions of law enforcement were inadequate to suppress the volume of anger or the genuine appetite for real change. On the other side of the Iron Curtain, there was clear evidence of similar expressions of dissatisfaction and a desire for fresh change. Although the uprising in what was then Czechoslovakia was put down at the time, the seeds of the ultimate demise of the repressive version of Czechoslovakia's Communist Party were well and truly sown in this period. The majority of European colonial territories across Asia and Africa had finally achieved their independence by the mid 1960s, and by 1968, it was obvious that pre-World War II colonialism was unsustainable. It may be only a slight exaggeration to state that history accelerated in the years leading up to 1970. This was a turbulent time, but also an incredibly fertile one for political thought and action. It is with humility that we take on the responsibility of introducing readers to *Pakistan Left Review* (*PLR*), a short-lived leftist journal, produced in the maelstrom of this momentous period in history. The journal was the creation of Pakistani postgraduate students under the auspices of the University of London Union (ULU) Pakistan Society in the late 1960s in London.

The contributors to the five issues of this journal were serious people, including Hamza Alavi, Salima Hashmi, Feroz Ahmed, Tariq Ali, and Rehman Sobhan, to name just a few. They were wrestling with issues that belied their youth and status at the time. The journal was launched as a means of protest. It laid out a manifesto for Pakistan's model of socialism by raising political consciousness among the masses. The journal offered an action plan for a new concept of society to implement when it became possible to dominate the political culture of Pakistan.

As the inaugural issue boldly argues, the rosy economic statistics that Pakistan enjoyed at the time, touting strong growth, expanding industrialisation, and improvements in health and education, masked profound inequalities and injustices. The contributors to the *Pakistan Left Review* were perhaps above all concerned with social justice. Throughout the journal's limited run, the contributors posed awkward questions and challenged official narratives. The power of such intellectual narration should not be underestimated. Kamran Asdar Ali's account of the rise and fall of the Communist Party of Pakistan (CPP) illustrates the importance of literary and cultural production throughout the life of the Party.[1] In a very real sense, the CPP aimed to shape the ideas of history and the nation in ways that shed light on class struggles. The *PLR*, although not formally part of the CPP, sought to achieve comparable goals. They tried to question, challenge, and disrupt dominant capitalist narratives through an engagement with philosophy, journalism, literary studies, and social sciences.

To be sure, leftist challenges to state-sanctioned 'official' narratives continue to the present day. The military-dominated Pakistani establishment guards and promotes official narratives arguably more aggressively than it did in the 1960s. The military establishment may, in fact, be more determined in the twenty-first century than it was in the 1960s. In part, this is because of the insecurity triggered by the dismemberment of East Pakistan, but also because the military has

---

1. Kamran Asdar Ali, *Communism in Pakistan: Politics and Class Activism 1947–1972*. Library of South Asian History and Culture 10 (London: I. B. Tauris, 2015).

become even more deeply entrenched in the wider economic structures of the country. Moreover, the experience of democracy since the 1970 elections has increased both the aspiration and the demand for the sovereignty of democratic institutions that have the authority and power to effectively challenge the military-industrial establishment.

The *PLR* editors and contributors did not shy away from criticism of a country for which they clearly cared deeply. The editors were also aware of sensitivities over where they were located. As they clarified in the first editorial:

> ... the aim of such criticism will not be to ridicule our own people, to show our superiority over them (a charge often justifiably made against those in the West) nor will it be to undermine the faith of our people in their country. (Aziz Kurtha and Iqbal Khan, Volume 1, Issue 1 of *PLR*)

Similar charges have more recently been levelled at Pakistani academics based in Europe and the US. They are accused of damaging the image of the country through their criticism. Far from wanting to damage the reputation of Pakistan, however, it is clear that the need for critical voices from outside the country is probably more pronounced now than it was in the 1960s. In the 1960s, perhaps, the potential for a different future for Pakistan seemed more attainable, and therefore critical friendships may have seemed all the more necessary and worthwhile. The space for progressive debate and action has undergone significant reduction *within* Pakistan in recent decades, while there has been a corresponding increase in global information flows. Overseas Pakistanis, consequently, not only have greater liberty to voice criticism of the government, they also have up-to-date information about diverse narratives from a variety of sources. Social media is a powerful channel for communication that has transformed Pakistan's intellectual networks into geographically dispersed, real-time 'communities'. While the writers in the *PLR* were well-connected with political activities in Pakistan, they relied heavily on personal networks. The twenty-first century inheritors of the *PLR* agenda must contend with the barrage of contradictory sources of information that is more characteristic of being *in situ*. We therefore suggest that the role of critical friends of Pakistan is not only as important as ever, it may actually be critical for ensuring that the leftist voice in the country is not allowed to be drowned out by the 'noise' generated by groups with a vested interest in propping up establishment narratives. It can be painful to read these issues of the *PLR* because the promise that is written across

every issue has evidently not been fulfilled in the ensuing fifty years. As
Anushay Malik, a labour historian, writes:

> The radical promise of the late 1960s did not deliver. The reasons for why
> the dreams of revolution were not fulfilled merit analysis and debate.
> However, it is essential to begin by noting and commemorating the fact
> that indeed these dreams existed. The demands of radicals of the time
> are a part of the political history of Pakistan. Centring the importance
> of workers and the demand for social and economic equality is the only
> way to truly commemorate the struggles of those who, in the late 1960s,
> thought a better, more equal future for Pakistan was possible.[2]

The demand for the restoration of democracy has been a common
denominator of the movements against Generals Ayub's, Zia's, and more
recently Musharraf's regimes. However, the anti-Ayub Khan movement
in the late 1960s encapsulated broader socio-economic issues and
subsequently resulted in a wider elevation of the political consciousness
of the masses. The Toba Tek Singh Kissan Conference is exemplary, as
covered in the Spring 1970 issue of *PLR* by Ahmed Bashir. There was a
wide range of leftist groups involved with the struggle. Feroz Ahmed, a
sociologist, provides comprehensive details of these groups and of the
divisions among them in his article, 'The Leftist Debate in West Pakistan',
in the last issue of the *PLR*.[3]

Another common denominator of the three dictatorships (Ayub, Zia,
and Musharraf) was their alliance with the West in the Cold War and
the War Against Terror that followed the attacks of 11 September 2001.
Therefore, the movements against military dictatorships in Pakistan
included an articulated resistance against Western imperialism. In
the 1960s this discourse was aligned with global movements against
imperialism and the Vietnam War. In the *PLR* we see the linkages
through people like Tariq Ali, who was a leader of the anti-Vietnam
War movement and then went on to be a principal advocate in the Stop
the War Coalition after 9/11. The Stop the War Coalition, however, also
led some to endorse reactionary elements like the Taliban who resisted

---

2. Anushay Malik, 'Radical Demands of the 1960s and Lessons for Our Present,' *Pakistan Left Review*, 2020.
3. Feroz Ahmed also forms a common link between *PLR* (1968–70) in the UK and *Pakistan Forum* (1970–3), a similar initiative by left-leaning postgraduate Pakistani scholars across the Atlantic in North America. Feroz Ahmed, Eqbal Ahmad, and Aijaz Ahmad were the editors of the *Pakistan Forum*. The *Pakistan Forum* volumes have been preserved and are available on JSTOR.

American imperialism. This is a sensitive subject because several 1960s-vintage Marxists have openly or subtly supported the Taliban as a resistance movement. They argue that the Taliban offer resistance to imperialism and some have also pointed out that the Taliban come from underprivileged communities who have managed to stand up to the traditional Khans. The Taliban, they argue, represent a movement of social justice. To be sure, these arguments are frequently contextualised within broader geopolitical conflicts. Tariq Ali, for example, in an interview with Australian broadcaster Philip Adams, recognised the violence and authoritarianism of the Afghan Taliban but sees it as a product of Cold War interference led by the US through its regional proxies of Saudi Arabia and Pakistan. The Taliban, he has argued, would not exist without the support of the Pakistan Army, but they are clearly not simple puppets of a US-led neo-imperial hegemony. The Taliban have figuratively bitten the hands that fed them.[4] While we recognise that the Taliban encompass aspects of resistance and social justice, it is difficult to follow these arguments to a conclusion that would lead us to either explicitly or tacitly endorsing the Taliban as a welcome force in the region, and it is clear that many, if not most, Pakistani leftists are cognisant of the complex and contradictory role played by the Taliban and other insurgent organisations. The exact role and character of the Taliban continues to be something decidedly more complex and unpredictable following the unexpectedly rapid collapse of the American-backed Afghan regime in the summer of 2021. On the one hand, the rhetoric of social justice and adherence to an Islamic rule of law is consistent and clear from the leadership. On the other, the reports of capricious vindictiveness and brutality from the ground are hard to ignore. Regardless of how the Taliban govern, or indeed whether they are able to do so in the long run, the appetite for social justice is undeniably present among the people of Afghanistan and Pakistan. The students who produced the *PLR* found a vehicle for both understanding and addressing that notion of social justice through the intellectual tradition inspired by Marx. Support for the Taliban may similarly be understood as a desire for comparable aspirations for social justice. We are persuaded that the Taliban are ultimately not able, or indeed willing, to deliver social justice for all segments of society, so while the Marxists and the Taliban may share

---

4. Tariq Ali on Pakistan, Afghanistan and the US. By Phillip Adams on Late Night Live. Broadcast: 19 December 2001.

overlapping rhetorical goals, it would be unwise to naively conflate the two as a consequence.

The alliances of Pakistan's military dictators with the West were rewarded by certain types of economic aid. Niaz makes prescient predictions in his article, 'The Stranglehold of "Aid"', in *PLR* Autumn 1969. He explained how an aid-dependent model can create negative political and economic consequences in the long run. Many of his broader conclusions remain pertinent. It is strange how little things have changed in Pakistan. Both Zia's and Musharraf's regimes received large inflows of aid as rewards for their alliance and to support their role as a stalwart 'missionary' army coordinating the 'Green Belt' in the war against the Soviet Union and later the Taliban. The argument of high GDP growth rates during military regimes, spurred by heavy aid inflows, is used to characterise civilian regimes as inept and unfit for economic leadership.

Intellectuals Abroad

London, the home of the *PLR*, had provided the base for political activities related to the colonies during the era of the British empire. In the case of India, the leaderships of both political parties, the Muslim League and the Indian National Congress, were the products of the British education system. The tradition continued with students from privileged backgrounds coming to London, Oxford, and Cambridge after Independence. London has long been known as a home for political exiles from around the world, and Pakistan is no exception. The editors and contributors to the *PLR* were not, for the most part, in political exile, the one exception being Tariq Ali who claimed to be in a form of clandestine exile. Tariq Ali's rise to the global stage of the movement against the Vietnam War took him beyond a focus on Pakistan, though as his contribution to the *PLR* demonstrate, he never lost an intense interest in the country. His interview with Maulana Bhashani is one of the most insightful contributions in the *PLR*. It is remarkable to find Bhashani directly admitting that the military dictatorship could not be opposed for fear of offending China. One can easily forget the extent to which Mao and Zhou, alongside Nixon and Kissinger, backed Yahya Khan in his repression of East Pakistan. In an open letter to Zulfikar Bhutto published in the *PLR*'s Autumn 1968 issue, Tariq Ali questioned the justification of another socialist political party alongside the NAP and challenged Bhutto's role during General Ayub Khan's regime.

London again emerged as the hub of political activities in the movement against the military regime of General Musharraf, particularly when the movement was at its peak in 2007–8. The focus shifted to London because major political leaders like Nawaz Sharif, Benazir Bhutto, and Altaf Husain were in exile in London. Although Benazir was based in UAE, all her political activities took place in London, a pattern that continued from her 1980s exile in London. Imran Khan had a huge following among the British Pakistani diaspora. Interestingly, students and academic staff at the SOAS University of London provided a neutral platform for the political parties and activist groups to coordinate the movement against Musharraf. SOAS, interestingly, is very close to the ULU building, whose Malet Street correspondence address was used by the *PLR*.

The *PLR* group were engaged in rigorous debates on socio-economic issues and were working to formulate a model of a new society in Pakistan. Youth activism against Musharraf in London, in contrast, was more narrowly focused on the restoration of democracy. Unlike their counterparts in the 1960s, their activism lacked a vision for a coherent socio-economic programme. The absence of such a programme meant that the movement was unlikely to trigger any fundamental social change. Politicising the youth was a major achievement of the movement against Musharraf, which reversed to some extent the depoliticisation of youth under Zia. An expanded civil society also emerged out of the movement against Musharraf. However, this too, failed to translate into coherent mass political consciousness.

The London Group was active in London around same time as the *PLR* was published there. Ahmed Rashid, Asad Rahman, Najam Sethi, Dilip Das, and Humayun Talat were some of its prominent members. The London Group convened at 81 Onslow Gardens in South Kensington and produced a pamphlet called *Pakistan Zindabad*. Their focus was more on activism. Some members of the *PLR* organising team, for example Salima Hashmi, attended a few meetings of the Group. The prominent members of the Group mentioned above went back to Pakistan and were involved with the insurgency in Balochistan during the 1970s and were captured by the security agencies. Dilip Das disappeared and his body was never found. Unfortunately, the issue of missing persons in Balochistan is even more pronounced at present. The London Group, members were released by General Zia's regime after the coup in 1977.

The *PLR* organising team often met at the Ganges restaurant at 40 Gerrard Street in Soho run by Tassaduq Ahmad. Tassaduq warmly welcomed the team because he too was a political activist. Salima Hashmi recalls Tassaduq refusing to charge her for food out of reverence for her father, Faiz Ahmed Faiz. Tassaduq was from East Pakistan, where he had gained prominence as a journalist. The language tensions of the time between Bengali and Urdu were proxies for much more significant political and economic competition between the two parts of the country, and Tassaduq had been forced to flee to avoid arrest and prosecution for his pro-East Pakistan and leftist journalism. He continued to campaign on social and political issues impacting Britain's Bangladeshi community in London until his death in 2002. One of the remarkable things about this generation of students and activists was that not only did they take themselves seriously, they were taken seriously by others. Tassaduq, for example, befriended Prince Charles through his volunteer initiatives—a genuine testament to the respect he had earned.

Within a couple of hundred yards of the Ganges restaurant, at the Nanking restaurant on Denmark Street, 'one of South Asia's most influential literary movements, the leftist Indian Progressive Writers' Association [PWA], was founded on 24 November, 1934'.[5] The PWA was established by Indian writers and intellectuals, including Mulk Raj Anand, Sajjad Zaheer, and Jyotirmaya Ghosh, with the encouragement and support of some British literary figures. The *PLR* introductory editorial resonates with the manifesto of the PWA: 'Radical changes are taking place in Indian society ... We believe that the new literature of India must deal with the basic problems of our existence to-day—the problems of hunger and poverty, social backwardness, and political subjection. All that drags us down to passivity, inaction and un-reason we reject as reactionary. All that arouses in us the critical spirit, which examines institutions and customs in the light of reason, which helps us to act, to organise ourselves, to transform, we accept as progressive.'[6]

These progressive Indians had close associations with the members of the Bloomsbury Set. This collection of English writers, intellectuals, and artists were particularly successful and productive in the early part of the twentieth century.[7] Its members included, among others, E. M.

5. Andrew Whitehead, 'Downstairs at the Nanking Restaurant,' 28 January 2016. https://www.andrewwhitehead.net/blog/downstairs-at-the-nanking-restaurant.

6. Mulk Raj Anand, 'On the Progressive Writers' Movement,' in *Marxist Cultural Movement in India*, Vol. 1, ed. S. Pradhan (Calcutta: National Book Agency, 1979).

7. Stanford Patrick Rosenbaum, ed., *The Bloomsbury Group: A Collection of Memoirs and Commentary*, rev. ed. (Toronto; Buffalo: University of Toronto Press, 1995).

Forster, Virginia Woolf, and John Maynard Keynes. The Indians within this Set were referred to as the 'Bloomsbury Indians' and considered a Bloomsbury subset. The *PLR*, therefore, was continuing a tradition of South Asian progressives in London, particularly focused on adjoining areas of Bloomsbury and Soho.

Aziz Kurtha, the co-editor of the *PLR*, was also pursuing a PhD in law at the LSE. Unlike Feroz Ahmed, he did not pursue academia but worked as a lawyer. Kurtha's exclusive and detailed interview with Zulfikar Bhutto in 1968 was the main contribution in the first issue of the *PLR*. Kurtha managed to unnerve Bhutto with his poignant questions ranging from Basic Democracies to his stance on the Vietnam War. Kurtha recalls how a few years later Bhutto, now prime minister, recognised him from the stage in a big Pakistan Peoples Party (PPP) public gathering in Karachi. Bhutto's aides arranged a meeting. Bhutto told Kurtha that he had been rude during the interview but also acknowledged that he was clever. Bhutto asked Kurtha whether he would work for the PPP. He was sent on three trips to the US to speak at Asian Studies department at universities—he spoke at Harvard, Dallas, UCLA, Vancouver, Calgary. He said the purpose was to release the Pakistani POWs being held in India.

Salima Hashmi recalls how Aziz Kurtha dropped a bombshell one evening at the ULU. The Pakistan High Commissioner, Mahmoud Haroon, had sent a message asking him to pay a visit to his office. The *PLR* organising team deliberated about the purpose and possible consequences of the meeting. The team waited outside the High Commission having fortified Kurtha with all kinds of advice. He reported that Mahmoud Haroon was a very clever man and had offered him a ten pounds contribution for the *PLR*, which Kurtha refused. Strikingly, this is a consistent pattern of Pakistan High Commission officials in London till this day. They attempt to penetrate Pakistani student organisations in the UK in order to maintain surveillance and to patronise students so as to promote a pro-establishment narrative through helping to sponsor events. More recently, they have been successful in coercing students to cancel events such as the one on Balochistan. The establishment's paranoia with dissenting voices at university campuses is partly driven by the movement for the independence of Bangladesh, which started at the University of Dhaka.

Salima Hashmi has contributed a detailed account of her *PLR* days for this volume. Her reflections summarise a half-century journey by a member of the *PLR* organising team as well as her own writings on art. She has inspired a whole generation of young activists and artists; her essay titled, 'A Distant Encounter', takes us back to her own youthful idealism.

In the Spring 1969 issue of the *PLR*, Aziz Kurtha published a critique of the 1962 Constitution. Some of the issues he raised persist even today, such as the debate around the presidential or parliamentary form of government, provincial autonomy, and the role of the army in the political system. He astutely pointed out that the 1962 Constitution allocated too much authority to the President and thus failed to put a check on his untrammelled authority. The judiciary had not started to assert itself at that time, a new phenomenon that was witnessed in the movement against Musharraf. The Lawyers' Movement in 2007 galvanised the public against Musharraf by rallying behind the Chief Justice, Iftikhar Chaudhry. However, the movement also unleashed judicial activism in the form of suo moto actions which can infringe upon the functioning of democratic regimes. The disqualification of elected public representatives, including former prime minister Nawaz Sharif, for example, presents a troubling example of the power of an activist court to potentially disrupt a sitting government. While such court decisions may be legitimate in law, there can be no doubt that the result is a strong push towards the party politicisation of the courts. Ultimately, this seems both dangerous and reckless for the establishment of stable democratic institutions.

Iqbal Khan, the other co-editor of the *PLR*, was studying philosophy at Birkbeck College. He continued producing left-leaning publication for the remainder of his time in the UK and also after he returned to Pakistan in 1990. In Lahore he was also the editor of Mashal Books until he passed away in 1993. Aziz Kurtha recalls that Iqbal had a very good command of both Urdu and English. Dr Mubarak Ali has contributed a brief biography of Iqbal Khan for this volume. Among his other contributions, Iqbal clearly laid out the demands of East Pakistan in his article, 'On the Question of East Pakistan', in the Spring 1969 issue of the *PLR*.

Rehman Sobhan was another person who encouraged Aziz Kurtha to continue producing the *PLR*. Sobhan abandoned his PhD studies in Economics in England in order to support the independence movement of Bangladesh, convinced that the emancipation of his country had to take precedence over a doctoral research degree. He went on to become the economic advisor to Mujibur Rahman following the creation of Bangladesh, and has continued to play an active role as an economist, public intellectual, and pillar of Bangladeshi civil society. Sobhan had continued his activism for a progressive South Asia from his undergraduate days at the Cambridge University during the 1950s, as Amartya Sen recalls in his recently published memoir, *Home in the World: A Memoir*. Sobhan was the president of the Majlis, the South Asian students society founded in 1891 at the Cambridge University (the Oxford Majlis was founded five years later). Amartya Sen was its treasurer during Sobhan's presidential term, as he reminisces, 'Rehman is probably the closest lifelong friend I have ever had, and the Majlis had a role in bringing us constantly together in the mid-1950s.'[8]

Kamal Hussain was the president of the Oxford Majlis at the same time. He played a very active role in the formation of Bangladesh and became the first Foreign Minister of independent Bangladesh in 1971. Before Indian independence, both the India Office and New Scotland Yard had kept a keen eye on the Majlis in the early part of the twentieth century. They were particularly concerned about its members' communist sympathies in the late 1920s and 1930s. It is worth noting that the anti-colonial struggle of like-minded students in the earlier period morphed into struggles for a progressive East and West Pakistan after independence, and eventually led to the creation of Bangladesh.

Sobhan's article, 'The Economic Basis of the Current Crisis', in the Spring 1969 issue of the *PLR* drew attention to the socio-economic disparities that were central to the economic policies of the 1960s. Ayub Khan is lauded for the economic prosperity achieved by some segments of society, though perhaps not the contributors to the *PLR*, with scant mention of democratic dispensation. The 1960s economic model in Pakistan is often given the credit for having been replicated in South Korea, a statement repeatedly cited as a fact also by former prime minister Imran Khan. The South Korean economic model led to something akin to an economic miracle. However, the view that Pakistan inspired economic policies led to the phenomenal economic growth is a misconception as Meghnad Desai explains.[9] The inaugural *PLR* editorial, however, had

---

8. Amartya Sen, *Home in the World: A Memoir* (London: Allen Lane, 2021).

9. 'I learned from Mahbub ul Haq and accords with economic history that South Koreans were encouraged by the World Bank in late 1950s, to visit both India and Pakistan, to learn about their planning strategy. They decided never to follow the South Asian self-sufficiency, import substitution strategy. They followed instead the Japanese model despite Japan having been their cruel imperial master. They sought cooperation of their business houses, Chaebol and encouraged them to export by giving them incentives.' (Desai, personal communication)

sharply criticised the policies of Mahbub ul Haq, Ayub Khan's Finance Minister. These policies, Sobhan argued, had led to widening inequalities. In hindsight, it appears clear that these inequalities not only made the dismemberment of East Pakistan more likely, they may well have made it inevitable. This is certainly one of the rare instances when an economist made an accurate forecast of the complex relationship between the economy and politics of a nation. In the current volume, we invited Sobhan to reflect on the development of Pakistan, India, and Bangladesh since Independence. In his insightful analysis of identity and exclusion, he charts some of the areas in which Pakistan in particular has fallen short of the ideals to which the *PLR* contributors subscribed. Pakistan's maintenance of what he sees as an exclusionary religious identity, he argues, effectively resulted in the abandonment of genuine democracy. Similar arguments have been made by others, but it is telling that such an approach was anticipated by Sobhan's contributions in the late 1960s and has only become more evident and compelling over time.

Instead of paying heed to such calls, Ayub Khan celebrated the 'Decade of Development' in 1968. This outraged the citizens and marked the beginning of the movement against Ayub Khan. Had the *PLR* contributors been able to see the persistence of high levels of economic inequality in the twenty-first century, they would no doubt have been profoundly saddened at the exacerbation of disparities along regional lines and between provinces and areas such as Balochistan, South Punjab, and erstwhile FATA. Clearly, few, if any, lessons have been learnt from the dismemberment of East Pakistan.

The clarity with which the *PLR* contributors describe the greatest challenges facing Pakistan's transition to a democratic and just society and their willingness to speak truth to power, both through their own articles as well as interviews with prominent leaders, is humbling. Simultaneously, their ambition for a Pakistani model of a socialist state that could somehow avoid the authoritarian directions of Stalinist and Maoist-inspired states is endearing and bittersweet. With the benefit of hindsight, we now know how unsuccessful Bhutto's Islamic Socialism really was. Tariq Ali challenged Bhutto directly in his open letter in the Autumn 1968 issue of the *PLR*, saying, 'We do not believe that a supernatural "Being" can in any way be a substitute for a real socialist struggle.' The editors frequently returned to the issue of Islamic Socialism, including publishing a review of Maxime Rodinson's *Islam and Capitalism* in the final issue of the *PLR* in early 1970. The term Islamic Socialism, to be sure, is salient beyond the borders of Pakistan. It has become a global slogan that takes on distinct forms in different locations. A recent series of online seminars demonstrates the variation in forms and meanings of the term across different parts of the Muslim world.[10] The translations of sections of books, such as by Herbert Marcuse, show that the editors were sophisticated readers of contemporary Marxist thought and were not doctrinaire in their approach.

The end of the Cold War led to the transformation of formerly command economies to hybrid liberal market and authoritarian control systems. Perhaps most tragically, we now know that Pakistan's economic growth, industrialisation, and expansion of education and health services have not only done little to help the country's poorest, but have arguably exacerbated the inequalities and rendered what was already a grotesquely unfair distribution of wealth in 1968 into an obscenity that the contributors to the *PLR* might never have imagined possible.

The military coup of 1977, led by Ziaul Haq, is an easy target to identify as the source of many of the problems Pakistan confronts today. Much of the current insurgency and increased availability of weapons can be linked directly to his policies of courting mujahideen groups as part of the American-led resistance to the Soviet invasion of Afghanistan. His appeals to Pakistan's religious groups reinforced the notion of the country as an Islamic Republic, with an increasingly narrow definition of what constituted 'true' Islam. Zia's close relationship with Wahabi leaders in the Arabian Gulf was both ideological and material. He seemingly had no difficulty in aligning himself with the most conservative Sunni groups both in and out of the country. A great deal has been written about the corruption of the military that can be attributed to decisions and actions during the Zia era.

There is no doubt that Zia's government did more to crush what had been a vibrant Marxist debate than any other regime before or since. He was the perfect person to collaborate with Reagan in hammering the final nails into the socialist coffin both in Pakistan as well as across Asia. There is good reason to dwell on the damage inflicted by Zia, but the truth is that it would be a mistake to give excessive credit to the high-profile celebrities of history. If Marxism teaches us nothing else, it should drive home the need to pay close attention to the broader economic and historical contexts that give shape and meaning to the relationships

---

10. Layli Uddin and Simon Fuchs, eds., *Series of Webinars on "Islamic Socialism in the Global South"*, 2020.

of production. The *PLR* is an extraordinary time capsule that allows us to delve into a unique moment in history. Its pages lay out in black and white a cogent leftist view of Pakistan that challenges accepted historical narratives that many of us have absorbed both consciously and unconsciously. The national curriculum of Pakistan's government schools has little to say about the rich leftist history of Pakistani politics. National curricula are all too often an exercise in narrow nation-building and the establishment of useful 'bad guys' (both historical and contemporary), that can serve to rally and motivate the masses without threatening *status quo* power relations. The current policy proposal of Single National Curriculum (SNC) is another manifestation of the ideology of narrow nation-building by ironing out diversity.

Reprinting the *PLR* today gives us an opportunity to take stock of where we were, and, equally importantly, where we *are*. It has become somewhat trite to say that those who do not learn from history are condemned to repeat it, but there is truth in that overused saying. We are, indeed, repeating aspects of history from the 1960s. The military dictatorship of General Ayub Khan may perhaps bear more resemblance to that of General Pervez Musharraf than that of General Ziaul Haq. If so, then understanding what happened then, and what happened to the political movements that both supported and opposed the military and the state, may prove instrumental in making sense of how the current generation can both understand and act in our own time of profound and even existential crisis.

Promises Unfulfilled

Throughout the pages of the *PLR*, the bitterness of the contributors comes through. They see what Pakistan could have become. They see the promise of a new country that could have forged a bold new path in the world and set an example for equitable distribution of resources and respect for ethnic, linguistic, and religious diversity. Instead, they see the energies of the Pakistani people being squandered to prop up an elite that has no interest in losing privilege, however much it costs the masses *and* the nation. In the Spring issue of 1969, Kurtha and Khan, the co-editors, pen an editorial entitled, 'Pakistan Usurped'. They lament the repetition of yet another instance of the military assuming control of the government. This time, from one military leader to another. General Ayub Khan handed over control of the government to General Yahya Khan. The justification for this transition was based on what Ayub called a breakdown in law and order. The disappointment for East and West Pakistanis who had been protesting for a return to democratically elected government must have been extreme. The editors do not hold back in sharing their views, and openly blame the 'leeches of Ayub Khan's administration who had been sucking the blood of helpless peasants for years'.[11] Rather than representing a breakdown in law and order, the editors say, the violence and protests were a desperate plea from the people for a *return* to law and order.

The earlier coup, in 1958, had been premised on a similar narrative of dysfunctional democratic institutions. The writers in the *PLR* are having none of it. The future, they say, is for a socialist Pakistan. One that is neither dependent on the West, nor overwhelmed by the Soviet bloc or Maoist China. They seek a novel manifestation of socialism that retains what we would call today a progressive social agenda of inclusivity and tolerance, but with explicit demands for a radical redistribution of wealth that had been accumulated by a tiny minority of the country.

In 1999, General Musharraf came to power making very similar claims. He has gone to great lengths to sanitise both his motives and his actions in public interviews and his autobiography, and to some extent he has been successful both in and out of the country in persuading some people that his regime was benign. The objections to a military disruption to democratically elected governments may be entirely sound while the lived reality may be somewhat murkier. It may be instructive to look at some of the actions and motives for resistance to these military interventions comparatively. In General Ayub's and General Yahya's day, UK-based students might enjoy a certain degree of insulation from the possible consequences of their public dissent. In the early days of social media, the activists and protesters in Musharraf's era must have certainly known that they could not count on their words and actions being unnoticed. In both periods, however, it seems that the protesters and critics *wanted* their ideas to get to Pakistan. The messages may have been broadcast from London, but the principal audiences were in Pakistan. The message of the 2000s echoed that of the late 1960s—Pakistan was not living up to its promise. The government was not serving the people in the way that it claimed it would. Such disappointment is true, at some level, of every government in every time, but there is something especially bitter when the country is young and its leaders espoused an idealism that raises hope and expectations. So perhaps the anger

---

11. *PLR* Spring 1969.

in the pages of the *PLR* is more pronounced and strident because the contrast with what might have been was so great. By the turn of the millennium, Pakistan's disappointing programmes of social justice and inadequate attempts to control corruption and sectarian fragmentation were not *new* phenomena. Additionally, the *PLR* generation had not yet seen the extent of moral and ideological bankruptcy that was rampant across those countries that had embraced the socialist experiment. The commitment to a genuine socialist state and economy is honest and resilient. By 2000, the shine of socialism was decidedly less pristine and had suffered decades of persistent attack by those forces who, rightly or wrongly, perceived socialism, and by extension anything left wing, as an existential threat.

The Pakistan Left and London

London has long held a special place in the imagination of Pakistani intellectuals. Prior to Independence, young people from South Asia studied in Britain's best universities, including the diverse collection of colleges that form the University of London. Post-Independence, this trend continued and young Pakistani scholars came in a steady stream to the Universities of Oxford, Cambridge, and London, and elsewhere as well. When General Ayub Khan led the coup in 1958, students and activists who opposed the military regime found that London could be a relatively safe harbour from which to voice their dissent and formulate alternative governance models. Some of Pakistan's most famous, and infamous, opposition activists have found themselves in exile from their home country in London. Many of Pakistan's heads of state have found themselves living out a period of exile in and around London. The Pakistan student organisations that rise and fall in the UK have proved a vital channel for the exiled voice to be heard and to resonate in Pakistan itself. Pakistan's student populations in the UK have demonstrated an admirable courage in standing up to authoritarian leaders, both military and non-military, despite potential risk to their scholarships or genuine risk of imprisonment and harassment upon their return home. The *PLR* is a wonderful example of such bravery. The contributors wrote their articles in full knowledge that there might come a day of reckoning in which they and their families could suffer real material consequences. The civil unrest in East Pakistan and the outbreak of war only a short period after the publication of the final issue of the *PLR* is testament to the severity of the situation at that time. London might have been a temporary safe harbour where young scholars could express their discontent, but it offered little protection once those same scholars returned home. The question of language had defined Pakistan's politics since its inception when Urdu was declared the sole national language. Bengali speakers in East Pakistan understandably objected, and the protests against the imposition of Urdu led to riots and killings of hundreds of Bengalis on 21 February 1952. Such is the significance of this day that in 1999 UNESCO declared 21 February to be International Mother Language Day at the suggestion of Bangladesh and as a tribute to the language movement by the Bangladeshis (then the East Pakistanis).

The inclusion of both Urdu and Bengali in the *PLR* was an intentional statement of inclusivity and solidarity across the fragile halves of a divided country that we now know would not endure in its original form. The contributors to the *PLR* came from both East and West Pakistan and its preoccupations encompassed the totality of this geographically divided country. Tellingly, the editors stated categorically that West Pakistan could never thrive on its own without East Pakistan, now Bangladesh. Obviously, the two countries have survived and will continue to do so, but the challenges facing both countries are profound, although Bangladesh's economy has outperformed Pakistan's economy. The editors accurately forecast that their separation in 1971 would severely restrict each country's ability to overcome the economic and social hurdles that faced them. Equally insightfully, Feroz Ahmed, in the final issue of the *PLR,* offered a wide-ranging analysis of debates among leftists in West Pakistan in which he identifies some of the regional and ethnic tensions that we now know were not only major obstacles to coherent leftist mobilisation but also major sources of friction within modern Pakistan.

The Twenty-first Century Left

What now for the left? The Cold War did tremendous damage to it, but it is far from gone. The collapse of the socialist command economies in the 1990s seemingly cut adrift much of the institutionalised networks that leftist organisations and sympathisers might use to facilitate mobilisation and communication. For a time, it looked as if the left, at least in the US and the UK, had moved irrevocably towards the centre. Tariq Ali's warning about the extreme centre highlighted the dangers of allowing a vacuum to develop in the party political landscape in both countries, and for a time that seemed to happen.[12] The popularity of Bernie Sanders in the US and Jeremy Corbyn in the UK is proof that there is widespread appetite for a socialist agenda in spite of the lack of obvious institutional homes in which such agendas might flourish. Their lack of electoral success, conversely, is proof that there remains substantial mistrust and animosity towards both socialist rhetoric and leftist agendas more broadly. The calls for profound transformation of society that ring loud and clear across the pages of the *PLR* might resonate well with students in London universities today. The extent to which Pakistani students have taken up the cause is mixed but certainly not completely absent. A concern for social justice appears to be as strong as it ever was. The faith that Marxist solutions can bring about the desired world has perhaps faded to the point that it has become a distraction. So, what would today's leftist graduate students argue is the solution? Anti-corruption rhetoric may offer useful rallying devices, but they lack the concrete action plans of an ideologically committed socialist student union. We do not subscribe to the fantasy that somehow earlier generations were *more* intellectual or *more* engaged politically, but it can be very difficult to compare levels of engagement across generations. Lyon's generation came of age in the 1980s and was notoriously apathetic and conservative (with a little c), but that did not mean they did not care about their world. The forms of expression that were fashionable and available were perhaps more narcissistic and fragmented. Cheema's came of age after the departure of Reagan and Thatcher when student unions and political involvement were back on the table. In the 1960s, a student who did not get overtly involved in politics was the oddball. In the 1980s, it was the reverse. Many of those committed political activists in the 1960s turned out to be decidedly more self-orientated than one might have imagined from listening to their youthful selves. Similarly, we wonder if the absence of a coherent political rhetoric of subsequent generations may reflect a shift in fashion rather than a shift in commitment.

The writers in the *PLR* would have been politically aware and engaged regardless of the fashions around them. Their sincerity is beyond question, but the social context matters and it shaped the expression of their politics. Had they been graduate students in the 1980s, they would have been the ones on the ramparts (so to speak) demanding divestment from South Africa, an end to covert military operations around the world and, in Pakistan, a rollback of the Zia policies that we now know have

12. Tariq Ali, *The Extreme Centre: A Warning* (London: Verso Books, 2015).

done so much long-term damage to the country. In the 2000s, they would no doubt have been leading the calls for a restoration of democracy. Would they have been calling for a Marxist transformation of Pakistan? Perhaps. Or maybe the fervent ideological positions they articulated so cogently between 1968–70 channelled a particular rhetoric that was in the air at that time. If they had come of age in a different period, the passion and compassion for humanity would still have been present, but the details might have been radically altered.

We are not magicians so cannot know with any certainty what individuals might say or do if they had grown up in a different environment or time. However, we do have the issues of the *PLR,* which serve as something of a time machine. We do not need to rely on the memories of the people who were there, because their younger selves can speak for themselves. Repeating history is the threat so often made to those who refuse to learn from history. In the pages of this short-lived journal, we have the opportunity to learn more about the aspirations and tactics of a collection of earnest Pakistani leftists writing at a tumultuous time of uncertainty and change. Let us learn from these voices so as not to blindly sleepwalk into the same disappointments and unfulfilled promises that all too often characterise national and international politics and economics.

* * * * *

References

Anand, Mulk Raj. 'On the Progressive Writers' Movement'. In *Marxist Cultural Movement in India*, Vol. 1. Edited by S. Pradhan. Calcutta: National Book Agency, 1979.

Ali, Kamran Asdar. *Communism in Pakistan: Politics and Class Activism 1947–1972*. Library of South Asian History and Culture 10. London: I. B. Tauris, 2015.

Ali, Tariq. *The Extreme Centre: A Warning*. London: Verso Books, 2015.

Malik, Anushay. 'Radical Demands of the 1960s and Lessons for Our Present.' *Pakistan Left Review*, 2020.

Rosenbaum, Stanford Patrick, ed. *The Bloomsbury Group: A Collection of Memoirs and Commentary*. Rev. ed. Toronto; Buffalo: University of Toronto Press, 1995.

Uddin, Layli, and Simon Fuchs, eds. *Series of Webinars on "Islamic Socialism in the Global South."* 2020.

Whitehead, Andrew. 'Downstairs at the Nanking Restaurant.' 28 January 2016. See: https://www.andrewwhitehead.net/blog/downstairs-at-the-nanking-restaurant.

A Distant Encounter: *PLR* Days and Early Art Writing

Salima Hashmi

Encountering a piece of one's writing from half a century ago can be a sobering experience. Entirely forgotten until very recently, the appearance of 'Reflections on Art' from the fourth edition of the *Pakistan Left Review* (*PLR*) in the 1960s was a sudden reminder of a tumultuous time. Never considering myself anything but a visual artist, painter, or photographer with a covert passion for teaching, pontificating on art in print was not a priority. True, the theoretical implications of the way an artist assembles images or the meanings and ambiguities they embody are part of one's practice but words were rarely summoned to explain the visual process.

This first venture in pondering on and writing an overview of Pakistani art, aeons ago, was owed entirely to editor Iqbal Khan's powers of persuasion and commitment to the scope of the *PLR*'s agenda. It grew out of abundant animated discussions on politics, history, and culture in London in the late 1960s, debates and conversations which preceded the appearance of the *PLR*. Deliberations, meetings, and arguments surrounded us, many taking place in the basement of the Ganges restaurant in Gerrard Street in Soho, owned by Tassaduq Ahmad, a leftist friend of Faiz Ahmed Faiz with a large heart in the right place.

Rehman Sobhan was among the many East Pakistani students who met up with those from other parts of Pakistan in intense dialogues and crossfire. When Faiz was in town the leftists who had departed Pakistan in the 1950s after the first wave of incarcerations would join the powwows, including Muhammad Afzal and Eric Rahim.

Somewhere along the way, an offshoot of these groups propelled itself off to meet regularly at the University of London Union (ULU). A sense of purpose slowly emerged which was the genesis of the *PLR*. Very occasionally we would adjourn to our flat in Muswell Hill, in the house of Muhammad Afzal and Joan, where Faiz often stayed.

Iqbal Khan, energised by Aziz Kurtha, was the instigator of the idea of documenting the deeply felt concerns and postulations being voiced and fought over around us. Every Sunday afternoon we sat in protest against apartheid in front of the South Africa House in Trafalgar Square. We marched for the Campaign for Nuclear Disarmament. We tussled with police on horseback in Grosvenor Square in the biggest anti-Vietnam War march the world had ever seen.

Those were the days of sit-ins at London School of Economics, the art schools, and universities across Britain. Paris came to a standstill in May 1968, and Rudi Dutschke was spurring on the students after the killing of one by a policeman in 1967.

The news from a restive Pakistan was gripping. Ayub Khan's 'Decade of Development' was coming apart at the seams, as were his tiers of governance and publicity machines. Iqbal Khan and Aziz Kurtha dwelt on the discussions surrounding this news and on the emerging fractures across Pakistan. They began listing and contacting possible writers while simultaneously agonising over how to raise resources to pay for the printing and distribution of the journal. Everyone subsisted on a shoestring budget of scholarships, stipends, and modest pay cheques which routinely ran out before payday. Aziz's younger brother, Ali, somewhat distanced from our fervour, was corralled into approaching sponsors, starting from his own family. Despite being on the periphery, he was nevertheless devoted to buttressing our ideals. Tasked with the most mundane aspects of putting a journal to bed, he painstakingly patched together resources, from securing cheap paper to the use of an electric typewriter.

The word spread across the student community. Aziz managed an interview with Zulfikar Ali Bhutto on his visit to London. Bhutto had created waves after falling out with Ayub Khan and forming his own party, adding a new element to the Pakistan political landscape.

In the midst of putting together the first issue, Aziz dropped a bombshell one evening at the University of London Union. The Pakistan High Commissioner had sent a message asking Aziz to pay a visit to his office. There was some consternation. Had he heard about the *PLR*? Was this because of Aziz's interview with Bhutto? He was nervous. His was a modest business family from Karachi, not given to dabbling in politics of any kind, let alone the kind he was embracing, though they were now settled in Britain and out of reach of Ayub Khan's hoodlums.

It was decided that Aziz would take up the High Commissioner's invitation. He was none other than the wily, urbane politician Mahmoud Haroon. A small group of us waited outside the building in Lowndes Square, having fortified Aziz with all kinds of advice. He was to avoid discussion on the *PLR*, especially names of contributors and contents of the upcoming journal. He was to act the earnest young intellectual eager for an innocuous discussion with a seasoned politician.

We waited outside for thirty minutes or so, after which a giggling, nonplussed Aziz appeared, scratching his head. It transpired that the shrewd politician-cum-diplomat had made nonchalant conversation for a while, after which he made it apparent that he was aware of most of the individuals contributing to the journal. He expressed his interest in fresh political thinking among students and intellectuals in London. The drift of the conversation left Aziz somewhat mystified. This was amplified when Haroon pressed a ten-pound note into Aziz's palm when he was leaving as 'my contribution towards your journal'. As he emerged from the embassy, Aziz appeared baffled as to whether he should have accepted 'the ten quid', much needed for the near-empty kitty, or whether acceptance would embarrass the *PLR*, leaving it vulnerable to accusations of 'selling out' to the embassy, i.e. the government. Our motley group, no less disconcerted, eventually decided that the 'bribe' was not generous enough to cause embarrassment but indicated instead what one always knew—a crafty politician always hedges his bets when he senses the balance of power tilting away from his position. The writing was on the wall, perhaps? Or was Aziz's conversation with Bhutto more significant than we realised and we were being given an inkling of the future?

Iqbal Khan was working on aesthetics as part of his Philosophy studies at the Birkbeck College and often probed some of the underlying aesthetic forms and nuances in Pakistani art. He was specifically interested in bridging the divides between empirical writings on aesthetics and the process of practice. He closely questioned the artistic framework in the oeuvre of Pakistani artists in our many conversations.

I recall our discussions on Chughtai and the contradictions embedded in nostalgic nationalism. Khan was an admirer of Chughtai's palette, believing it to be close to the hues and aesthetics reflected in ancient manuscripts of the subcontinent. My arguments centred around the more robust explorations of form in the works of the early cubists of the Lahore Art Circle. Their struggles were more potent in the quest for a 'post-colonial identity'—a phrase not yet in common usage. Many arguments later, at Khan's insistence, I attempted to organise the many threads in our conversations. Unfamiliar with the developments in art school curriculums which were influencing young artists at the time, Khan was keen on the article reflecting the 'here and now' of Pakistani art. Thus 'Reflections on Art' was written.

Today, the first part of the essay seems the most naive. There are far too many generalisations regarding form, content, and clichéd art history references. However, the historical context more or less holds good fifty years later, if a little rudimentary in its articulation. There are some embarrassing oversimplifications regarding societal and cultural development, but one is cognisant of the artist's voice in this narrative, which quite necessarily differs from that of the art historian or scholar.

The prickly debate of the time—the question of a 'distinctive Pakistani style'—lingers on after five decades. Five decades which have been reasonably fertile insofar as scholarly research and publications in South Asia are concerned. Art histories, post-colonial identities, and a prolific body of art making has been spawned over this period.

Apart from scholarly investigations, artists have grappled with negotiating the international art world, art academia in the West, and the multiple challenges of art exchange. Visual culture has altered exponentially in this half century. Artists have attempted to address the continuities and discontinuities of traditions, new materials, and fresh images which reflect the multiple dimensions of social life. Intertwined with all this has been continuous political turmoil, with all the startling and immense consequences of a truncated Pakistan after the 1971 military action in East Pakistan.

The essay in the *PLR* carried portents of the events that followed its publication. The effect of the separation of East Pakistan on the visual arts was particularly marked. The essay, penned in 1969, notes the influential status of Zainul Abedin. In his seminal work, 'Modernism and the Art of Muslim South Asia', published in 2010, Iftikhar Dadi reiterates the importance of Zainul Abedin as an artist of deep humanism and one of the most dominating figures in Pakistani culture. With hindsight one is aware of how little this truly meant to the Pakistani state. Dadi notes:

> The national prominence accorded to Zainul Abedin and other Pakistan artists overcompensated in the cultural realm for actual economic and political inequalities that persisted and increasingly alienated large sections of the East Pakistani populace from Pakistan nationhood.[1]

The mainstream history of Pakistani art widely disseminated today in art schools and in artists' conversations barely acknowledges the years from 1947–71 in terms of artistic exchange between both wings of the

---

1. Iftikhar Dadi, *Modernism and the Art of Muslim South Asia* (Chapel Hill, NC: University of North Carolina Press, 2010, p. 109).

country. The All Pakistan National Exhibitions in the 1960s leaned heavily towards the artists from Dhaka and Chittagong as well as artists such Murtaza Bashir (Murtaja Baseer), Qamarul Hassan, Saifuddin Ahmed, and Muhammed Jehangir who came to exhibit their work and were part of the 'art scene'.

Among these was the unusual presence of the sculptor, Novera Ahmed, all but forgotten in Pakistan today. The essay highlights her importance as a 'highly original and radically inclined sculptress(!) whose frustration at the hands of the establishment and society eventually drove her out of the country'.[2] It is only very recently that scholars, art historians, and artists in Bangladesh have reclaimed and restored Novera Ahmed to her rightful status as an artist of critical importance and a pioneering sculptor of the subcontinent.

'Reflections on Art' focuses on the relationship between folk art and contemporary art and design professionals, an awareness which emerged forcefully in the early 1960s and which owed a great deal to the East wing of the country. The curriculum of the newly-established National College of Art (NCA), formerly Mayo School of Art, was embracing the enriching connections of forms with new directions in art making and modern design. Even in those early days, the role of the NCA in investigating the architecture, textiles, jewellery, furniture, and related artefacts of what were once remote areas—such as the Swat Valley, Cholistan, and Thar—was an effort to broaden the visual vocabulary and experience of would-be artists and designers.

Written long before the setting up of the National Institute of Folk Heritage (now Lok Virsa) and the Folk Art Museum, the essay muses on the possibility of such an entity and its importance in founding a library of folk motifs and forms. It makes a case for compiling an index of indigenous folk design, pointing out its future role in serving and inspiring local industry, specifically the textile industry. This indeed has come to pass.

'Reflections' draws attention to Shakir Ali's role as mentor to artists such as Zahoor ul Akhlaq, then a young artist spending long hours poring over the Indian miniatures in the British Museum and the Victoria and Albert Museum. A student at the Hornsey College of Art and Royal College of Art, he was yet to attain the status of arguably Pakistan's finest contemporary visual practitioner. He was beginning to extrapolate

---

2. Quotation from the essay.

exactly what the essay bemoans, the distance between the past and life as it was being lived.

One had feared at the time that connections between tradition, history, and the contemporary reality was very fragile in art practice. Sadequain is mentioned as an artist who was drawn to all of these threads but seemed susceptible, even at that time, to the 'demands of the new philistine class without whose patronage the artists can't survive'.[3]

This indeed proved to be the case in Sadequain's highly illustrious, popular, frenzied career. It was marked by continuous prolific bursts of ambitious works—public murals, exhibitions, museum shows, ambitious commissions both national and international. If anything, Sadequain's penchant for showmanship matched by his energy and skill came to validate the 'idea' of an artist in the public imagination.

The fear expressed in 'Reflections on Art' of the Pakistani artist falling short of what could be expected of him or her has been more than vindicated by the last three decades of art making in Pakistan. The oppressive times in Pakistan from 1977 onwards have been subverted by artists, writers, poets, and activists of every genre. These decades have witnessed the significant role played by women artists in responding to military regimes through their work, taking up themes like violence against women, and nurturing young artists in finding their artistic voices. The contemporary miniaturist has been inventive in connecting visual histories to new narratives and devised vocabularies which are radical and profoundly reflective of the social and political stresses of life in Pakistan.

The last sentence of the essay pessimistically reads: 'More than anything else, it is this moral quality, this human concern, this spirit of challenge expressed in visual form that one finds sadly absent in Pakistani art'.

This has been firmly repudiated by the fearless, adventurous, and highly courageous trajectory of Pakistani contemporary art. With hindsight, this author acknowledges the superiority of the human artistic force in Pakistan.

---

3. Quotation from the essay.

Identity and Exclusion: The Making of Three Nations

Rehman Sobhan

INTRODUCTION

This chapter addresses the issue of identity and exclusion in the making of the Pakistani state. The failure to resolve the issue of inclusion precipitated the Partition of India. The very same issues of unresolved identity conflicts and its exclusionary implications for state-building culminated in the emergence of an independent Bangladesh. In yet another path-setting essay, 'Identity and Violence: The Illusion of Destiny', Amartya Sen has pointed out that conflict and violence across the world and over time are sustained by the illusion of a unique identity that seeks to divide people. In contemporary times, this division has increasingly focused on religion, and has inspired the belief that we are confronted with a 'clash of civilisations'. Sen argues that this compulsion to invest people with a unique religious identity ignored the multiple identities around which the lives of most people are constructed, in the way of gender, class, profession, language, literature, sciences, morals, or politics and has thus served to provoke confrontation and violence. If we were to recognise the pluralism in our identities we would then work to construct a society that constitutes a mosaic of people who connect with each other through a network of relationships that compel people of different creeds, communities, genders, and political persuasions to live in harmony.

Among our multiple identities very few precipitate violent conflict. It is usually those identities that involve competition over resources or power, and thereby intrude into the political domain, which are likely to generate conflict. It is within the political domain that potential conflicts of identity are both accentuated and mediated. Bangladesh, as with any other society, accommodates a variety of identities, some of which have been historically conflictual. Indeed, the very genesis of Bangladesh originated in successive conflicts related to different sets of identities.

26

The first of these conflicts, associated with religious identity, led to our separation from the body politic of India and from West Bengal, and our association in the state of Pakistan. The second conflict, associated with our political, linguistic, and cultural identity, culminated in the division of Pakistan and the creation of Bangladesh.

Bangladesh's experience of two such bloody and divisive conflicts, associated with the particularisation of an identity, inspired our founding fathers to build a society that projected our pluralism rather than our singularity. We sought to build a genuinely inclusive society, which could democratise opportunities for the poor and dispossessed, as well as religious and ethnic minorities, who could participate equitably in the political processes and share in the benefits of development. This conceptualisation of our identity was captured in the declaratory principles of Bangladesh's constitution: nationalism, democracy, secularism, and socialism. Our nationalism was designed to recognise both our inclusive identity as well as our territorial boundaries. Our commitment to democracy originated in our need to build an inclusive political sphere. Our concept of socialism visualised a commitment to democratise economic opportunities for all, but particularly for the marginalised and dispossessed. Our commitment to secularism was designed to put an end to the politicisation of communal identities. This compulsion to construct an inclusive identity was inspired by our experience as citizens of a largely exclusionary Pakistani state, where identity conflicts were built into the very nature of the state and eventually precipitated its breaking up.

Identity and the Emergence of Pakistan

Pakistan's raison d'être was built around the construction of a unique identity—associated with religion. Pakistan's founding fathers visualised the Indian state as being constructed around a set of conflicting religious identities. India was perceived as a federation of religious communities—Hindu, Sikh, Muslim, Christian, Buddhist, and Parsi. This communal construct of identity was in considerable measure promoted by our British imperial masters, who believed in the political strategy of divide and rule. While religion was always an important part of the social and cultural life of the people of India, the introduction by the British of separate electorates, denominated by religion, institutionalised the communalisation of politics in imperial India. This overriding identification of religion as the basis of identity overlooked the multiple identities that go to make up a state. Culture, language, ethnicity, tribe, class, caste, gender were all no less significant identities and exercised enormous influence over the lives of the people of India. It would, for example, have been interesting to speculate on how India would have evolved if the British had introduced separate electorates on the basis of language, ethnicity, gender, or even class.

In the post-colonial era after 1947, both India and Pakistan were confronted with conflicts, where the various identities that had been overlooked in the Partition of the subcontinent asserted themselves. The Indian states were reconstructed on the basis of language and, in the case of North East India and more recently Jharkand, by tribal identity. The Indian political process, even after over 70 years of democracy, votes in some measure based on communal identities, with caste and religion often determining the selection of candidates and voting behaviour. Insurrectionary and communal violence remain a by-product of such identity conflicts. The emphasis on religious identity in determining the composition of the two states that emerged from imperial India placed the fate of the religious minorities left within the boundaries of the partitioned states as the first major problem to confront the two states. When Mohammed Ali Jinnah, the founder and first Governor General of Pakistan, argued for Pakistan as the homeland of the Indian Mussulmans, he could not have been paying close attention to the geography of India. The concept of a homeland for the Muslims of India originated in the ideological belief that religion is the dominant identity that defines a state. Jinnah invested this ideology with a political agenda, which sought to create a series of territorial enclaves where Muslims were in a majority. In his original conception of Pakistan, this included NWFP, Sindh, Punjab, and in the eastern region, Bengal as well as Assam, which were conceived as one political unit. However, the most populous of the Muslim majority areas (Punjab and Bengal/Assam) had non-Muslim populations, of which 40–45 per cent were Hindus and Sikhs in the Punjab, and Hindus, Buddhists, Christians, and Animists in Bengal and Assam. In the residual 'Hindu' majority states of India, sizeable Muslim minorities resided in the United Provinces (now known as Uttar Pradesh), Bihar, and the Central Provinces (now Madhya Pradesh), while enclaves of Muslims were indeed living for centuries in many other states in Western and Southern India.

Thus, whilst the political rhetoric behind Pakistan was built on a separatist ideology dominated by religious identity, the realities of politics, economics, and geography demanded an integrated society even within the three separated regions of India, that could accommodate the historical coexistence of peoples with different religious identities. The Muslims of India were in fact distributed all over India so that a homeland for the Muslims would have implied many homelands. The concept of Pakistan could thus, at best, seek homelands distributed across India where Muslims were at least in a numerical majority. This meant that Pakistan would have to be a multi-religious as well as a multi-lingual and multi-ethnic state. The constitutional implications of the demand for Pakistan that inspired the political negotiations for independence, mediated by successive Viceroys of India, the Lords Wavell and Mountbatten, thus developed into a reconceptualisation of the Indian state as a federation of states accommodating people with plural religions as well as other identities. The negotiations for Independence were thus not about creating separate sovereign states based on religious identity, but about the sharing of power between component federating provinces and the centre within an independent Indian federation. It was the impasse in these negotiations that led to the eventual Partition of India.

It should be remembered that Jinnah had accepted the plan of the Cabinet Mission led by Lord Stafford Cripps in 1946 for an Indian federation, which was to be constructed around three highly autonomous regions in North West India, Central India, and Eastern India. This would have given a high degree of autonomy to the two Muslim-majority areas of NWFP, Punjab, and Sindh in the North West and to Bengal and Assam in the Eastern part of India. However, within these autonomous regions, with their respective Hindu and Muslim majorities, sizeable minorities would expect to have their political, economic, and human rights guaranteed, which would have had to ensure a secular social order and the retention of an integrated economy built upon a unified social and political infrastructure. The political obligation to accommodate sizeable religious minorities on both sides of the divide should have compelled both India and Pakistan to build a secular and inclusive state where religious identity was no longer part of the instrumental dynamic of political life. The tragedy of Pakistan, and to a lesser extent India, was their failure to transcend the divisive inheritance of communalised politics. The unleashing of massive communal violence on the eve of the Partition of India directed against religious minorities on both sides of the Partition line led to one of the first encounters with ethnic cleansing in the post-war world. The massacre of religious minorities in East and West Punjab exceeded in scale similar to episodes in Bosnia, Rwanda, and Darfur. As a result of these massacres, the sizeable minority of Sikhs and Hindus who were left behind in West Punjab and urban Sindh, and controlled a significant share of the economy, were compelled to flee their ancestral homes. A similar flow of refugees entered West Pakistan from East Punjab, as well as from UP and Bihar, whose Muslim minorities feared for their lives and livelihoods. Many of the Bihari Muslims ended up in East Bengal. The two Bengals were spared the large-scale ethnic cleansing that ravaged Punjab. However, there were episodes of communal violence in Calcutta and Noakhali, which encouraged a relatively smaller exodus of Muslims from India and Hindus from East Bengal.

The Exclusionary Pakistani State

Pakistan's birth was thus caught between two tensions. Its multi-religious inheritance obligated it to establish a plural and inclusive society. Such was indeed the expectation of its founder, Mohammed Ali Jinnah, who in his historic address to the country at the time of Independence argued that Pakistanis should no longer define their identity by their religion but should embrace a more inclusive identity, which demanded that Pakistan should recreate itself as a secular society. However, as he spoke, ethnic cleansing in West Punjab was ensuring that its well-integrated population of Sikhs and Hindus would no longer find it safe to live in Pakistan. As a consequence of this massive exodus of religious minorities, West Pakistan could revert to the more exclusive identity of a Muslim state even though its founder wished it to be a multi-faith country.

In contrast to West Pakistan, East Bengal, now Bangladesh, did not cleanse itself of religious minorities. At the time of partition, 28 per cent of its population was composed of Hindus, while around 1 per cent were Buddhists and Christians. Bangladesh thus, both by choice and necessity, was compelled to build a plural society that would provide equal opportunities for people of all faiths. In practice this meant that Jinnah's hope that religion would not be the basis for defining identity was more likely to remain relevant for what was then East Bengal.

If Pakistan had evolved as a genuine democracy in which the 54 per cent of its population in the East wing could exercise a political voice commensurate with their numbers, there may still have been scope for building a more plural society, since at least a quarter of East Bengal's population were non-Muslims. However, the malign legacy of violence at its birth infected the pathology not just of West Pakistan, but the very construction of the Pakistani state. From the outset, power at the centre was usurped by an alliance of the feudal elite of West Pakistan, the armed forces, and the bureaucracy. In none of these fractions of the elite was there any representation of Bengalis or of religious minorities. This exclusive elite dominated the state and used its power to create a society that excluded Bengalis as a whole, excluded the common people of both East and West Pakistan, marginalised women and, because of its re-emphasis on religious identity, discriminated against religious minorities.

To build and sustain such an exclusionary state demanded the denial of democracy, the centralisation of power, and an inegalitarian development strategy. Such a state could never sustain popular legitimacy and thereby needed to depend on military power to coerce its citizens to accept such an exclusionary social order. However, military power in poor countries such as Pakistan lacks the resource base to suppress all of its citizens all of the time. To build and sustain this coercive apparatus and retain the loyalty of the ruling elite demands external support to provide both military assistance, as well as development aid. Such an externally dependent elite was thus compelled to barter the nationalism of the state. As and when this external patronage weakened, the survival of the state came under threat.

The cohesion of such an exclusionary and externally dependent state was always fragile. To build such a state, the commitment to sharing power between the provinces and centre, which inspired the Pakistan movement and eventually led to the Partition of India, had to be abandoned. The Bengalis, whose commitment to Pakistan was predicated on the assumption that they would exercise autonomy at the regional level and share power at the federal level, found themselves betrayed virtually from the earliest days of Pakistan. Power was centralised and the centre was monopolised by the West Pakistan-based elite. This elite used its power to extract resources from East Bengal, monopolise external aid and channelled state resources to build an inegalitarian society both socially and at the regional levels.

Such an inequitable social order demanded the suppression of democracy as well as the denial of autonomy to the provinces, and particularly to Bangladesh. But it also demanded the subordination of the democratic aspirations of the less privileged majority of the population, even in West Pakistan.

The emphasis on a religious identity was used as a facade to conceal the emerging elitist and Punjab-centric identity of the Pakistani state. The struggle for democracy, regional autonomy, social justice, secularism, and the nationalist struggle thus coalesced within the struggle for self-rule for the people of Bangladesh. The creation of our national identity thus always needs to be viewed within the historical context that led to our national liberation.

It could thus be argued that the exclusionary nature of the Pakistani state, built on a non-inclusive identity, doomed it from its birth. The 24 years of a united Pakistan were invested in an unfinished struggle by the Bengalis for democracy and for the self-rule that had originally inspired them to support the demand for Pakistan. When, in fact, the democratic process led to an overwhelming vote by the Bengalis in December 1970 for the Six-Point programme for self-rule that had been presented by the Awami League under the leadership of Bangabandhu Sheikh Mujibur Rahman, the Pakistani elite chose to challenge this electoral mandate through a declaration of war on the people of Bangladesh. The resultant genocide inspired our liberation struggle, which culminated in an independent Bangladesh.

The Exclusion of the Religious Minorities

During Pakistani rule, we witnessed not just the denial of democracy to the people of Pakistan and the denial of self-rule for Bangladeshis, but the emergence of a highly inegalitarian society, where wealth was monopolised by a narrow, West Pakistan-based elite. The religious minorities, overwhelmingly located in Bangladesh, were marginalised. They were largely excluded from the practise of administrative authority, whilst a state-centred development strategy denied access to financial resources to the minorities among the business community. Opportunities for professional advancement for the minorities were limited. At the lower level of the economic ladder, pressure to sell off land, backed by political coercion and threats of violence, led to a gradual alienation of minority properties. During the War of 1965 between India and Pakistan, a special legislation was enacted under the Enemy Properties Act, which effectively declared the Hindus of Pakistan to be enemies of Pakistan. The act was used to seize the commercial and landed properties of the Hindu community on a large scale. The progressive denial of opportunities and erosion of their property rights accentuated this sense of insecurity and alienation from the Pakistani state among minorities, which led to a steady exodus of Hindus from East Bengal to India. The share of Hindus in the population of East Pakistan came down from 28 per cent in 1941 to 21 per cent in 1951, 18.5 per cent in 1961, and 13.5 per cent in 1974 at the first census after the emergence of an independent Bangladesh.

During the period of Pakistani rule, particularly after the proclamation of martial law in 1958 and the formal ascent to power of a West Pakistani dominated elite, emphasis on a Muslim identity was reasserted. The 1962 Constitution declared that only a Muslim could aspire to be elected as President of Pakistan. The ruling elite of Pakistan were far from being ideologically inspired believers in an Islamic state and most of its leaders, ranging from Field Marshal Ayub Khan to General Yahya Khan, had largely secular appetites for power and material gain. Yet both leaders chose to exploit the name and symbols of Islam in the belief that this would legitimise their autocratic rule in the eyes of the people.

The Pakistani elite used the idea of a religious identity to undermine the Bengalis' cultural rights by proclaiming Urdu as the state language, which inspired the historic Bengali language movement of 1952. The emphasis on a religious identity was used as an instrument to marginalise the cultural identity of the Bengalis, and to divert attention from the assault on their democratic rights as well as their exclusion from economic opportunities. The final chapter of Pakistani rule ended in a genocide. Pakistan, which was born in violence inflicted on religious minorities, eventually met its end in violence aimed not just at its alienated minorities, but eventually at the majority Bengali population, most of whom were Muslims. Pakistan's communalisation of its identity has continued to haunt its society and politics long after its division. Today religious sectarianism has precipitated sever[e] violence between Sunnis and Shias and contributed to the rise of fundamentalist political forces committed to the use of force as an instrument of political change, not just in Pakistan, but in its two neighbouring countries.

Constructing the Bangladesh State

The constitution of an independent Bangladesh was built around the commitment to correct the injustices associated with the phase of Pakistani rule. Democracy, which had been denied to the people of Pakistan, was seen as the central pillar of the Bangladesh state. Secularism, which was once intended by the founder of Pakistan as a pillar of the Pakistani state, was proclaimed as another founding principle of Bangladesh. The period of Pakistani rule had witnessed a sustained assault on the secular assumptions of the founding father and had elevated a religious identity to the position of a dominant feature of the Pakistani state. It was again expected that an independent Bangladesh would attempt to put an end to the abuse of religion for political and material gain. A secular state demanded that the progressive marginalisation of minorities, whether denominated by religion or ethnic group, should end and all such identities should be submerged within a shared Bangladeshi national identity.

The Pakistani state had been built upon social, interpersonal, and regional inequality. To sustain these inequalities demanded an assault on democracy. An independent Bangladesh built upon the blood of large numbers of common people was thus bound by a duty to build a society committed to correcting the injustices and inequalities associated with the Pakistani state. A state committed to democracy, secularism, and social justice needed to ensure that it retained it distinct national identity and territorial integrity. Such a state needed to challenge the hegemonic influence of the external patrons that had supported the era of Pakistani rule. At the same time, Bangladesh had to proclaim its distinctive identity in relation to its larger-than-life neighbour, which surrounded her on all sides. Hence the commitment to nationalism as part of the distinctive identity of an independent Bangladesh.

Bangladesh's Developmental Journey Towards an Inclusive Society

After fifty years of existence as an independent entity it merits closer examination as to how far Bangladesh has managed to accommodate those multiple elements which constitute the nation within an inclusive state that democratises opportunities for all communities. This remains part of another story with its admixture of realised hopes and disappointments which have become part of the narrative of many post-colonial states.

Bangladesh has certainly emerged as something of a developmental success story compared to Pakistan. Its robust economic growth rate, particularly in recent years, has seen its GDP level of $318 billion rise above Pakistan's level of $287 billion. Bangladesh's per capita income (PCI) rose from $120 in 1973 to $1,888 in 2020. In this same period Pakistan's PCI grew from $150 (25 per cent higher than Bangladesh's) in 1973 to $1,378 in 2019. Indeed, in 2020, Bangladesh's PCI was even higher than India's ($1,877).

Over the years, Bangladesh's level of poverty has also come down from around 70 per cent in 1972 to 20 per cent in 2019. If we look at the human development indicators in 2020, Bangladesh ranked 133rd compared to Pakistan's rank of 154. In such areas as reduced fertility, longer life expectancy, higher female labour force participation, lower infant and maternal mortality, higher rates of female education and levels of women's empowerment, Bangladesh's performance has, over the years, moved well ahead of Pakistan. All these measures of economic advancement indicate that political independence has significantly enhanced Bangladesh's development potential to the extent that it is today well ahead of Pakistan in areas where it had lagged behind in 1971.

One of the less attractive features of the Bangladesh development story has been its inability to build a more egalitarian society. Such a goal had been integral to the vision of its founding father, Bangabandhu Sheikh Mujibur Rahman. But over the years, this vision has been subordinated to the goals of private enterprise-oriented growth.

Bangladesh has also remained, notwithstanding some setbacks, a more secular society than Pakistan and perhaps even compared to India today. Though much more needs to be done in this sphere to improve the condition of minorities in Bangladesh. However, Bangladesh's democratic journey has faced interruptions and its elective bodies have been exposed to elite capture. Its governance indicators are also far from satisfactory, though here again Pakistan ranks below Bangladesh in most indicators. Both countries need to address their governance and democratic deficits if they aspire to build truly inclusive societies.

A Brief Biography of Iqbal Khan (co-editor of *Pakistan Left Review*)

Mubarak Ali

Progressive writer, social and political activist, Iqbal Khan died on 26 April 1993 at the age of 60. His younger brother told me that his date of birth was also the same and the year was 1933. His family belonged to Rampur and after Partition he migrated to Pakistan and settled in Hyderabad, Sindh.

He graduated from City College Hyderabad, University of Sindh. As a student he was active in extracurricular activities and took part in organising musical, dramatic, and all-Pakistan English, Urdu, and Sindhi debates. After graduation, he left for England and did his MA in Philosophy from Birkbeck College, University of London. As he was a private person, and quite reticent about his personal life, we know very little about private affairs—he was married to an English lady and had a daughter but unfortunately the marriage did not last long, and the couple separated.

Afterwards, Iqbal Khan left for the Bahamas to teach English. During his stay there, he married a local resident. The couple came back to England and settled in Oxford where Khan taught in a community school while his wife worked at the Bahamas University.

In 1990, he decided to come back to Pakistan to create political consciousness among the youth. When I was offered the post of Resident Director at the Goethe Institute, Lahore, he replaced me as the Editor of *Mashal*, a publication NGO, where he worked until he passed away.

He remained very active during his stay in Pakistan. He started to publish a quarterly magazine, *Badalti Dunya*, which lasted only a year and halted publication due to lack of funds. He later organised a group of young people known as 'Young Thinkers'. There were weekly meetings in which he invited some of the progressive intellectual to address the youth, and from time to time, he contributed to introducing the left ideology.

Iqbal Khan also contributed articles to the daily, *Frontier Post*, which were highly appreciated in the leftist circles. Following are his works except his book titled, *Fresh Perspectives on India and Pakistan*, which is an anthology of articles written by prominent writers on India and Pakistan. The book was self-published by him in London His other books are in Urdu and all of them were published from Lahore.

- *Azadi Ki Talash*
- *Urdu aur Secularism*
- *Pakistan America Ke Chungal Mein*
- *Pakistan: Siasat, Falsafa aur Taleem*

Pakistan Left Review

Autumn, 1968

Contents

A View from the Left

Editorial

This journal is a means of protest. It is being launched out of great concern for our fellow-countrymen in Pakistan and a deep anxiety about the way the destiny of our country is being shaped. In this, our first issue, and subsequent issues, there will be much criticism of Pakistan, its society, its institutions, and even of its people. It is necessary to make it clear at the very outset that the aim of such criticism will not be to ridicule our own people, to show our superiority over them (a charge often justifiably made against those educated in the West) nor will it be to undermine the faith of our people in their country. On the contrary, our criticism will be motivated by the desire to see in Pakistan an end to the humiliations and injustices that are inflicted daily upon our people, an end to poverty and ignorance, and an end also to the greed, the vulgarity and the unreason which are perpetuated in the names of economic progress and religion by a handful of exploiters, upstarts and mullahs.

Of course, if you look at official surveys and statistics, listen to the politicians, or read those foreign journalists and authors who have a vested interest in the existing state of affairs in Pakistan, there would seem to be hardly any cause for concern. Has Pakistan not made very good progress in industrialisation? Has it not achieved an annual growth rate which is probably the highest among the underdeveloped countries? Indeed, the success of economic planning in Pakistan seems to have been such that the Chief Economist of the Planning Commission could confidently predict that the increase in the number of jobs in the coming year will be 'a little higher than the population rise'—a goal, in his own words, 'made possible by the tremendous development in every department, in every nook and corner of Pakistan!' Similar success stories are told about the health services, education, and foreign affairs. In short, as the President has said,

> In spite of the handicaps with which Pakistan began its life, the throes of birth and teething troubles, and the fact that this little infant was born in

the teeth of bitter opposition from powerful sources, this country has by the grace of Allah gone from strength to strength.

But, if the picture of Pakistan depicted by such claims and statistics is true, how can one explain the fact that, judging by the per capita annual income, Pakistan still remains, even after twenty years, one of the poorest countries in the world? Nor do figures for per capita income paint an unduly pessimistic picture; for the inequalities of income distribution are so great in Pakistan that about 66 per cent of the of the country's insurance fund and 70 per cent of its industrial effort is in the hands of twenty families!

And how can one also explain the fact (if the success story of Pakistan is correct) that even after twenty years cholera, small-pox, plague and a host of other diseases are as endemic in the country as ever; that a vast number of people remain all their lives either semi-starved or ill-nourished; that the health facilities are so abysmally inadequate that, until only three years ago, there was no more than *one doctor* for every *seven thousand* of the population, *one hospital bed* for every *three thousand*, and one nurse for *thirty thousand*? Again, the real horror of our situation is barely indicated by such statistics. These cannot tell us of the actual suffering of our people: what it must be like to suffer all one's life from poverty, disease and hunger all at the same time. For that one must go, of course, not to the economists and politicians but to poets and writers; but here is an account of an experience an American educationalist had while visiting East Pakistan:

As we were leaving East Pakistan for Lahore, I had one of those experiences which color and shape one's views about a whole country and a whole range of problems. As I was coming out of a drug store, having made my purchases, I saw the figure of a woman silhouetted in the doorway, her hand outstretched for alms. The sun was behind her, and I could not see her face, but from her shape and posture I judged her to be young, perhaps twenty. When I approached her I saw there was another reason why I could not see her face. She did not have one. The bitter ravages of disease, most likely a consequence of typhoid or dysentery, had so eroded her flesh that nose and cheeks were all gone. Nothing was left but tone, gristle, teeth, and hurt, desperate eyes. I had seen this condition before, and I have seen it many times since, but somehow this particular young woman became for me symbolic of the sufferings of a nation.

It is this, the lived experience of millions of our countrymen, that gives the final lie to all claims of 'progress' and 'economic growth'.

Nor does the 'progress' of Pakistan appear so admirable when one looks at the efforts made by our successive governments to reduce ignorance, and to provide a more viable type of education. About 80 per cent of people aged fifteen or over are still illiterate; and, what is more, in a country whose future, indeed whose very survival, depends on skilled manpower, as few as 6 per cent of the annual secondary school leavers have technical and vocational training! This situation has been described even by one government official as 'disgraceful', though this is not the only respect in which our educational system deserves such an epithet. For example, both the quality and the salaries of our teachers, from primary level to that of university, can only be described as appalling; the almost phenomenal scarcity of books on all subjects has made a mockery of our university education; school fees, and the cost of books and stationery (especially at the secondary stage) are so high that it is amazing that even a small minority of parents can keep their children at school; it is of little wonder that in these conditions teachers and students alike show an astonishing lack of personal integrity, curiosity and industry. And, to top it all, the whole system is distorted at every level by an elitist bias in favour of the moneyed and the professional classes—a bias which the educational thinking in our country (if the Report of the Commission on National Education is any guide) appears to be in favour of preserving rather than reducing!

Such is the *real* face of Pakistan: the face which, in the hot pursuit of wealth and power in which the 'leaders' of our country have been engaged ever since its inception, is conveniently ignored. This is the principal outrage against which we are raising our voices in protest. We know that twenty years is perhaps too short a time to allow for any spectacular advances, especially as the problems we are concerned with here are so enormous and so complex. But what pains and angers us—as we are sure it does any Pakistani who loves his country—is not that disease and hunger and poverty have not been totally eliminated in Pakistan; it is that, in these twenty years, even the institutional and organisational foundations have not been laid from which one day a just, rational and more prosperous society could emerge. If anything, the policies and priorities of our rulers and policymakers point in the opposite direction. The examples of some countries—notably those of Russia and China—demonstrate without any doubt that even in twenty years, a short time as it is, the conditions of living of the entire mass of our people (and not merely a handful of politicians and businessmen) could have been improved, or at least the necessary foundations for achieving this could have been secured through socialisation of wealth, and by diverting very much greater resources into the population control programmes and health and educational services. But far from trying to do this, what is actually happening in Pakistan is that, under the influence of Western economists, our 'leaders' and planners have embraced the philosophy of 'economic growth'. According to this philosophy (in the words of Dr Mahbub ul Haq, the Chief Economist of the Planning Commission) the salvation of the country lies not in 'vague ideas of a welfare state' but in creating 'surplus value'; and the suffering of the masses are more or less *necessary* hazards on the road of progress:

> It is well to recognise (says Dr Haq) that economic growth is a brutal, sordid process. There are no short cuts to it. The essence of it lies in making the labourer produce more than he is allowed to consume for his immediate needs, and to invest and reinvest the surplus thus obtained. … It is … immaterial who owns this surplus—whether the 'capitalists' as in free enterprise economy, or the 'state', as in a communist economy.

Dr Haq goes on to point out that 'the clamour for better distribution and "vague" "welfare state" ideas undermine a firm commitment to growth philosophy' and concludes:

> There exists a functional justification for inequality of income if this raises production for all and not consumption for a few. The road to eventual equalities may inevitably lie through inequalities.

Since the happiness and future of millions of people are involved, we believe it is absolutely crucial to be clear about the validity of the kind of philosophy espoused by Dr Haq and others who are guiding the fate of our nation. We are convinced that neither social justice nor social welfare need be sacrificed for the sake of economic development; and it is precisely here that the experiences of Russia and China become relevant. What these examples show is that industrial progress and improvement in living conditions can go hand in hand; and what is more that each is indispensable to the other and neither can proceed successfully without the socialisation of wealth and the means of production.

Nevertheless, let us also be on our guard against idealising the communist system too much. In alluding to the achievements of Russia and China in economic and social spheres we are only pointing to a *method* for improving the conditions of the masses in our country; we are not selling an *ideology*. It is not that we consider the question of ideology unimportant for Pakistan; far from it. The lack of an inspiring vision capable of binding men together against a common enemy or misfortune has often been pointed out, and by Pakistanis themselves. But is ideology, in the sense of a complete system of life embracing explanations about its origin and prophecies about its destiny, really needed in Pakistan? If what is required is something to fire the people with enthusiasm, to release their creative and constructive energies to the full, surely nothing can attain this better than a programme of action which promised them a life not so accursed—a life free from hunger and fear and injustices? What could better spur them to action than the full realisation of their own plight and a *real* chance of alleviating it? What, in our view, is *immediately* lacking in Pakistan is just this kind of moral consciousness—the sensitivity among the people towards each other's suffering and a sense of outrage against the forces, human and material, which are preventing them from putting an end to it.

But there is a sense of 'ideology' in which the question is relevant to our situation. For we in Pakistan are still not clear as to what kind of society we should be trying to create in our country. The concept of an Islamic society with which we started twenty-one years ago does not seem now to be as promising as it once did, and we must face anew the task of formulating the basic principles and structure of our future society.

Here indeed is our greatest opportunity. For, as it happens, the formative years of our society coincide with what might turn out to be the twilight of western civilization. Increasingly the institutions which the western civilization created, its culture, its ideas and ideals are all being questioned and criticised. Similarly, the events and researches of the past two decades have thrown much unfavourable light upon the workings of communist societies. We know now (as no one could even fifty years ago) that both the western democracies and the communist states tend to develop, in their different ways, into totalitarian and deeply conservative systems: repressive, and impervious to change and to fresh ideas; that both, in their actual workings, turn out to be little more than power-games; that neither has succeeded in producing a rational, responsible and mature society. We know also how excessive concern for progress produces a society in which human beings are treated as mere tools; how emphasis on performance, 'behaviourism', leads to human waste; how individualism results in social and moral anarchy; how the society which works by compromise loses all lustre and breeds cynicism; how competitiveness, when it becomes a philosophy of life, creates an army of failures, maladjusted and alienated persons. Because we are able to look objectively at both communism and the West we can, in transforming Pakistan from a medieval society into a modern one, go a step beyond the two 'models', provided we have the imagination and zeal to take advantage of the opportunity our historical situation offers us.

It is too much to expect (need it be said?) that such a complex and utterly altruistic task can be performed by a regime that has become corrupt to the core and whose claim to lead the nation rests on physical force and a phoney democracy. Pakistan's greatest need is for new men and women—for persons whom power and privilege has not corrupted, and who are capable of action as well as of vision. This journal is an invitation to such men and women to make their voices heard: to lay down, through these pages, an agreed programme of action, and to formulate an original concept of society. There are indeed people who are trying, both here and in Pakistan, to develop political consciousness among the masses. We believe that the work of analysis and clarification we will be carrying out in this journal will have little value if not seen by such brave people as relevant to their task, just as their work cannot achieve any lasting results without the kind of society whose idea we will be formulating in this journal. It is indeed to those who are engaged in active social and political work, as well as to the more theoretically inclined friends both at home and abroad, that the following pages, and the following numbers, of this journal are essentially addressed.

WRITE FOR THIS JOURNAL

Have you anything to say about our national institutions? If you have, send your articles, comments, etc. to *PLR* c/o Pakistan Society, University of London Union, Malet St., London, W.C.I.

An Exclusive Interview with Z. A. Bhutto

Aziz Kurtha

A. Kurtha: Since you left the Government in 1966 Mr Bhutto you seem to have criticised it on several points and policies. You have said that it is an undemocratic regime, that it is an oppressive bureaucracy etc. Why then were you in the Government for eight years? Do you think the Ayub Government made any significant progressive changes at all?

Z. Bhutto: Since opening was made, facilitating in the future certain what you may regard to be true reforms. A direction was set in the agrarian field; it may have been very little it may have been negligible, none the less from 600 landowners numerically you went to the ceiling of 500 and far over and now you can bring about further reforms; ... it was a step forward. But you are asking me the problem in a different context, you are asking me the question why I was in the Ayub Government. I give you not this one reason but this among many other reasons. I am not now discussing the merits of land reforms separately. In answer to your question I said that there was chaos in the land. I was a member of the Government also because the country welcomed it. There were promises then of bringing back democracy. I was not one of those persons who broke the previous constitution. And then at that time also there was not an opposition party. If I had thrown up my hands as a professor and protested then what contribution would I have made even inside the government to bring about certain changes in the foreign policy of the country?

A. Kurtha: As there have been so many ministers in and out of the Government how do you regard the view of the ultra left that it is in fact hopeless to expect any fundamental reforms for instance by way of complete nationalisation, basic land reform, handing back plots of land to peasants etc. through the parliamentary system and that one must now start hoping not to permeate the Ayub system but start attacking it from outside.

Z. Bhutto: It is very difficult. It is very difficult because of a number of reasons. Our traditions—we do not have a revolutionary background. That is an important consideration, our people are not I would say inherently conservative but they are excessively conservative. The bureaucracy is very conservative.

A. Kurtha: Do you think that matters? Do you not think that it is a superficial structure, only a superficial minority that is conservative and the vast majority of the population just do not know what the real situation is like anyway?

Z. Bhutto: But it comes to the same thing. The small minority that holds power in the country controls it so effectively with its power in its hands, it is so complete that it can exercise its control and perpetuate it for a long time to come, unless there are some external factors, external I mean not from outside Pakistan but external from the Government.

THE ARMY

A. Kurtha: Is there any element in the army which you think will give you support in the future?

Z. Bhutto: I cannot say. It is a very sensitive subject. I have no access to their thinking. I have no contact with them either.

A. Kurtha: Is there a general impression then that they would always toe president Ayub's line or are there some dissidents within the army?

Z. Bhutto: I really cannot say because I am not in touch with the thinking of the armed forces and nor is that possible, and nor have I made the effort to find out because my work is in the political field and I have to do my political work.

A. Kurtha: But surely the two things are rather combined in Pakistan. I mean politics and the army are not easily divisible in our country are they?

Z. Bhutto: But in any case as I said I have not made the effort to find out.

A. Kurtha: You have mentioned the need for reforms and particularly those relating to property and to ownership of land. Now we read Dr Mahbub ul Haq's recent report, which as you know says 79 per cent of the country's insurance funds and 66 per cent of its total industrial effort is in the hands of about twenty families. Now what would you do about this if you were President? How would you go about changing that situation? Or do you think the situation is beyond change?

Z. Bhutto: But this also facilitates change; because when there is so much concentration in a few hands it is easier if you want to bring about reforms to bring about the change also. If it is diffused it is sometimes more difficult.

A. Kurtha: I hope that is a rationalisation of the situation and not a justification.

Z. Bhutto: No—that is not a justification. It is sheer blunder it is ... capitalism. It does not exist anywhere else in the world. I am not justifying the system but I am also not pessimistic. You have to meet a situation as it exists. You cannot hope for the ideal and want it to work. For instance when we don't have freedom of the press we can't just go home saying 'What a pity we don't have freedom of the press' and then lock ourselves up. O.K. so if we don't have freedom of the press we have to overcome the problem by communicating to the people through other means. So also if this is the situation into which the country has been brought then we can't just become alarmist and say that the country is being plundered, the nation is being sapped by robber barons—some of them millionaires with fortunes comparable to those of multi-millionaires in the U.S. You judge a country not by its millionaires, you judge a country by the condition of the poor. So from that point of view it is a depressing situation. You must see the situation and try to overcome it. So if there is a reformative Government in some ways it will find it easier to level the wealth which is concentrated in a few hands.

A. Kurtha: Turning to the forthcoming elections in 1970. Do you hope to stand as an independent candidate for the Democratic Front or do you hope to unite the other opposition parties behind you?

Z. Bhutto: But you assume that I am going to be a candidate and I have not given you any reason for making that assumption. I can say yes or no about my candidature, and I can be evasive. But as far as your question is concerned the decision is partly mine and partly it is not mine. In one sense I can say yes I am going to contest the election and I am a candidate as there were some last time, like Mr Bashir. On the other hand I must say no if my effort is to offer a united opposition. That decision does not remain mine alone. I must try to seek a consensus.

KASHMIR

A. Kurtha: In your small book called, 'The United Nations and Peacekeeping operations' (1965), you seem rather pessimistic about the role of the United Nations (UN) in maintaining peace. Are you then very pessimistic about the role of the UN in ever being able to bring about a settlement of the Kashmir problem?

Z. Bhutto: Well I feel that the UN has to be radically reformed before it can play an effective role in bringing about peace. Today the role of the UN is only to freeze the *status quo* and in this way it is a deception against those who repose hope and confidence in it. What is happening to us has a striking similarity to what is in the Middle East. So much so that the same man with the same briefcase is running around in the Middle East as came running around to Pakistan in 1965. This problem of Kashmir is affected by many things. For instance, the East-West detente the fact that the UN is being exploited by the Great Powers behind the curtain of the Security Council, so that they can co-operate to extend their hegemony … it is a loaded question.

A. Kurtha: Now I would also like to ask you one or two questions which you were not able to answer after your speech at Conway Hall in July.

Z. Bhutto: Now it is one thing to have an interview and quite another to conduct an interrogation—to be subjected to a cross-examination.

A. Kurtha: I have no intention of cross-examining you. However, during your speech at Conway Hall you said that you were concerned about Vietnam; that most foreign policy issues could be related back to Vietnam and that the people of Vietnam were fighting for Asia. Now if you really are so concerned about this why do you say nothing about recognising the National Liberation Front [NLF] or the Democratic Republic of Vietnam [DRV] as the only spokesmen for the Vietnamese people?

Z. Bhutto: Wherever I go I speak about Vietnam I regard that to be the most cardinal problem (in foreign policy).

A. Kurtha: Will you therefore go to the extent of recognising the NLF or the DRV?

Z. Bhutto: Well naturally when I speak about the sacrifices of the Vietnamese people I speak of their sacrifices because the other party is not really struggling against them, it is the U.S.A. which is struggling against them.

A. Kurtha: O.K. We will leave that. We also know that the Pakistani delegation in SEATO has consistently abstained on the issue of Vietnam. It has not voted for resolutions condemning the so called aggression of the Vietnamese.

Z. Bhutto: You know this is an absurd situation—I mean the view that we are making a contribution to world peace by taking a point of view which is not taken by other nations in SEATO. That is an eye-wash. It is not only an eye-wash it is just a big joke. We are not making any contribution because the U.S. does what it wants to outside SEATO without consulting the South East Asian Treaty Organisation. Secondly even within SEATO if a dissident voice is heard it makes no difference at all to the situation. Now this is not only a consolation but it is in fact a deception to the people of Pakistan. We are only endangering our interest unilaterally by remaining in SEATO. Recently Arshad Husain has said that in these things there is not need for a *Talak* (divorce) that this a romance which can be terminated gradually. I am very pained to hear a Foreign Minister of a Muslim country saying this. It is a very absurd thing to say. If we indulge in these types of jokes the country is going to face far greater chaos.

A. Kurtha: Would you say then that we ought to quit SEATO immediately?

Z. Bhutto: I said it long ago.

DEPARTURE FROM FOREIGN OFFICE

A. Kurtha: As you know rumours have circulated that you were ousted as Foreign Minister largely due to American pressure on the President.

Z. Bhutto: I was not ousted, nor was I thrown out, nor was I kicked out. I resigned; three times, before the Tashkent Agreement. After the ceasefire I put in my resignation but not in a letter because obviously in a war-time situation you do not send letters. The enemy is sitting on your territory and there is no precedent for that. But I told Ayub Khan that as soon as the situation returns to normal and the war ends, I would like to go, and he said that if you do that it will be a betrayal. Then again after Tashkent in February I told him I would like to go but he said you cannot because as long as I am President you will always occupy the highest position; but I said I am not interested in positions. I did not want to do anything precipitous. The enemy was on our territory. God forbid if as a consequence of that certain complications had arisen and the Indians had occupied Lahore. The full blame would have gone on me. It is all very well now to say 'why did you not make some declarations at that time'—because at that time the Indians were fearing me, if I had gone from the scene they would have been encouraged and others would have been encouraged to do something. The Chinese and all the other Great Powers were all considering my role and the same tables would have been turned on me. You must therefore take everything into account. So there was no question of my being ousted or thrown out or kicked out. I resigned myself, but at the same time there *was* great American pressure on the President.

A. Kurtha: Was this American antagonism towards you due to any personal differences with any foreign politicians?

Z. Bhutto: Personal incidents do not come into policies of Great Powers. The question was about my policies, that is to say my wanting to be on good terms with China, and a desire to take on an independent foreign policy line on Kashmir, to take a position like a brave and heroic nation should take instead of talk, talk, talk and passing resolutions at the UN and again further deception etc. etc.—and so they (the Americans) came to know that this man and the policies that he is pursuing are of such a nature that they are not in our interest. So there is no question of any personal differences, and if on personal differences a Government changes its foreign minister then that Government does not deserve its sovereignty.

CHINA

A. Kurtha: Coming to something rather different, there has been talk among the National Awami Party members that the relationship with China, this flirtation with China, is no more than a facade; it is there to mesmerise most of the opposition into thinking that this is part of a socialist alliance. Is it in your opinion anything more than a facade?

Z. Bhutto: Some people might want to make it a facade but the fact is that the door has been opened. You may open it with one intention someone else may open or maintain it with another intention, but the objective conditions are then given an opening. Some people may take a cynical approach, other people may take an opportunistic approach but the objective conditions have been facilitated.

A. Kurtha: What was *your* position on China, how do *you* see the relationship with China?

Z. Bhutto: I have always seen it as a relationship between two sovereign states. I do not go beyond the social structure of countries because I do not believe in interference in another country's foreign policy. At the same time I believe that China's policies are based on principles of socialism and those principles of socialism are valid. So from that point of view the fact that it happens to be a socialist state contributes to the valid decisions that it takes on certain matters. It would not have taken the same position on self-determination on Kashmir as it has if it was not a socialist state. There are certain positions that it has to take on the basis of its ideology. Like we are Muslims we have to take certain decisions because of our ideology on certain matters.

A. Kurtha: Your reference to socialism worries me now and again. Because, for instance I heard you speak at your convention in Conway Hall ... You said there that our type of capitalism in Pakistan is not even a humanitarian type of capitalism. Now do you seriously think that there can ever be a humanitarian type of capitalism?

Z. Bhutto: No—not at all. But you also must get out of the rut of an academic approach and taken into account a political speech made by a practical politician in the political arena. He has to see his audience, he has to see the kind of people there are. He has to see that he is in a foreign country. But what I have written on the subject of socialism is quite clear, but that is for internal education. You must not look at it from a very narrow and limited point of view. I didn't even go into the details of the subject. I just made a passing reference to it.

A. Kurtha: Well—the reason why I brought this up was that I saw some basic contradictions in what you said at the meeting.

Z. Bhutto: Which contradictions?

A. Kurtha: Well—this was one (re: humanitarian capitalism!)

Z. Bhutto: No—that was not contradiction. What I was saying was that these people, these criminals are not even practising capitalism. Theirs is a form of capitalism of 1848 or 1890. They are not even following the American or British form of capitalism—they are worse culprits.

BASIC DEMOCRACIES

A. Kurtha: The other point that seemed to me contradictory was that you said that Basic Democracies [BDs] is another word for fascism. Well I thought to myself this is a very progressive thing to say. But on the other hand the inconsistency is that if you feel that one part of the system is fascist then are you not necessarily strengthening that system by saying that you are a candidate who will fight an election along the lines laid down by that system? More than that, how could you ever acquiesce, for eight years, in a system one part of which was in fact fascist?

Z. Bhutto: The point is this, that originally the Basic Democracies were not meant to be what they have turned out to be. In the beginning Ayub Khan said that he wanted a system to replace political parties. He did not want to give it the political responsibility which it has now got. He did not want a vacuum by abolishing political parties. He wanted to replace it by a system where people take interest and take part in local development and keep the administration under control and check. That was the original concept of it.

A. Kurtha: Did not a man of your intelligence see the potential of repression in the whole concept of BDs?

Z. Bhutto: At that time the President was also simultaneously of the view that he would restore democracy in the sense of its real restoration. He, and Iskander Mirza more so, were really thinking in terms of weeks and months. There was also American pressure that there should be some kind of democracy but when the Americans saw that this was fine and dandy then the pressure was withdrawn—on the contrary they then encouraged this thing. So it started as one thing and ended as quite a different thing. As far as your second point is concerned on the basis of hair-splitting I would say 'yes', how can you approve and reprove! But the point is, either we pick up the gun and go into the mountains like the Baluchs have done or else we have some political activity within the confines. We don't like the game but this is the only game he wants to play. Now if we don't play this game we don't exhaust him either. A dictator is not removed by democratic means, by polls. You eat into him. You chop into him and this is one of the opportunities that is given to eat into him and chop at him. If Miss Jinnah had not contested that 1965 election he would have been in a much stronger position. Now he is in a much weaker position. Slowly, slowly there is an erosion taking place. We know what the technical results will be but an election is not just a matter of winning or losing. In these circumstances it is also educating the people. It gives us an opportunity to say things and do things which you could not do in normal circumstances. It is an opportunity to weaken a dictator, to make him run from pillar to post, to unnerve him and his administration and then contribute to the process. There are some in the mountains like the Baluchs: there are others that are doing this. If we just say one or the other we either shut ourselves and all forget our responsibilities because it is hopeless and you must boycott (the election), and the other alternative is just fighting. In that case they are also finished, you are also finished, and the perpetuation of tyranny continues. So there has to be this combination of factors in the situation.

ELECTION OR REVOLUTION?

A. Kurtha: People who are really interested in a revolutionary change in Pakistan think that you represent a posture of compromise and that you have been too long a diplomat to really understand that the system that exists there is something that cannot be compromised with.

Z. Bhutto: How am I representing a compromise?

A. Kurtha: Well by fighting a system along the lines that it has laid down, that is a compromise.

Z. Bhutto: What do you want me to do?

A. Kurtha: Go into the fields as a revolutionary.

Z. Bhutto: Why not go to London and lecture?

A. Kurtha: No, be in Pakistan but represent a revolutionary body and say that you will not fight the election. Boycott the election.

Z. Bhutto: But he would love it!

A. Kurtha: But you would lose it anyway.

Z. Bhutto: But he would love a boycott. With a boycott what will happen is that he will take over the greater reins of authority. He will control further papers—the one or two that are left over. He will demoralise the people. He will externally say, 'look what a great hero I am, there was nobody in the field!' People outside would not know the details of things. He would have greater Western support and that would suit him ideally. I think it would only strengthen the forces of tyranny and oppression, there is no doubt of it. As far as revolutionary traditions are concerned we don't have a revolutionary tradition in our past. To start one is a different thing. But historically we don't have it. You may give me one historical example here and there, but I am talking of a real revolutionary tradition, and you know even at the time of the Khilafat Movement we preferred to go to Afghanistan rather than to fight at home. But as far as risks are concerned I think I have taken more risks than anyone else. I have used stronger language than anyone else. I have suffered more than anyone else as regards losses of every nature. Now this in itself is a revolution. Because I have the lead in many things; I went out, I addressed the people in Multan where there were 5 lakh people. We went to Khanabad. There were attacks and attempts on my life. There were in fact three attempts on my life. They first tried to get me bumped off in a jeep accident, then they sent Goondas to kill.

A. Kurtha: Who are 'they'?

Z. Bhutto: Well I wouldn't like to say who 'they' were but it is obvious who they are. I don't know their names but I know that they can only come from one source. So the whole gauntlet has been covered. So I think I have done my duty, my conscience is clear—if you people are not satisfied, it is unfortunate.

A. Kurtha: It is not just that we are not satisfied, we think you have a tremendous potential which you are not exploiting.

Z. Bhutto: I am doing my very best. In politics you need team work. Other things you can do alone, you can be an author or a lawyer alone. But in politics you need people and I am trying to build that up. I am trying to broaden my base; I am trying all the time to bring people out. Now things are moving.

A. Kurtha: So you don't think that by going along with the existing system you are necessarily strengthening it by making it appear respectable and liberal?

Z. Bhutto: I don't deny that danger, but taking everything into account if we can really muster up a massive support of the opposition, if we can put up a formidable fight then there are other possibilities also, which I would not like to talk about here. Once things start going many other things open up. I know the dice are loaded against me and that there are many things against me—the bureaucracy, the money, the big business. But there is also a gradual decomposition (of the system).

EAST PAKISTAN

A. Kurtha: We know that now all the opposition parties support the move for autonomy for East Pakistan. But how would you yourself try to ameliorate the situation? Have you any definite plans or approaches that you would like to tell us about?

Z. Bhutto: You can really only know that when you are in power. You have to assess to what extent the damage has been done, to what extent the disparity has increased and how the disparity can be reversed. Immediately I would strengthen the East Pakistan Industrial

Development Corporation. Secondly there would be certain immediate measures taken in relation to banking and other matters. I don't want to go into details here because again elections are coming. But there is, of course, the problem of public transport and natural resources. Once we have taken some immediate steps we will have a little time to consolidate and look into the situation. Some of the steps which I have in mind even a capitalist Government would take but, that would not be an answer, as this is not an answer. I think many things can be done in the economy to bring about a situation where disparity can be removed. We can bring about capital formation on the right lines—and this system of credit formation is not really capital formation. The way it comes and goes, it is not being ploughed into the country. The people are not benefitting from it.

A. Kurtha: At your meeting in Conway Hall some people were shouting that Assam is a part of East Pakistan. What is your opinion on that?

Z. Bhutto: I have already written a long article on that I don't want to repeat all that here.

TASHKENT

A. Kurtha: On Tashkent you have already said that you can't tell us about your differences with the President—But do you think the Russians are in fact violating the Tashkent Agreement by supplying arms to India although they are doing the same to us now. Did they first violate the agreement by supplying arms to India, after the war?

Z. Bhutto: You must take the agreement in its totality. There was a deadlock over its progress and that was inevitable, but now that the Soviet Union has given arms to Pakistan, I would like to see what the nature of these arms is and whether it is a long-term agreement and the conditions attached to it. Because we need arms and I would not like to say anything that would jeopardise that possibility—to say more would raise unnecessary complications.

INDIA

A. Kurtha: Do you think that by sticking to our position on Kashmir, that is, supporting the right of self-determination which, needless to say,

I do support, we are jeopardising our relationship with India to such an extent that it is not in fact worthwhile?

Z. Bhutto: I can never be of that opinion till all the cows come home.

A. Kurtha: What about the view that there is a potential of a third World Power if we had an alliance with India?

Z. Bhutto: There is no such potential of a third World Power. Take first things first. First you must do justice to your own people before you go to the moon, and I will not have the people of Jammu and Kashmir sitting in bondage, and coming to a settlement with a country which keeps the people of Jammu and Kashmir in oppression.

A. Kurtha: Finally, if you were in power as President, how would you view a revolutionary movement in Pakistan which would not simply support your party or any other party but would be intent on bringing about complete and real socialism, as opposed to the half-hearted measures which are laid down in your manifesto.

Z. Bhutto: My manifesto is not a holy book and it has its limitations in terms of time and with time there will be a corresponding change made in our approach and thinking. Our efforts would be directed towards increasing the pace towards progress.

A. Kurtha: How would you view people who are trying to increase the pace by boycotting the party-system and hoping to start or join some revolutionary movement in the field as opposed to trying to fight an election?

Z. Bhutto: Well—if they have something to quarrel about and get into the field. You are assuming we would have a situation which would call for a revolution. I do not take that assumption into account, I believe we will do things which will satisfy the bulk of our people. Of course there may be one or two people there wanting to quarrel all the time, there may be some anarchists who are not satisfied with anything—but we will get the overwhelming support of the people and if again the people are not satisfied we will move again according to the people's wishes because they are supreme; and if we don't then we will be thrown out.

An Open Letter to Zulfikar Ali Bhutto

Tariq Ali

Dear Mr Bhutto:

This is a frank letter so please don't take it as a personal attack on yourself. I am more interested in ideas rather than personalities. You have formed a new political party; you have presumably drafted and approved its manifesto and you have declared that your new party is a socialist party.

As a result a lot of interest has been aroused among many Pakistani socialists living abroad in self-imposed exile as to what this new party is all about.

We would like to ask you the following questions:

Why was it felt necessary to found a NEW party when the National Awami Party [NAP] is already in existence? Could it be, perhaps, that the reason for this was that the NAP was not keen on the ideas of using Islam to deceive and fool the people? For too long in Pakistan Islam has become a vested interest wedded to material values. For too long Islam has been used by politicians as the answer to every problem. As socialists we are freethinkers. We do not believe that a supernatural 'Being' can in anyway be a substitute for a real socialist struggle. Therefore, we regard all this talk of 'Pakistan's foundations resting firmly on an ideology defined by the principles of Islam ...' as a load of hypocritical cant. A new socialist party in the year 1968 can have no truck with religious hypocrisies. Religion has misled our people for too long. As socialists it is our duty to demystify the whole bogus process. Of course, it is not an easy job; of course it requires courage and determination; but then that is what socialism is all about.

We also find your answers to questions regarding your participation in the Ayub Government from 1958 till 1966 extremely unsatisfactory. It is no good telling us that things went wrong. It is much more complicated than that. How could any socialist co-operate with a military regime? Of course, the system which prevailed before martial law was corrupt in

58

every sense of the word, but was martial law any better? We say: NO. It was worse because of its repression and curtailment of civil liberties. It was a hundred times worse because it tried to put the clock backwards. Basic Democracies were always meant to be a farce. For you to pretend that they could have been different is to deceive yourself. Why did the Ayub regime become 'fascist' only after you left? It is facile to think that the presence or absence of personalities can in any way alter the structure of the regime in which they participate. We agree that the 'destiny' of Pakistan is in the hands of a few families but then this was true even when you were in the Ayub cabinet. Why did we not hear a murmur of protest in those days when students were being butchered on the streets of Dacca and Karachi? Admittedly you were responsible for moving Pakistan's foreign policy 'leftwards' but can we presume that Ayub did not support this 'change'?

No, Comrade Bhutto, we are not yet convinced that either you or your party are socialist. Your manifesto talks about 'mixed economy'—this is simply a social-democratic stance. Do not confuse it with socialism. Socialism, as Marx envisaged it, is about ownership and control by the workers and peasants. In a socialist society there is no place for a 'private sector'. And you talk about a 'neutral' foreign policy. Neutral between whom? Between the United States and Vietnam? Between the United States and China? NO! There is no such thing as 'neutrality'. It was always a bogus concept advanced by countries who retained their capitalist economy, who were dependent on American imperialism and who at the same time wanted aid from the Soviet Union. We do not want this fake 'neutrality'. In the struggle today between U.S. imperialism and the liberation movements we would like a Socialist Pakistan to be on the side of the oppressed, giving them support moral and material.

These are just two main objections. There are many more and we can discuss them later, but till then let's open a discussion on the nature of socialism in Pakistan. A free and wide-ranging discussion in which all socialists can take part and which will go a long way towards uniting the many socialist Pakistanis living abroad in exile. An exile, let me add, which is only temporary. Some day we will return, but while we are abroad we should clarify our theories and an important part of the clarification would be an answer from you.

Yours sincerely,
Tariq Ali

* * * * *

Note: The interview with Mr Bhutto and Tariq Ali's article went to Press before Mr Bhutto's arrest and detention. Whilst criticism of Mr Bhutto's past record must remain as must also disagreement with some of his proposed policies, we would uphold his right to make his views known. Consequently, we deplore his recent arrest together with other members of the opposition.

We would condemn even more strongly the repressive and brutal measures taken against students and other demonstrators in West Pakistan in recent weeks. It is obvious that the more oppressive the present regime becomes the more violent will be the reactions against it.

Book Reviews

Anwar Khan

Gandhi: A Study in Revolution by Geoffrey Ashe (London: Heineman, 1968).

Non-Violence and Aggression by H. J. N. Horsburgh (Oxford U.P., 1968).

In the wake of a national hysteria about Commonwealth citizens allegedly reversing the colonial strategy by immigration it may seem ironic, if not hypocritical, that a British Premier should recently unveil a statue commemorating the centenary of, perhaps, the greatest rebel in the unforgotten Empire. Churchill after all had said that 'Gandhi and all that he stands for, must be crushed'. But as Mr Ashe's absorbing biography shows us, Gandhi was educated at the Inner Temple in London, and ever since those early days he maintained such a benevolent view of British imperial motives that one could almost surmise that his famous steel-rimmed spectacles were supplied, rose-tinted, under the National Health Service. But without his benign assumptions posterity may never have known his doctrine of *satyagraha* (non-violent resistance, or more correctly, Truth-Force).

Gandhi was an astute politician but he was also, in quintessence, a spiritual leader. Many of his Hindu followers saw him as an avatar, and this may explain why despite several setbacks in his campaign for swaraj (home rule) his leadership was never really in question. The author has produced a solid, well-written but largely uncritical, account of the Mahatma's personal and political life covering almost everything from his peculiar sex life to his less well-known struggles against racism in South Africa. The book also, briefly, traces the history of the Muslim League and describes Quaid-i-Azam in the following terms: 'Austere and arrogant, upper-crust, well dressed in European style, Jinnah did not suggest a demagogue. Yet possibly he was helped by being so wildly unlike Gandhi.' The Mahatma, we are shown, was quite amicable with Muslims in his early days but his feelings about the nascent nation

61

which was fighting to be delivered from the womb of Mother India, is summed up as follows: 'The demands Jinnah (had first) put were only a beginning. A new word, a new slogan was being uttered, so monstrous to him (Gandhi) that his mind reeled from it in helpless dismay: *Pakistan.*'

For a more thorough and critical analysis of Gandhi's non-violent philosophy and its implications and prospects today, we must turn to Mr Horsburgh's work. The author begins with 'a critique of armed force as an instrument of justice' and goes on to examine the claims of Gandhian *satyagraha* as a morally preferable method of achieving the ends to be achieved by warfare. It contains a fascinating discussion of the relation of ends and means and demonstrates clearly that 'means dominate ends in Gandhi's thought'. This crucial feature combined with the Mahatma's persistent attempts to create a favourable dialogue with his opponents tends to show that whilst his techniques were revolutionary his objectives were not. The book outlines the ethico-religious foundations of the doctrine, traces its development and illustrates certain forms of action like strikes and boycotts (but not generally sit-ins) which fitted into Gandhi's non-violent campaign. But Mr Horsburgh seems to forget that Gandhi permitted violence when the alternative was cowardice and in 1947 he even envisaged war with Pakistan if that was 'the only way left'. The author writes lucidly and has produced a highly interesting work, but I fear that he is over-optimistic when he states that 'a resolute non-violent community can hope to emerge successfully from even a protracted struggle against a ruthless opponent'; and as Arthur Koestler suggested through his main character in *Darkness at Noon*, Gandhi's philosophy of absolute non-violence may, unwittingly, have hindered further liberation struggles because 'such chasteness in the choice of means leads to political impotence'.

* * * * *

The Indo-Pakistani Conflict by **Russell Brines (London: Pall Mall, 1968).**
Pakistan's Relations with India by **G. W. Choudhury (London: Pall Mall, 1968).**

The books by Messrs. Brines and Choudhury have several features in common a viz. the subject matter, the Pall Mall Press, the partisanship. Mr Brines is a very pro-Indian journalist and the blurb tells us, unabashedly, that he was able to observe the 1965 Indo-Pakistan conflict 'from the Indian side'. Add to this the later assertion that 'for material on the (same) hostilities the author has depended primarily upon sources that must remain anonymous', and you have the makings of an almost propagandist work which eludes verification. In the first 300 pages he outlines the background of the conflict and reviews among other things, the granting of independence and the ensuing troubles in 1947, the problem of Kashmir, the Cold War and the Chinese Attack on India. The chapter on the partition of India is written in the same racy journalese which characterises the book as a whole. He refers to the 'discipline' of British rule and regrets 'the hasty and bloody amputation of British India'.

The lengthy discussions of 'Soviet policy' and 'Peking policy' reflect an apparent obsession with 'communist expansion' and allegedly ubiquitous 'infiltration'. Describing the 1965 hostilities as 'the biggest tank-battle since World War II', he deprecates Pakistani strategy and claims that contemporary anti-government demonstrations in India were communist inspired. Mr Brines has apparently visited Pakistan but is content with making the most ludicrous generalisations like, 'The Bengalis' (in the East) are small rice-eating men from humid river and jungle areas ... (and the West Pakistanis ... are big-boned wheat eaters from the dry plains and deserts' (p. 232). Does the author know that the Amazon jungle and the Sahara Desert are *not* included within Pakistan's frontiers?

Professor Choudhury's experience as a Pakistani delegate to the United Nations seems to colour the views expressed in his book. But he writes clearly and concisely and states, somewhat truistically, that Indo-Pakistan relations since 1947 have 'pivoted mainly on the issue of Kashmir'. He asserts that India has retracted its own original pledges in denying a plebiscite to the people of Kashmir and this much seems common ground between him and Mr Brines. In an interesting chapter on religious minorities he expresses deep concern over religious persecution but seems unduly critical of (Indian) secularism as such.

We are at least spared an itinerary of the paths followed by the forces of both India and Pakistan during the 1965 war. As neither Mr Choudhury nor other reporters were allowed anywhere near the front-line, his remarks could only have amounted to the guess-work espoused by contemporary journalists. Nevertheless, it is in his chapter on 'Armed Conflict, 1965' that Professor Choudhury's qualities as a professional apologist for the government are clearly revealed. For instance, nothing whatever is said about the outcry and the many demonstrations against the Government which followed the conclusion of the Tashkent

Agreement. We are only told that there 'were expressions of dismay and frustration ... But when Ayub explained its significance to the nation, the movement subsided'!

It may be appropriate here to make a general point about the 1965 war. Whatever honourable ultimate objectives it was supposed to achieve, the fact that it was a tragedy in terms of the suffering caused is surely platitudinous. But having once embarked on that course it was (paradoxically) an even greater pity to call a halt so soon after the Russian conciliatory initiative on September 7th [1968]. This is because not only might the end result have been even more favourable for us but the true significance and horror of a sub-continental war would once and for all have been driven home to the bulk of the population. As it is, and as Mr Choudhury knows, the conflict has evoked if anything only rosy reminiscences about bravery among those who were comfortably remote from the line of combat.

It is a pity that he only makes fleeting references to the sufferance of the two States' economies under the strain of intermittent conflicts, because in countries where the vast majority of the population is (kept!) perpetually poor, if not poorer, the real need is to abandon revival of mutual hostilities and to strive for a common social revolution.

Ethics and Revolution: Extracts from Bengali and Urdu translations

Herbert Marcuse

নীতি এবং বিপ্লব

হারবার্ট মারকিউম

নীতি এবং বিপ্লবের মধ্যে কি সম্পর্ক তা আলোচনা করার জন্য আমি এই প্রশ্নটি করতে চাই : যুক্তি দিয়ে কি বোঝান যায় যে বিপ্লব ন্যায়সঙ্গত, শুভ এবং এমনকি বোধহয় প্রয়োজনীয়? এই যৌক্তিকতা শুধু রাজনৈতিক দিক থেকে নয় (কোন বিশেষ স্বার্থের সুবিধার জন্য) নীতিশাস্ত্রের দিক থেকেও প্রয়োজন। অথবা অন্যভাবে বলতে গেলে মানুষের অবস্থার এবং কোন ঐতিহাসিক মুহূর্তে তার সুপ্ত সম্ভাবনার দিক থেকে বিচার করলে কি বিপ্লবের সমর্থন করা যায়? অর্থাৎ নীতিশাস্ত্রের ভাষায় 'ন্যায়' এবং 'শুভ' ব্যবহার করা হবে রাজনৈতিক ও সামাজিক আন্দোলনের অর্থে, এবং সেইজন্য এই অনুমান করা হবে যে এই ধরণের আন্দোলনের নৈতিক মূল্যবিচার (যার সংজ্ঞা দেওয়া প্রয়োজন) ব্যক্তিগত বিচারের এবং পছন্দের বাইরে। এই অনুমান অনুযায়ী 'শুভ' এবং 'ন্যায়' এর অর্থ হবে সাধারণতন্ত্রে সুখ ও স্বাধীনতার প্রতিষ্ঠা করা এবং উন্নতি করা অথবা প্রসার করা, তা সে যে প্রকারের সরকারের দ্বারাই হোক না কেন। এই প্রাথমিক সংজ্ঞা যুক্তভাবে ব্যক্তির ও সমষ্টির মঙ্গল বোঝায়। এই চিন্তাধারার মধ্যে প্রাচীন রাজনৈতিক দর্শনের এক অবহেলিত মূল আদর্শকে খুঁজে পাই, যথা সরকারের উদ্দেশ্য শুধু মানুষকে চরম স্বাধীনতা দেওয়া নয় নয়, তাকে চরম সুখ দেওয়াও — বলতে গেলে তার জন্য এক ভয় এবং দুঃখ বর্জিত জীবন, এক শান্তির জীবন প্রতিষ্ঠা করা।

এখন আমাদের সামনে এক অস্বস্তিকর প্রশ্নের বাধা, যেমন কে এবং কোন অধিকারে সাধারণতন্ত্রের সমষ্টির স্বার্থ নির্ধারিত করে এবং সেইথেকে ব্যক্তির স্বাধীনতা এবং সুখের পরিধি ও সীমা নির্ণয় করে? সাধারণতন্ত্রের নামে ও পক্ষ থেকে কে স্থির করে ব্যক্তির কতটুকু স্বাধীনতা এবং সুখের ত্যাগ সমাজের দাবী? কারণ যতক্ষণ না পর্যন্ত সমষ্টির এবং ব্যক্তির মঙ্গল একরূপ হয়, ব্যক্তির মঙ্গলকে বলপূর্বক সাধারণের মঙ্গলের অনুরূপ করা হবে। উপরোক্ত প্রশ্ন করিলে আমরা আরেক সমান গুরুত্বপূর্ণ এবং অস্বস্তিকর সমস্যার সম্মুখীন হই। যদি ধরেও নিই স্বাধীনতা শুধু ব্যক্তিগত ব্যাপার নয়, এবং তাহা সমাজের দ্বারা বা যে রাষ্ট্রে বাস করি তার দ্বারা নির্ধারিত, তাহলেও 'সুখ' সম্বন্ধে আমরা কি করতে পারি? ব্যক্তির সুখ কি তার নিজস্ব ব্যাপার, একান্ত ব্যক্তিগত বিষয় এবং সেরকমই থাকা উচিত, এই চরম মত কিন্তু কিছুক্ষণ চিন্তা করলেই আর সমর্থন করা যায় না। এমন অনেক প্রকারের ব্যক্তিগত সুখ আছে যা কোন সাধারণতন্ত্রই সহ্য করতে পারে না। এটা সম্পূর্ণভাবে সম্ভব এবং ঘটনা থেকে আমরা জানি এটা সত্য - যে হিটলারের নির্যাতন করার বন্দীশালায় যারা সর্বাপেক্ষা জঘন্য অত্যাচারী ছিল তারা নিজেদের কর্মে বেশ সুখীই ছিল। বহু নজীরের মধ্যে এটা একটা যেখানে আমরা দ্বিধাহীনভাবে বলতে পারি যে ব্যক্তিগত সুখের ব্যাপারে কোন ব্যক্তি নিজের বিচারক হতে পারে না। এখানে আমরা অনুমান করে নিই এক বিচারক মণ্ডলী বা আদালত যার অধিকার আছে (প্রকৃতপক্ষে অথবা নৈতিকভাবে) ব্যক্তির সুখের সংজ্ঞা দেওয়ার।

65

এবার প্রারম্ভিক বক্তব্য পরিষ্কার করে বলার পর 'বিপ্লব' বলতে আমি কি বুঝি তা আমাকে ব্যাখ্যা করতে দিন। বিপ্লব বলতে আমি বুঝি সামাজিক এবং রাজনৈতিক গঠনের পরিবর্তন করার উদ্দেশ্যে কোন এক সামাজিক শ্রেণীর অথবা আন্দোলনের দ্বারা কোন আইনসঙ্গতভাবে প্রতিষ্ঠিত সরকার এবং সংবিধানের উচ্ছেদ সাধন। সব সামরিক অভ্যুত্থান, প্রাসাদ-বিপ্লব এবং নিবারণকারী প্রতিবিপ্লব (যেমন ফ্যাসিস্টবাদ এবং নাৎসীবাদ) এই সংজ্ঞার সীমা বহির্ভূত কারণ তারা সমাজের মূল আকৃতি এবং গঠনের পরিবর্তন সাধিত করে না। বিপ্লবকে এইভাবে ব্যাখ্যা করলে আমরা এই বলে আর একটু অগ্রসর হতে পারি যে এই ধরনের আমূল এবং গুণগত পরিবর্তন বলতে বলপ্রয়োগ বোঝাবে। শান্তিপূর্ণ বিপ্লব, যদি সেরকম কিছু থাকে বা সম্ভব হয়, কোন সমস্যার সৃষ্টি করে না। সুতরাং আমরা শুরুতেই যে প্রশ্ন করেছি তাকে নূতনভাবে সাজিয়ে জিজ্ঞাসা করতে পারি : মানুষের স্বাধীনতা ও সুখ প্রতিষ্ঠিত এবং বৃদ্ধি করার হাতিয়ার হিসাবে হিংসার বিপ্লবাত্মক প্রয়োগ কি যুক্তিসঙ্গত? এই প্রশ্ন বিশেষ অনুমানের ওপর নির্ভর করে, যেমন কোন নির্দিষ্ট ঐতিহাসিক অবস্থায় কোন সমাজে মানুষের কতখানি স্বাধীনতা ও সুখ আয়ত্বাধীন তার সম্ভাবনা নির্ধারণ করার কোন যুক্তিসঙ্গত মান আছে। যদি সে রকম কোন মানা না থাকে তবে সমাজে অধিকতর অথবা উচ্চস্তরের স্বাধীনতা এবং সুখ অর্জন করার সুযোগের দিক থেকে কোন রাজনৈতিক আন্দোলনের বিচার করা বা মূল্য নিরূপণ করা অসম্ভব হবে। মানুষের স্বাধীনতা ও সুখের কোন নির্দিষ্ট সম্ভাবনা বিচার করার আদর্শ এবং পরিমাপ করার মান আয়ত্বাধীন ধরে নিলে এই বোঝায় যে সব নীতিশাস্ত্রগত এবং নৈতিক মানই ঐতিহাসিক। যদি তা না হয় তবে তারা অর্থহীন ও বস্তুহীন। তাই যদি হয় তবে আমাদের প্রশ্নের এই অর্থ হয় যে কোন বৈপ্লবিক আন্দোলনের পক্ষে নৈতিক অধিকার দাবী করতে হলে তার পক্ষে যুক্তিসঙ্গত কারণ দিয়ে অবশ্যই দেখান প্রয়োজন যে মানুষের স্বাধীনতা এবং সুখের সত্যকার সম্ভাবনা আয়ত্বে আনার সুযোগ বিপ্লবের আছে, এবং সেই আন্দোলন অভীষ্ট ফল লাভের পক্ষে যথেষ্ট। এই সমস্যার যুক্তিসঙ্গত আলোচনা তখনই সম্ভব যখন তাকে আমরা ইতিহাসের পরিপ্রেক্ষিতে দেখতে পারি। তা নাহলে, শুধুমাত্র দুটি পথ খোলা থাকে, যেমন সব বিপ্লব এবং বিপ্লবাত্মক হিংসাকে স্বতঃসিদ্ধভাবে অস্বীকার করা, অথবা অনুমোদন করা। এই দুই সংস্থিতিই – স্বীকৃতি বা অস্বীকৃতি — ঐতিহাসিক ঘটনাবলীর বিরুদ্ধে যায়। যেমন ইহা বলা অর্থহীন যে ইংরাজদেশীয়, আমেরিকাদেশীয় ও ফরাসী বিপ্লব ছাড়াও আধুনিক সমাজ গড়ে উঠতে পারত। আবার এ বলাও নিরর্থক যে সব বিপ্লবাত্মক বল প্রয়োগাই সামাজিক ক্ষেত্রে সমান কার্যকরী এবং ফলদায়ক হয়েছে। সপ্তদশ শতাব্দীর ইংরাজদেশীয় সশস্ত্র গৃহযুদ্ধের এবং প্রথম সহিংস ফরাসী বিপ্লবের ফলাফল বলশেভিক বিপ্লবের পরিণাম হতে অবশ্যই খুবই পৃথক, এবং নাৎসী ও ফ্যাসিস্ট দলের বিপ্লববিরোধী বল-প্রয়োগের ফল থেকে সম্পূর্ণ অন্যরূপ হয়েছিল। তাছাড়া সামাজিক ও রাজনৈতিক হিংসাত্মক কার্যকলাপকে স্বতঃসিদ্ধভাবে অস্বীকার অথবা স্বীকার করা এক অবস্থার সৃষ্টি করে যেখানে ইতিহাসে যেকোন পরিবর্তনই, তা সে উন্নতিশীলই হোক বা নিম্নগামীই হোক, মুক্তকারীই হোক বা ক্রীতদাসকারীই হোক, অনুমোদনযোগ্য।

বাস্তব প্রয়োগের দিক থেকে এক রাজনৈতিক মতবাদ কোনো কোনো ঐতিহাসিক পরিস্থিতি স্বীকার করে নিয়েছে যেখানে বলপ্রয়োগ ছাড়া সমাজের উন্নতি অসম্ভব। এই চিন্তাধারা সর্বাত্মক ক্ষমতাধারী গণতন্ত্রের নীতি নির্ধারণের ব্যাপারে এবং কার্য পরিচালনার ক্ষেত্রে হাতিয়ার বিশেষ। বোবসপিয়ের-এর কথায় অত্যাচারের স্বেচ্ছাতন্ত্রের বিরুদ্ধে মুক্তির স্বেচ্ছাতন্ত্র। স্বাধীনতার সংগ্রামে অত্যাচারের বিশিষ্ট স্বার্থের বিরুদ্ধে সমষ্টির স্বার্থের খাতিরে সন্ত্রাস সৃষ্টি শুধু অবশ্য প্রয়োজনীয় নয়, দায়িত্বও হয়ে দাঁড়াতে পারে। এখানে বলপ্রয়োগ, বৈপ্লবিক শক্তি প্রয়োগ, শুধুমাত্র রাজনৈতিক পন্থা হিসাবে নয়, নৈতিক দায়িত্ব ও কর্তব্য হিসাবে প্রতিভাত হয়। এখানে সন্ত্রাসকে প্রতিক্রিয়া-সঞ্জাত বলপ্রয়োগ হিসাবে বর্ণনা করা হয়। এই সন্ত্রাসেরবৈধতা শুধু অত্যাচারীদের বিরুদ্ধে প্রতিরক্ষার জন্য এবং তাদের পরাজয় না হওয়া পর্যন্ত। সেই একই যুক্তিতে মার্কসীয় চিন্তাধারা অনুযায়ী সর্বহারার কর্তৃত্ব কেবলমাত্র সাময়িক নিয়ম, যার প্রয়োজন উদ্দেশ্যসিদ্ধির সাথে সাথে শেষ হয়ে যাবে। তার কারণ এই ধরে নেওয়া হয় যে এই কর্তৃত্বের প্রয়োজন ততদিনই থাকবে যতদিন পুরাতন শাসক-গোষ্ঠীর শক্তির প্রয়োগ বন্ধ করতে হবে। এখানেও বিপ্লবাত্মক শক্তি প্রয়োগকে হিংসার প্রতিক্রিয়া হিসাবে বর্ণনা করা হচ্ছে। মার্ক্সীয় চিন্তাধারা এই ধরে নেয়, যে পুরাতন শাসক-শ্রেণীগুলি কখনই স্বেচ্ছায়তাদের ক্ষমতা হারাবে না, এমনকি তারাই বিপ্লবের বিরুদ্ধে প্রথমে শক্তি প্রয়োগ করবে, এবং বিপ্লবাত্মক বলপ্রয়োগ হবে বিপ্লব প্রতিহতকারী শক্তির বিরুদ্ধে প্রতিরক্ষা।

অনন্যাধীন বিপ্লবী-সরকার গঠনের মূল উদ্দেশ্য হবে জন-সাধারণকে এক নতুন ধরনের শিক্ষা দেওয়া। শিক্ষামূলক ও সাময়িক কর্তৃত্বে স্বপক্ষে বক্তব্য হচ্ছে : 'মানুষকে স্বাধীন করতে হলে বল প্রয়োগের প্রয়োজন।' এটা আপাতদৃষ্টিতে অস্বাভাবিক মনে হয়। রাজনৈতিক দর্শন চিরকালই মানুষের বাধ্যতা স্বীকারের পশ্চাতে শক্তিপ্রয়োগকে নৈতিক ক্রিয়া বলে স্বীকার করে নিয়েছে। কিন্তু রুশোর যুক্তি সম্পূর্ণ নূতন। মানুষকে দুর্নীতি-পরায়ণ ও অত্যাচারপূর্ণ পরিবেশ থেকে মুক্ত করার জন্য বলপ্রয়োগ প্রয়োজনীয়। কিন্তু যারা নিজেরাই জানে না যে তারা ক্রীতদাস তারা কিভাবে নিজেদের মুক্ত করতে পারে? তাদের অবশ্যই শিক্ষা দিতে হবে এবং স্বাধীনতার দিকে চালিত করতে হবে। যাদের প্রতি এই যুক্তি যত বেশী প্রযোজ্য তাদের অন্য কোনো জীবনযাত্রা বা চিন্তাধারার সম্ভাবনা সম্বন্ধে অজ্ঞ রাখার জন্য তাদের জ্ঞান-বুদ্ধি বিকৃতভাবে গড়ে তুলতে সমাজ আর আয়ত্বাধীন সব পন্থা বিশেষভাবে অবলম্বন করবে। এই শিক্ষামূলক এবং ভিত্তিগঠনকারী সর্বময় কর্তৃত্বের চিন্তাধারা আজ বিপ্লবের অবিচ্ছেদ্য অঙ্গ এবং বিপ্লবে দমননীতি প্রয়োগের যুক্তি হয়ে দাঁড়িয়েছে।

পরিবর্তন-সমন্বিত এবং সাময়িক অনন্যাধীন সরকারের বিরুদ্ধে প্রধান যুক্তি এই প্রশ্নে পাওয়াযায় : যারা শিক্ষা দেবে তাদের শিক্ষা দেয় কে? যারা প্রকৃতপক্ষে অনন্যাধীন ক্ষমতা প্রয়োগ করে তারা কোন অধিকারে স্বাধীনতা ও সুখের নামে - সাধারণ সর্ত হিসাবে কথা বলে? কিন্তু এই যুক্তি যথেষ্ট নয়। যে সমাজে নিয়ম-সৃষ্টিকারী উচ্চস্তরের ব্যক্তিরা কর্তৃত্ব-বিধায়ক নয় এবং সর্বদা নিচের স্তরের বা শ্রেণীর জনগণের দ্বারা কার্যকরী ভাবে নিয়ন্ত্রিত হয় না, সেখানেও অল্পবিস্তরভাবে একই যুক্তি খাটিয়া থাকে। যাইহোক, যদি আমরা স্বীকার করেও নিই যে সংখ্যাগরিষ্ঠ লোক আজ স্বাধীন নয় এবং তাদের মুক্তি স্বতঃস্ফূর্তভাবে হবে না, তাহলেও প্রশ্ন থেকে যায় যে বাধ্যকারী পন্থা উদ্দেশ্য সিদ্ধির পক্ষে, অর্থাৎ মুক্তির জন্য যথেষ্ট কিনা। অন্যভাবে বলতে গেলে, পরিবর্তন সমন্বিত অনন্যাধীন সরকারের প্রয়োজনীয়তার প্রশ্ন, এবং বিপ্লবে দমননীতির ও বলপ্রয়োগের নৈতিক যৌক্তিকতার প্রশ্ন একই সমস্যার দুটি দিক।

স্বাধীনতার নামেই সব ঐতিহাসিক বিপ্লবের সমর্থন করা হয়েছে এবং তাদের সুপক্ষ হয় সেই কারণেই। অথবা সঠিকভাবে বলতে গেলে আরো অধিক সংখ্যক মানুষের জন্য আরো বেশি স্বাধীনতার নামে। আমরা প্রথমে অভিজ্ঞতার ভিত্তিতে এই দাবী কঠোরভাবে পরিবর্তনশীল স্বাধীনতা নির্ভর করে ঐতিহাসিক পরিস্থিতি এবং প্রক্রিয়ার ওপর যার ফলে অনেকসময় অভ্যস্ত জীবনযাত্রার আমূলপরিবর্তন ঘটে থাকে, এবং যা প্রচলিত ধারণার বিরুদ্ধে যায়। সভ্যতার ক্রমবিকাশের প্রতি নূতন স্তরে মানব ও প্রকৃতির ওপর মানুষের ক্রমবর্ধমান প্রভুত্বের ফলে স্বাধীনতার আকৃতি ও প্রকৃতির পরিবর্তন হয়। উভয় দিক হতেই প্রভুত্বের অর্থ শাসন এবং নিয়ন্ত্রণ। প্রকৃতপক্ষে আজ শিল্পভিত্তিক উন্নত সমাজে মানুষের স্বাধীনতার সম্ভাবনার সাথে ইতিহাসের বিগত অধ্যায়গুলিতে মানুষের আত্নহীন বা সম্ভাব্য স্বাধীনতার কোন মতেই তুলনা করা চলে না। এইভাবে মানব স্বাধীনতার আকৃতি, বিস্তার, মাত্রা এবং প্রকৃতিরদিক থেকে বিচার করলে আমরা একান্তই ঐতিহাসিক এবং পরিবর্তনশীল অবস্থা নিয়ে কারবারকরি। সত্যকার সম্ভাব্য স্বাধীনতার সাথে তুলনা করলে, আমরা সর্বদাই এক অপেক্ষাকৃত অস্বাধীন অবস্থায় বাস করি। স্বাধীনতার ব্যাপারে আমলের সাথে সত্যকার সম্ভাবনার, অথবা যুক্তিসঙ্গতর সাথে প্রকৃতর যে প্রচন্ড ব্যবধান তা কখনই মিলিয়ে যায় নাই। স্বাধীনতা সব সময়ই ধরে নেয় মুক্তি করা, অথবা এক রকমের স্বাধীনতা এবং অস্বাধীনতা হতে পরবর্তী আরেক স্তরে যাওয়া, কারিগরী উন্নতির অগ্রগতির সাথে সাথে সম্ভাবনার দিক থেকে পরবর্তী অধ্যায় গুণগত ও পরিমাণ বিষয়কভাবে এক উচ্চতর স্তরের। কিন্তু তাই যদি সত্য হয়, যদি স্বাধীনতা বলতে সর্বদাই ধরে নিই অস্বাধীন এবং অসুখী অবস্থা থেকে মুক্ত করা তবে তার মানে এই হয় যে এই বন্ধন-মুক্তির প্রক্রিয়া সব সময়ই স্থায়ী এবং অনুমোদিত প্রতিষ্ঠানগুলির এবং স্বার্থের বিরুদ্ধে আঘাত করে এবং অবশেষে তাদের বিনষ্ট করে। ইতিহাসে দেখা যায় না কেউ নিজের স্বার্থ স্বেচ্ছায় ছেড়ে দিয়েছে। এই যুক্তি দিয়েই কার্যকারিতার দিক থেকে সহিংস বিপ্লবকে প্রতিরোধকারী শক্তি হিসাবে সমর্থন করা হয়েছে।

বিপ্লবের নীতি এইভাবে সাক্ষ্য দেয় দুই ঐতিহাসিক অধিকারের সংঘাত ও দ্বন্দ্ব : একদিকে প্রতিষ্ঠিত সাধারণতন্ত্রের অধিকার, যার ওপর ব্যক্তিদের জীবন এমনকি সুখ নির্ভর করে, এবং অন্যদিকে ন্যায়-এর অধিকার কারণ তা মানুষের শ্রম, দুঃখ এবং অবিচারলাঘব করতে পারে। অবশ্য যুক্তিপূর্ণ মানের সাহায্যে এই ভবিষ্যৎসুযোগকে সত্যকারের সম্ভাবনা হিসাবে দেখাতে হবে। কোন ঐতিহাসিক হিসাব-নিকাশের যুক্তিসঙ্গত

ভিত্তি দিতে হলে আমাদের হিসাব নিতে হবে বর্তমান সমাজের পক্ষ থেকে মানুষের কাছ থেকে কতখানি ত্যাগ দাবী করা হয়েছে; বাঁচার সংগ্রামে এবং সমাজের রক্ষার জন্য কত বলির প্রয়োজন হয়েছে। এই অঙ্কে আরো হিসেব নিতে হবে সমাজের বুদ্ধিঘাত এবং বস্তুজাত সম্পদের এবং কিভাবে এই আয়ত্বাধীন সম্পদের পূর্ণ সম্ভাবনার দিক থেকে তাদের মানুষের অবশ্য প্রয়োজনীয় চাহিদার তৃপ্তির এবং বাঁচার সংগ্রামের শান্তির জন্য ব্যবহার করা হয়। অন্যদিকে ওই একই হিসাবে দেখাতে হবে প্রতিযোগী বৈপ্লবিক আন্দোলনের পক্ষে বর্তমান অবস্থার উন্নতির সুযোগ, যেমন, বৈপ্লবিক পরিকল্পনা ও কর্মসূচী দ্বারা দেখান যে বিপ্লবের ফলে কারিগরী, বস্তুগত এবং মানসিক সম্ভাবনার দিক থেকে সমাজের ত্যাগের পরিমাণ এবং বলির সংখ্যা কমান সম্ভব।

বিপ্লবের নীতি যদি কিছু থাকে তবেতা ঐতিহাসিক মান-অনুযায়ী হবে কোন অনড় মান অনুযায়ী নয়। এই মান সেই সাধারণ মানসমূহের উপযোগিতা অস্বীকার করে না যা মানবতার দিকে মানবজাতির অগ্রসর হবার পক্ষে প্রয়োজনীয় সর্ত ঠিক করে। তবে কোন কোন প্রকারের হিংসাত্মক কার্য আছে যা কোন বৈপ্লবিক অবস্থাতেই সমর্থন করা যায় না, কারণ তারা সেই উদ্দেশ্যকেই অস্বীকার করে যার সিদ্ধির জন্য বিপ্লব একটি পন্থা। ইচ্ছানুযায়ী বলপ্রয়োগ নৃশংসতা এবং নির্বিচার সন্ত্রাস সৃষ্টি ইত্যাদি সেইসব কার্য। যাইহোক ঐতিহাসিক গতিশীলতার মধ্যে বিপ্লব নিজস্ব এক ধরনের নৈতিক এবং নীতিশাস্ত্রগত বিধির প্রতিষ্ঠা করে এবং নতুন মান এবং মূল্যবিচারের উৎস হয়ে দাঁড়ায়। প্রকৃতপক্ষে বর্তমানের বেশীর ভাগ সামাজিক গুণগুলির সৃষ্টি বিপ্লবে, যেমন ইংরাজদেশীয় গৃহযুদ্ধ সমূহের ফলে সহ্যগণও মানুষের জন্মগত অধিকার, আমেরিকাদেশীয় এবং ফরাসী বিপ্লবের ফলে। এই আদর্শগুলি ক্রমে ঐতিহাসিক শক্তিতে পর্যবসিত হয়। প্রথমে আংশিক আদর্শ হিসাবে এবং ক্রমে বিশেষ রাজনৈতিক উদ্দেশ্যসিদ্ধির জন্য বৈপ্লবিক আন্দোলনের হাতিয়ার হিসাবে। প্রথমে এই আদর্শগুলি বাস্তবে পরিণত করতে শক্তি প্রয়োগের প্রয়োজন হয়, পরে তারা কিছুটা রাজনৈতিক, তবে সাধারণভাবে নীতিশাস্ত্র সম্মত রূপ নিল এবং হিংসাকে অস্বীকার করল। এইভাবে সব বিপ্লবই নিজেদের নীতিশাস্ত্র সম্মত মানের অন্তর্ভুক্ত করে।

ঐতিহাসিক বিপ্লবের নেতারা কখনও শুধু হিংসার স্বার্থেই শক্তিপ্রয়োগকে বৈপ্লবিক মূল্য দেন নাই। জর্জ সোরেল-এর সমসাময়িক ব্যক্তিরা তার হিংসা ও যুক্তির মধ্যে যোগসূত্র ছিন্ন করার প্রয়াসকে অস্বীকার করেছিলেন। এই চেষ্টার সাথে সোরেল এর ইচ্ছা ছিল শ্রেণী-সংগ্রামকে সব নীতিগত বিচার থেকে মুক্ত করা। যুদ্ধে সামরিক শক্তিপ্রয়োগের সাথে শ্রেণী-সংগ্রামের বৈপ্লবিক অবস্থায় বলপ্রয়োগের তুলনা করতে গিয়ে তিনি শ্রেণী সংগ্রামকে যুদ্ধ কৌশলের পর্যায়ে ফেলেন। তার কাছে চরম উদ্দেশ্য হচ্ছে শত্রুর সর্বাত্মক পরাজয় এবং হিংসার প্রয়োগ শুধু সেই উদ্দেশ্য সাধনের হাতিয়ার হিসাবে। অন্যদিক থেকে হিংসাকে শুধু হিংসার খাতিরে সমর্থন করা হয় নাই। তাকে সমর্থিত করা হয়েছে যুক্তিসঙ্গত দমনের অংশ হিসাবে। প্রতিক্রিয়াশীল বিপ্লবের দমনের জন্য, প্রতিষ্ঠিত অধিকার এবং সুবিধাভোগ দূর করার জন্য, এক কথায় সমাজের বৃহত্তর স্বার্থের জন্য পার্থিব ও মানসিক প্রয়োজনের জন্য। বলিতে গেলে উপরোক্ত কারণগুলির জন্যই কৃচ্ছসাধন, বণ্টনের নিয়ন্ত্রণ, এবং মতপ্রকাশের নিয়ন্ত্রণ বলবৎ করা প্রয়োজন।

এখানে আমরা সমগ্র নীতিশাস্ত্রের এককঠিন সমস্যার সম্মুখীন হই, যেমন নৈতিক মানের চূড়ান্ত অনুজ্ঞার ব্যাপারে কে, এবং কোন রীতি, নীতি শাস্ত্র সম্মত মানের যোগ্যতা নির্ণয় করে? পাশ্চাত্য সভ্যতা বস্তুতান্ত্রিক হয়ে আসার সাথে সাথে এই প্রশ্ন ক্রমে গভীর হয়ে আসে। মধ্যযুগে এটা কোনো সমস্যা ছিল না, যতক্ষণ সমসাময়িক নীতির অনুজ্ঞাকে সবাই মেনে নিত। প্রতিবাদ সত্ত্বেও অবিশ্বাসীদের নির্মূল করা বা ধর্ম-বিরোধীদের পুড়িয়ে মারা ন্যায়বিচার বলে গণ্য করা হত। বর্তমানে নীতির অনুশাসন বা অনুজ্ঞা নির্ভর করে প্রচলিত রীতি, ভয় উপযোগিতা এবং ধর্মের সমন্বয়ে গঠিত এক বিপদজনক, অস্থায়ী এবং সুবিধার্থে নমনীয় অবস্থার ওপর।

এখন গতানুগতিক এবং প্রতিষ্ঠিত সমাজের সংখ্যা অনুযায়ী বিপ্লব নীতি বিগর্হিত, ইহা বর্তমান সাধারণতন্ত্রকে আঘাত করে, ইহা অনুমোদন করে এমনকি দাবী করে প্রবঞ্চনা, চাতুরী, দমন এবং জীবন ও সম্পত্তির বিনাশ। কিন্তু বিপ্লব যে সমাজ চায়, সেইসমাজ কি বর্তমান সমাজের চেয়ে স্বাধীনতার উন্নতির জন্য বেশী সুযোগ দিতে পারে? ঐতিহাসিক ভাবে আধুনিককালের মহাবিপ্লবগুলির বস্তুগত অভিপ্রায় ছিল, সামাজিক স্বাধীনতার প্রসার এবং চাহিদার বা অভাবের সন্তুষ্টির বিস্তার করা। ইংরাজদেশীয় এবং ফরাসী বিপ্লবের সামাজিক ব্যাখ্যা

যতই বিভিন্ন রকমের হোক না কেন, এক বিষয়ে সবাই একমত যে বিপ্লবের ফলে সামাজিক সম্পদের একপ্রকার পুনর্বন্টন সম্ভব হয়, যার ফলেপূর্বতন বঞ্চিত শ্রেণীগুলি সম্পদের দিক থেকে এবং/অথবা রাজনৈতিক দিক থেকে এই পরিবর্তনের ফলে উপকৃত হয়। বিপ্লবের নেতাদের উদ্দেশ্য এবং আদর্শ এবং জনগণের প্রেরণা ও অভিপ্রায় সম্পূর্ণ পৃথক হতে পারে। কিন্তু এই বিপ্লবগুলির বস্তুগত ক্রিয়ার গুণে মানুষের স্বাধীনতার প্রসার সম্ভব হয়। এইভাবে মানুষেরকাছ থেকে অবর্ণনীয় ত্যাগ দাবী করা সত্ত্বেও বিপ্লব সমস্ত রাজনৈতিক যুক্তির উর্ধ্বে নীতিসম্মত অধিকার প্রতিষ্ঠা করে। এখন আমি স্বীকার করছি যে, যখন বিপ্লবের ঐতিহাসিক ভূমিকা শুধু ঘটনার পরই চেনা যায়, তার সম্ভাবিত দিক বা গতিপথ, উন্নতির পথ বা অবনতির পথ, আগে থেকেই কম বেশি নিশ্চয়তার দ্বারা দেখান সম্ভব। তুলনা হিসাবে এটকা দেখান যেত এবং ঘটনার পূর্বে দেখান হয়েছিল – যে ১৭৮৯ খ্রিস্টাব্দের ফরাসী বিপ্লব প্রাক্তন রাজতন্ত্রের চেয়ে মানুষের স্বাধীনতার ক্রমবিকাশের জন্য অধিকতর সুযোগ দেবে। অন্যদিকে এটাও দেখান সম্ভব হত, এবং তা ঘটনার বহুপূর্বেই পরিস্ফুট হয়েছিল, যে ফ্যাসিস্ট এবং জাতীয় সমাজতন্ত্রী সরকার বা দলের সম্পূর্ণ বিপরীত অবস্থার সৃষ্টি করবে। আমাদের বৈজ্ঞানিক, কারিগরী ক্ষমতা ও বস্তুজাত সম্পদের বৃদ্ধির সাথে সাথে এবং মানুষ ও প্রকৃতির ওপর বৈজ্ঞানিক প্রভুত্বের পথে আমাদের অগ্রগতির ফলে, ঘটনার পূর্বে বিপ্লবের ঐতিহাসিক সুযোগ সৃষ্টি করার পক্ষে কতখানি সম্ভাবনা আছে তা দেখান যুক্তিসঙ্গত হয়ে আসছে। আজ স্বাধীনতার উপাদান ও সম্ভাবনা মানুষের নিয়ন্ত্রণের মধ্যে এবং তাদের পরিমাপ করাও ক্রমেই তার সাধ্যের মধ্যে আসছে। এবং এই কার্যকরী নিয়ন্ত্রণের এবং হিসাব করার ক্ষমতার অগ্রগতির সাথে সাথে এক ধরনের হিংসার সাথে আরেক প্রকারের হিংসাত্মক ব্যবহারের তুলনা করার এবং এক রকমের ত্যাগের সাথে আরেক প্রকারের ত্যাগের পার্থক্য খুঁজে বার করার অমানুষিকতা ক্রমবর্ধমানভাবে যুক্তিসঙ্গত হয়ে আসছে। কারণ সমগ্র ইতিহাসে মানুষের সুখ ও স্বাধীনতা এবং এমনকি ব্যক্তিদের জীবন বলি দেওয়ার প্রচুর উদাহরণ আছে। যদি মানুষের জীবনকে আমরা অবশই সর্বাবস্থায় পবিত্র ভাবি, তবে এই পৃথকীকরণ অর্থহীন। কিন্তু আমাদের স্বীকার করতে হবে যে ইতিহাস প্রধানত অনৈতিক এবং দুর্নীতি-পরায়ণ কারণ ইদা মানুষের জীবনকে কখনইপবিত্র হিসাবে শ্রদ্ধা করে নাই। কিন্তু প্রকৃতপক্ষে আমরা বৈধ এবং অবৈধ আত্মত্যাগের মধ্যে পার্থক্য দেখি। এই পার্থক্য ঐতিহাসিক এবং সেই সর্ত অনুসারে নীতিশাস্ত্রসম্মত মানসমূহ হিংসাত্মক ব্যবহারের প্রতি প্রযোজ্য।

এখন আমি একটি শেষ প্রশ্ন তুলে ধরতে চাই, যেমন, বিপ্লবের উদ্দেশ্য সাধনের জন্য কি সব পন্থাকেই যুক্তি দিয়ে সমর্থন করা যায়? আমরা কি যুক্তিপূর্ণ এবং যুক্তিহীন, প্রয়োজনীয় এবং ইচ্ছানুযায়ী দমননীতি অবলম্বন করার মধ্যে কোন পার্থক্য দেখতে পারি? কোন বিপ্লবের আদর্শ যুক্তি দিয়ে দমনকে সমর্থন করে? বলশেভিক বিপ্লবের উপমা দিয়ে আমি এই প্রশ্নের আলোচনা করতে চাই। বলশেভিক বিপ্লবের ব্যক্ত উদ্দেশ্য ছিল সমাজতন্ত্রের প্রতিষ্ঠা। তার দ্বারা বোঝান হয়েছিল শিল্প-দ্রব্য প্রস্তুতের জন্য প্রয়োজনীয় সমস্ত সম্পদের সমাজতন্ত্রীকরণ ও শ্রেণী-বিহীন সমাজ সৃষ্টির প্রথম সোপান হিসাবে সর্বহারাদের সর্বময় কর্তৃত্ব। যে বিশেষ ঐতিহাসিক অবস্থার মধ্যে বলশেভিক বিপ্লব ঘটে তাতে নতুন সমাজতান্ত্রিক দেশ শল্পীকরণের প্রয়োজনীয়তা উপলব্ধ করেছিল। পাশ্চাত্যের ধনতান্ত্রিক দেশগুলির সাথে প্রতিযোগিতার জন্য এই প্রয়োজন হয়। এর কারণ ছিল দুটি : প্রথমত, সশস্ত্র সৈন্যবাহিনী গড়ে তোলার জন্য এবং দ্বিতীয়, বিশ্বব্যাপী প্রচারের জন্য। এখন আমরা যৌক্তিকতা বা অযৌক্তিকতার দিক থেকে কতখানি দমননীতির প্রয়োজন ছিল তা দেখতে পারি। বিপ্লবের যুক্তি অনুযায়ী ক্রমবর্ধমানগতিতে শিল্পীকরণ বাঞ্ছনীয়, এবং দেশের অর্থনৈতিক কাঠামো থেকে অসহযোগী তত্ত্বাবধায়কদের অথবা মালিকদের নির্মূল করা, কর্মে নিয়মানুবর্তিতা বাধ্যমূলক করা ভারি শিল্পের প্রাথমিক প্রয়োজনের ফলে শিল্পীকরণের প্রথম স্তরে চাহিদার বা প্রয়োজনীয় সন্তুষ্টির ত্যাগ এবং এইসব উদ্দেশ্য যারা বিফল করতে চয় তাদের সব নাগরিক অধিকার স্থপিত করা ইত্যাদি অবশ্যই ইঙ্গিত হিসাবে স্বীকৃত হবে। আর বেশি আলোচনার মধ্যে না গিয়ে, আমরা যুক্তিহীন বলে এমনকি বিপ্লবের দিক থেকেও অস্বীকার করতে পারি : মস্কোবিচার, চিরস্থায়ী সন্ত্রাস, অত্যাচার শিবির, এবং শ্রমিক শ্রেণীদের ওপর 'দল'-এর প্রভুত্ব।

এখানেআমি একটি মন্তব্য যোগ করতে চাই। আমার কাছে প্রতিভাত শিল্প-ভিত্তিক সমাজের এক বিশেষ গুণ হচ্ছে এই যে শাসনযন্ত্র যতই সিাবযোগ্য এবং নিয়ন্ত্রণক্ষম হয়ে আসে, মানবজাতির অগ্রগতির সুযোগ ততই নির্ভর করে নেতাদের বুদ্ধিগত এবং নৈতিক গুণাবলীর উপর এবং নিয়ন্ত্রিত জনসাধারণকে শিক্ষিত করার

ইচ্ছা এবং ক্ষমতার ওপর, এবং তাদের শান্তি ও মানবতার সম্ভাবনা ও প্রয়োজনীয়তা বোঝাতে পারানোর ওপর। কারণ আজ, উন্নত, শিল্পভিত্তিক সমাজের জটিল শাসনযন্ত্র মাত্রেই প্রভুত্বব্যঞ্জক - তা চায় কর্ম, বশ্যতা, যান্ত্রিক প্রণালীর বস্তুগত ক্রিয়ার প্রতি অধীনতা স্বীকার। বলতে গেলে, যারা সেই যন্ত্র নিয়ন্ত্রণ করে তাদের অধীনতা স্বীকার। বর্তমানে কারিগরী বিদ্যাকে সুষ্ঠ শাসনের শক্তিশালী হাতিয়ার হিসাবে পরিণত করা হইয়াছে। এই শাসন-যন্ত্র যত বেশি যোগ্য এবং কর্মক্ষম হবে, ততবেশি আমাদের চাহিদার যোগান দিতে পারবে। আর এইভাবেই রাজনৈতিক প্রভুত্বের পথ আরো প্রশস্ত হবে।

আমি এবার সমাপ্তিতে আসছি। পন্থা এবং উদ্দেশ্য এই দুয়ের মধ্যে সম্পর্ক নিয়ে বিপ্লবের যতনীতিগত সমস্যা। এক অর্থে উদ্দেশ্য সিদ্ধি পন্থাকে সমর্থ ন করে যেমন, যদি অবলম্বিত পন্থা সুস্পষ্টভাবে স্বাধীনতার পথে মানুষের অগ্রগতিকে সাহায্য করে। এই বৈধ উদ্দেশ্য, একমাত্র বৈধ আদর্শ, এমন এক অবস্থার সৃষ্টির দাবী করে যার দ্বারা এই উদ্দেশ্য-সিদ্ধি ত্বরান্বিত হবে। এবং এই সামাজিক অবস্থার সৃষ্টির জন্য আত্মত্যাগ যুক্তিসঙ্গত হতে পারে। সমগ্র ইতিহাসে এই ত্যাগকে যুক্তি দিয়ে সমর্থন করা হয়েছে। কিন্তু স্থা এবং উদ্দেশ্য এই দুয়ের মধ্যে যুক্তিগত সম্পর্ক যুক্তি-তর্কের দ্বারা স্থির করা যায়। উদ্দেশ্যই পন্থাকে নিমন্ত্রণ করে আনে, সেইজন্য পন্থার অবলম্বনের সময় উদ্দেশ্যকে দৃষ্টি-বহির্ভূত করলে চলবে না। কিন্তু বিপ্লব যতই যুক্তিপূর্ণ, প্রয়োজনীয় এবং মুক্তিকারী হোক না কেন হিংসাকে দ দেওয়া যায় না। অহিংস ইতিহাস এক সমাজের সম্ভাবনার আশা দেয় যার জন্য এখনও সংগ্রাম করে যেতে হবে। বর্তমানে হিংসার জয় মনে হয়, অপরপক্ষে।

অনুবাদক
সুবীর কুমার মুখোপাধ্যায়

যেখান সম্ভব সেখানে শব্দানুবাদ করার চেষ্টা করেছি। অনেকক্ষেত্রে ভাবানুবাদ ছাড়া উপায় নেই। তাড়াতাড়িতে অনেক জায়গায় ভাষার গলদ রয়ে গেছে - আশাকরি পাঠকেরা বিষয়ের গুরুত্ব বুঝে ক্ষমা করবেন। যতদূর সম্ভব কথ্য ভাষা ব্যবহার করার চেষ্টা করেছি। কিছু ভ্রম সংশোধনের জন্য শ্রীযুক্তা গীতা সেনকে ধন্যবাদ। বাকী ভুলের জন্য দায়ী আমি।

انقلاب کی اخلاقی بنیاد : مارکیوز

ہر برٹ مارکیوز کے ایک مضمون سے اقتباس

انقلاب اور اخلاقیات میں کیا رشتہ ہے۔ اس پر میں مندرجہ ذیل سوال کی روشنی میں غور کرنا چاہتا ہوں: کیا یہ ثابت کیا جا سکتا ہے کہ انقلاب کا لانا نہ صرف درست اور اچھا ہے بلکہ لازمی ہے؟ اور لازمی بھی سیاسی اعتبار سے (یعنی کسی فرد یا گروہ کے وقتی اغراض کو پورا کرنے کے آلے کی حیثیت سے) نہیں بلکہ اخلاقی اعتبار سے؟ دوسرے الفاظ میں، کیا اس امر کی دلیل مل سکتی ہے کہ بغیر انقلاب کے حالتِ انسانی کی بہتری، یا انسان کی اُن صلاحیتوں کا استعمال جو اُسے ایک مخصوص تاریخی مقام رکھنے کے باعث حاصل ہوتی ہیں، ممکن نہیں؟ مندرجہ بالا مسئلے کو اس انداز سے پیش کرنے کا مقصد یہ ہے کہ اس طرح اخلاقی اصطلاحات مثلاً ''اچھا'' اور ''درست'' سیاسی اور سماجی تحریکات کے لیے استعمال کی جا سکیں، گو یہ فرض کرنا پڑے گا کہ ان تحریکات کی اچھائی کی پرکھ کرنا جذبات پر منحصر نہیں ہے بلکہ ذاتی پسند و ناپسند سے بالا تر ہے۔ اگر یہ فرضیہ تسلیم کر لیا جائے تو ''اچھا'' اور ''درست'' سے مراد ہو گا وہ کام جو کسی ریاست میں انسانی آسودگی (happiness) کو برقرار رکھنے، اس میں اضافہ کرنے یا اس کو زیادہ سے زیادہ افراد تک پھیلانے میں مدد گار ثابت ہو گا، خواہ اس ریاست کی طرزِ حکومت کچھ بھی ہو۔ اس ابتدائی تعریف میں انفرادی آسودگی بھی شامل ہے اور ذاتی بھی، نجی آسودگی بھی اور جماعتی بھی۔ دراصل اس تعریف کی مدد سے ہم کلاسیکی فلسفے کے ایک بنیادی خیالیہ (concept) کو، جسے اکثر و بیشتر ذہن دوز (repress) کر دیا جاتا ہے، ایک دفعہ پھر کام میں لا سکتے ہیں۔ وہ خیالیہ یہ ہے کہ حکومت کا منتہا انسان کے لیے ممکن ترین آزادی کا حاصل کرنا ہی نہیں بلکہ انسان کی ممکن ترین آسودگی بھی ہے۔ یعنی ایسے حالات کا فراہم کرنا جن میں انسان خوف اور مصائب سے آزاد، چین اور سکھ کی زندگی بسر کر سکیں۔

لیکن اس جگہ پہنچ کر ہمیں اپنے پہلے پریشان کن مسئلے سے سابقہ پڑتا ہے: ایک ریاست کی فلاح عام کس امر میں ہے اور کس میں نہیں، اس کا تعین کون کرتا ہے؟ کس کو یہ حق

پہنچتا ہے، بلکہ پہنچ سکتا ہے، کہ وہ اس بات کا فیصلہ کرے، اور پھر اپنے فیصلہ کے مطابق انفرادی آزادی اور آسودگی پر حدیں قائم کرے اور اُن قربانیوں کا تعین کرے جو ریاست کے نام پر اور ریاست کی خاطر افراد سے مانگی جاتی ہیں؟ بات یہ ہے کہ اگر جماعتی بہبودی اور انفرادی بہبودی میں شروع ہی سے مطابقت نہیں ہوگی تو انفرادی بہبودی کو جبر اً جماعتی بہبودی کے مطابق ڈھالنے کی کوشش کی جائے گی۔ لیکن اگر ہم نے یہ سوال اٹھایا تو فوراً ہی ہمیں ایک اور مسئلے سے دو چار ہونا پڑے گا جو اتنا ہی دقیق اور پریشان کن ہے: اگر مان بھی لیا جائے کہ آزادی انفرادی اور ذاتی معاملہ نہیں، بلکہ اس کی حدود کا تعین کرنا ریاست کے اختیار میں ہے، تب بھی انسان کی آسودگی کا مسئلہ رہ جاتا ہے۔ کیا ایک شخص کی خوشی اس کا اپنا ذاتی معاملہ ہے یا اس کے حدود اور معنے بھی مطلقاً ریاست ہی مقرر کرتی ہے؟ لیکن اگر ہم صرف چند لمحوں کے لیے ہی اس انتہائی نظریے پر غور کریں جس کے مطابق انسانی خوشی انفرادی ہے اور ہر فرد کا ذاتی معاملہ نہ صرف ہے بلکہ رہنا چاہیے تو پتہ چلے گا کہ اس نظریے کی موافقت میں ہمیں کوئی دلیل نہیں مل سکتی۔ یہ یقینی طور پر کہا جاسکتا ہے کہ انفرادی خوشی کی کچھ ایسی صورتیں ہیں اور یہ کبھی کبھی ایسے رنگ اختیار کرتی ہے کہ کوئی ریاست بھی اسے برداشت نہیں کرسکتی۔ یہ قطعی ممکن ہے، بلکہ ہمیں معلوم ہے کہ یہ امر واقعہ ہے کہ وہ لوگ جو ہٹلر کی تعذیبی چھاؤنیوں (concentration camps) میں جلاد خاص تھے وہ اکثر اپنے کام کی انجام دہی میں خوش تھے۔ اس قسم کی خوشی ان انفرادی آسودگیوں میں سے ہے جن کے متعلق یہ کہتے ہوئے ہمیں کوئی ہچکچاہٹ محسوس نہیں ہوتی کہ کوئی فرد بذاتِ خود نہ تو طے کرسکتا ہے، نہ اسے طے کرنے کا اختیار ہونا چاہیے کہ اس کی خوشی کس امر میں ہے اور کس میں نہیں اور ہمیں ایک ایسی عدالت کا (درحقیقت یا اخلاقی اعتبار سے) وجود فرض کرنا پڑتا ہے جسے انفرادی آسودگی کو متعین کرنے کا حق پہنچتا ہو۔

ان تمہیدی وضاحتوں کے بعد اب میں یہ عرض کرنا چاہتا ہوں کہ "انقلاب" سے میری کیا مراد ہے۔ میری نظر میں جب کوئی سماجی طبقہ یا تحریک سیاسی معاشی اور سیاسی نظام کو بدلنے کی غرض سے کسی قانونی آئین اور حکومت کا تختہ الٹ دیتی ہے تو اسے "انقلاب" کہتے ہیں۔ اس تعریف کے مطابق فوجی انقلابات، محلاتی انقلابات، اور "مزاحمی" جوابی انقلابات

(مثلاً فسطائیت اور ناتسیت) دراصل انقلاب کہلانے کے مستحق نہیں ہیں کیوں کہ اس قسم کے انقلابات معاشرے کے بنیادی نظام کو نہیں بدلتے۔ اب اگر انقلاب کی یہ تعریف تسلیم کر لی جائے تو ہم مزید یہ کہہ سکتے ہیں کہ اس قسم کا بنیادی اور صفاتی تغیر (qualitative change) اپنے ساتھ تشدد لاتا ہے... چنانچہ اب ہم اپنے ابتدائی سوال کو دوسرے الفاظ میں اس طرح پیش کر سکتے ہیں۔ کیا تشدد کا انقلابی استعمال جائز ہے؟ یعنی ایسا استعمال جس سے انسانی آزادی مستحکم ہو سکے یا ان میں اضافہ ہو سکے؟ [اس سوال کا جواب اسی وقت دیا جا سکتا ہے جبکہ] اس مخصوص تاریخی معاشرے کو [جس کے بارے میں یہ سوال اٹھایا جا رہا ہے] ایسے عقلی معیار میسر ہوں جن کی مدد سے وہ معاشرہ یہ فیصلہ کر سکتا ہو کہ اس کے پاس انسانی آزادی اور آسودگی کو فراہم کرنے کے کیا امکانات ہیں۔ لیکن اب اگر ایسے عقلی معیار کا وجود ہی نہیں ہوا تو یہ اندازہ کرنا غیر ممکن ہو گا کہ کسی سیاسی تحریک کو انسانی آزادی اور آسودگی کی مزید توسیع کرنے یا ان میں اضافہ کرنے کے مواقع حاصل ہیں کہ نہیں۔

لیکن اگر انسانی آزادی اور آسودگی کے مجوزہ امکانات کا صحیح طور پر اندازہ لگانے کے لیے عقلی معیار ہیں تو ہمیں یہ بھی ماننا پڑے گا کہ اخلاقی معیار کی حیثیت تاریخی ہے، ورنہ یہ معیار بے معنی تصورات ہی رہیں گے۔ اب اگر اس امر کی روشنی میں ہم اپنے [مندرجہ بالا] سوال پر غور کریں تو یہ مطلب نکلے گا کہ اگر کوئی انقلابی تحریک یہ دعویٰ کرتی ہے کہ وہ اخلاقی اعتبار سے درست ہے تو اس میں عقلی طور پر یہ ثابت کرنے کی صلاحیت ہونا چاہیے کہ اس میں انسانی آزادی اور آسودگی کے اصلی مواقع حاصل کرنے کی اہلیت ہے۔ یعنی اس کے پاس اس بات کا عقلی جواز ہونا چاہیے کہ اسے جو وسائل میسر ہیں وہ اس کے مقاصد کو پانے کے لیے مناسب ہیں اور کافی ہیں۔ اس طرح تاریخی اعتبار سے جانچ پڑتال کرنے کے بعد ہی یہ ممکن ہے کہ ہمارے مسئلے پر عقلی بحث کی جا سکے۔' ورنہ صرف دو ہی صورتیں رہ جائیں

ا۔ مارکیوز کا مطلب یوں بیان کیا جا سکتا ہے: ایک انقلابی تحریک اخلاقی اعتبار سے درست ہے کہ نہیں، اس سوال کا غائبانہ طور پر جواب نہیں دیا جا سکتا۔ اس کا جواب دینے کے لیے ہمیں دیکھنا پڑے گا (الف) کہ آیا اس تحریک کے پاس انسانی آزادی اور خوشی کو حاصل کرنے کے ذرائع ہیں کہ نہیں اور (ب) کہ یہ ذرائع ان مخصوص تاریخی حالات میں جن میں یہ تحریک اٹھائی گئی ہے کافی ہیں یا نہیں۔ بالفاظِ دگر، مندرجہ بالا سوال کا جواب دینے کے لیے تاریخی حالات کا علم لازمی ہے۔ (مترجم)

گی: یا تو غائبانہ (a priori) طور پر سارے انقلابات اور انقلابی تشدد کی حمایت یا ان کی تردید۔ لیکن دونوں ہی صورتیں، اقراری بھی ہیں اور انکاری بھی، تاریخی حقیقتوں کے خلاف ہیں... مزید یہ کہ سماجی اور سیاسی تباہ کاریوں کی غائبانہ حمایت کرنا یہ کہنے کے مترادف ہو گا کہ تاریخ میں ہر ردو بدل جائز ہے، خواہ وہ ترقی کا معاون ہو یا رجعت کا، خواہ وہ آزادی کی خاطر کیا جائے یا غلامی کی...

چنانچہ انقلاب کا اخلاقی تجزیہ کرنے سے پتہ چلتا ہے کہ دو تاریخی حقوق کے مابین کشمکش اور تصادم رہتا ہے۔ ایک جانب حق اس کا ہے جس کا وجود ہے، یعنی مروجہ حکومت کا (جس پر افراد کی زندگیوں اور غالباً خوشیوں کا دار و مدار ہے) اور دوسری جانب حق اس کا ہے جس کا وجود ممکن ہے، بلکہ جس کا وجود ہونا چاہیے، تاکہ اس کے ذریعے سے مشقت اور صعوبت اور نا انصافیوں میں کمی لائی جا سکے (بشرطیکہ اس بات کا ثبوت مل سکے کہ ایسی صورتِ حال کا واقعی امکان ہے)۔ لازماً، ایسا ثبوت عقلی معیار پر مبنی ہوگا۔ بلکہ ہم یہ بھی کہہ سکتے ہیں کہ یہ معیار تاریخی معیار ہوں گے۔ بالفاظِ دگر، ان کی شکل ہو گی ایک تاریخی حساب کی، جس کی مدد سے صحیح طور پر اندازہ لگایا جا سکے گا کہ کسی مستقبل کے معاشرے کو موجودہ معاشرے کے مقابلے میں انسانی ترقی کے کیا مواقع حاصل ہیں — یعنی تکنیکی اور مادی ترقی کو اس طرح استعمال کرنے کے جس سے انسانی آزادی اور خوشی میں اضافہ ہو سکے۔ اب اگر اس قسم کے تاریخی حساب کی بنیاد ہے عقلی اصولوں پر تو ایک طرف تو شمار کرنا ہوگا ان قربانیوں کا جو موجودہ نسلوں کو مروجہ معاشرے، قانون اور نظام کی خاطر دینا پڑ رہی ہیں۔ ساتھ ہی ساتھ یہ دیکھنا پڑے گا کہ معاشرے کو کیا ذہنی اور مادی ذرائع میسر ہیں اور ان کا کس طرح استعمال کیا جا رہا ہے تاکہ یہ اندازہ لگایا جا سکے کہ آیا ان میں انسانی ضروریات کو پورا کرنے اور زندگی کی کشمکش میں کمی لانے کی جو صلاحیتیں ہیں ان کو پوری طرح کام میں لایا جا رہا ہے یا نہیں۔ دوسری طرف اس تاریخی حساب کو یہ اندازہ لگانا ہوگا کہ کسی انقلابی تحریک کو موجودہ صورتِ حال بہتر بنانے کے کیا مواقع حاصل ہیں۔ یعنی آیا انقلابی منصوبہ یا پروگرام اس بات کا ثبوت پیش کر سکتا ہے کہ اسے ایسے تکنیکی، مادی اور

ذہنی ذرائع حاصل ہیں جو قربانیوں اور مظلوموں کی تعداد میں کمی لاسکیں؟ پیشتر اس کے کہ یہ سوال پیدا ہو کہ ایسا تاریخی حساب ممکن ہے یا نہیں (اور مجھے یقین ہے کہ یہ ممکن ہے) اس کی غیر انسانی اور محض عددی خصوصیت ظاہر ہے۔ لیکن یہ غیر انسانیت ہے تاریخ کی اپنی، اس کی تجربی (empirical) اور عقلی بنیاد کی علامت۔ [اس حقیقت کو نظر انداز کرنا ہے] ریا کاری جو (تاریخی) تجربے کو ابتدا ہی سے مسخ کر دے گی۔ ساتھ ہی ساتھ، یہ بے رحم حساب محض کھلا کھلا تصور بھی نہیں، دراصل تاریخ خود ایک فیصلہ کن موڑ پر پہنچنے کے بعد اسی قسم کے بچے تلے تجربے کی صورت اختیار کر چکی ہے...

آیئے اب مندرجہ بالا بحث کو مختصر أ دہرائیں اور از سر نو پیش کریں۔ مطلقاً(absolute) اخلاقی اعتبار سے، یا مافوق التاریخ منطق(Suprahistorical validity) کے معیار پر تو ثابت نہیں کیا جا سکتا کہ مستقبل کی آزادی اور آسودگی کی خاطر کوئی ظلم اور قربانی، خواہ وہ انقلابی ہو یا نہیں، جائز ہے۔ لیکن تاریخی اعتبار سے ہمیں دو امور کے درمیان امتیاز کرنے اور فیصلہ کرنے کی ضرورت درپیش ہوتی ہے۔ ظلم اور قربانیاں روز مرہ معمول ہیں ہر معاشرے میں، اور یہ غلط ہو گا (میں اس بات کو جس قدر ممکن ہے زور دے کر کہوں گا) یہ غلط ہو گا کہ آپ ایک خود مقررہ اور مصلحت آمیز مقام پر پہنچ کر، یعنی اس مقام پر جہاں انقلاب کا ذکر آتا ہے، یکایک با اخلاق اور نیک بننا شروع کر دیں۔ کیا کوئی شخص ان قربانیوں کی تعداد مقرر کر سکتا ہے جو ایک مروجہ معاشرہ حاصل کرتا ہے اور ان کی جو اس معاشرے کو الٹنے کے باعث ہوتی ہیں؟ کیا ان دو قسم کی قربانیوں کے مابین امتیاز کیا جا سکتا ہے؟ کیا دس ہزار قربانیاں بیس ہزار قربانیوں کی نسبت زیادہ اخلاقی ہیں؟ بہرحال ایسا ہے تاریخ کا غیر انسانی حساب، اور اس غیر انسانی تاریخ کے اندر استعمال ہوتا ہے تاریخی حکم شمار۔ ایک معاشرے کے مادی اور ذہنی ذرائع کا، صنعتی اور تقسیمی سہولتوں کا، کس حد تک غیر لازمی ضروریات کی تکمیل کی جاتی ہے اور لازمی ضروریات کو نظر انداز کیا جاتا ہے، ان سب کا شمار کیا جا سکتا ہے۔ شمار کیا جا سکتا ہے آبادی کا بھی اور کام کرنے والوں کی تعداد کا بھی۔ یہ ہے تاریخی حساب جس کی تصدیق ممکن ہے، اور اس قابلِ شمار مواد کی بنا پر سوال کیا جاسکتا ہے کہ

آیا میسر ذرائع اور صلاحیتیں انتہائی دانشمندی کے ساتھ پوری طرح استعمال کی جا رہی ہیں یا نہیں۔ یعنی یہ کہ کیا اول لازمی ضروریات اور بعد ازاں دیگر ضروریات کی اس طرح تکمیل کی جا رہی ہے کہ کم سے کم مشقت، صعوبت اور ناانصافی کے ساتھ ان کی ممکن ترین تکمیل ہو سکے؟ اگر کسی مخصوص تاریخی صورتِ حال کا تجزیہ اس سوال کا جواب نفی میں دیتا ہے، اگر وہاں ایسے حالات کا وجود ہے جن کے باعث تکنیکی سمجھ بوجھ آگے نہیں بڑھ پاتی بلکہ جسے جبری سیاسی اور سماجی اغراض، جو فلاحِ عام کا نام اختیار کر لیتے ہیں، پس پشت ڈال دیتے ہیں، تو ان حالات میں انقلاب لانے سے آزادی کی ترقی کے امکانات میں اضافہ ممکن ہے، بشرطیکہ اس طرح میسر ذرائع کا بہتر طریقے پہ عقلی اور انسانی استعمال ہو سکے...

Poem (*Published in PLR for the first time*)

Faiz Ahmed Faiz

چاند نکلے کسی جانب تری زیبائی کا
رنگ بدلے کسی صورت شبِ تنہائی کا
دولتِ لب سے پھر اے خسرو شیریں دہناں
آج ارزاں ہو کوئی حرف شناسائی کا
گرئی رشک سے ہر انجمن گل بدناں
تذکرہ چھیڑے تری پیرہن آرائی کا
صحن گلشن میں کبھی اے شہِ شمشاد قداں
پھر نظر آئے سلیقہ تری رعنائی کا
ایک بار اور مسیحائے دِل دِل زدگاں
کوئی وعدہ کوئی اقرار مسیحائی کا
دیدہ و دِل کو سنبھالو کہ سرِ شام فراق
ساز و سامان بہم پہنچا ہے رسوائی کا
فیض

---

* Poem handwritten by Shoaib Hashmi

People ask us: Why do you want to start a journal about Pakistan in London? Why do you not go home and do something there? The answer was recently supplied by *The Times*:

... In contrast, the press in India's neighbour, Pakistan, has been relegated to the role of the publishing company of the Government information services. While there are no direct official controls or muzzling legislation, veiled pressures and threats have brought about a semi-official self-imposed censorship through the back door.

In most cases the major publications and news agencies are indirectly controlled financially by the Government press trust—ostensibly established to bolster newspapers in financial difficulties.

With the exception of a few popular papers—and notably the English language Pakistan Observer of East Pakistan—the major English and Urdu daily papers devote the greater part of their columns to glowing praise of President Ayub and his regime. It is not uncommon to find six photographs of the President in one edition of the morning paper.

Editors and publishers who remain outside the scope of Government financial ties usually toe the line. They know that official advertisements can be withdrawn while emergency rules give the Government the right to seize and close any press or publication.

Coverage of political news is confined to publication of the full text of official speeches. Opposition views are ignored and the names of political opponents of the regime only appear in print if they are under attack.

– from an article by Peter Hazelhurst, October 1968

PAKISTAN LEFT REVIEW

Spring, 1969

Contents

Pakistan Usurped

Editorial

So, the lights have gone out again in Pakistan. The tiny plant which had so miraculously appeared on the rock-face of the Ayub regime and had shattered that stony edifice of repression has been trampled by yet another self-styled saviour of the nation.

So it had happened in 1958. Then, as now, though to a considerably minor way, the course of history had been rudely interrupted and the nation's advance towards democracy had been blocked. Then as now the pretext of the army's intervention into the nation's affairs was that law and order had broken down and the country's economy was in danger of collapsing. 'Law and order'—but *whose* law and *whose* order? Certainly, the law that had made it possible for Ghulam Mohammad and Iskander Mirza to rape the country had been in peril in 1958. Even more certainly the law and order which propped Ayub's clan and the robber barons of Pakistan had crumbled in the face of popular revolt. But what about the law and the order which millions of people throughout the country clamoured in 1958 as in 1969, and for whose sake young men and women braved bullets in the streets of Rawalpindi, Dacca, and Karachi? Certainly during the past few months the economic life of the country had come to a halt. But what about the 'economic life' of the oppressed and ignored people in mills and offices, in schools, hospitals, docks, in villages and in isolated settlements which has never been allowed to move so that the economy of the few could gallop untrammelled?

It is no doubt true, as the world knows by now, that there has been violence and bloodshed during the past months. Yet rarely in the history of the oppressed people's struggle against tyranny was so much achieved with so little *innocent* blood. In West Pakistan there were rare cases of extreme mob violence. In East Pakistan where the people's fury could no longer be contained it is very well worth remembering that the violence was directed mainly against those leeches of Ayub's administration who had been sucking the blood of helpless peasants for years. And one must also put against the 'bloodshed' and 'violence' of the peasants—

81

which, however deliberate, was only retaliatory—the violence and crimes committed by Ayub and his regime and which range from fascist style torture and murder of political opponents to petty bullying of the masses.

In any case, and this is most important to remember, there was no need for Ayub to have handed over the entire government of the country to the army. The 'breakdown of law and order', the 'anarchy' and the 'violence' which is supposed to have forced Ayub to take this course could have been ended by the strong action backed by the police and perhaps the army; the situation did *not* call for the complete takeover of the country by the army. The riots were spontaneous and entirely unorganised; the rioters possessed no means of resisting a determined effort—had such an effort been made—by the authorities to restore order. The whole situation could have been brought under control by announcing severe penalties against acts of violence and looting. There was no justification whatever for inviting the military leaders to destroy the political life of the country. Ayub Khan's decision to do so had come not because, as he sanctimoniously put it in his letters to General Yahya, 'all possible civil and constitutional means to resolve the present crisis' had been exhausted, but because he had realised that no matter what he did he would no longer be able to stay in power. Or else why did he not resign sooner? It wasn't because the opposition leaders weren't united. It is contemptible nonsense to pretend that in a country such as ours which contains so many contradictions and diversities there could be full agreement among its various political forces. And yet there was a good deal of agreement among the more important parties—at least enough to provide a basis for action, provided Ayub were ready to play the political game in the way that was in the interest of the nation. All the important parties were agreed on an early election based on adult franchise, on the abolition of the BDs, but above all they all wanted Ayub to get out so that a provisional government could be formed and elections could be held. It was only because Ayub kept trying to the last minute to cling to every tiny bit of straw that offered hope for the continuance of this regime— from downright criminal acts like engineering clashes among political opponents to buying off of opposition leaders—that the heroic and most precious effort of our people was frittered away.

General Yahya has claimed that he has no personal ambition and would relinquish power as soon as the country has returned to normal. The words have a familiar ring: Is this not what Ayub said when he took over power ten years ago? Still, there is no reason to suppose General Yahya would prove as dishonest as Ayub—though well intentioned people seldom succumb to the lure of office on account of a change in their nature; they do so because they come or are led to believe that they have no alternative, indeed that the 'interest of the country' demands it. In any case, for anyone but a leader who has sprung from among the masses it should be difficult to distinguish between the interest of the country and the interest of the big business and the bureaucracy, both of which dread the transfer of power to the people and would not let it happen as long as it is in their power to do so.

It is, however, quite possible General Yahya will not allow himself to be influenced by such anti-democratic elements in the country and will keep his promise. But if he does, surely the parties and factions that manifested themselves this time will rear their head again? What will happen then? Will the General bring his jawans and his tanks rolling back again? And how long will this process go on?

Socialists Must Unite

While these and similar questions hang over the fate of our unfortunate country the socialists must try and learn from the experience of the past few months. What is absolutely obvious is that there is an urgent need for all the socialists of Pakistan to join hands and launch a vigorous movement with a clear programme. *PLR* is taking the first small step in this direction by proposing a conference of all Pakistani socialists living in Britain. Details of this are printed on a separate sheet enclosed in this issue. From now on our aim should be to put our forces together in order to clarify and propagate socialist ideas among Pakistanis. Time has come to subordinate our personal ambitions and rivalries to the greater cause of the people. We must try and formulate a socialist manifesto in the light of the realities that exist in Pakistan, so that when the opportunity arises again—as surely it will—we are able to offer our people a clear and acceptable alternative to the present social and political system. We must promise to ourselves that from now on we will be more selfless, more determined, and more organised. From now on our uncompromising slogans will be LAND TO THE PEASANTS! FACTORIES TO THE WORKERS! POWER TO THE PEOPLE!—and we will continue to raise these cries until the gilt and steel amour of the enemies of our people is shattered to pieces.

The Economic Basis of the Current Crisis

Rehman Sobhan

Two months ago the present popular upsurge in Pakistan was being
viewed by progressives with mixed feelings. A struggle against an
authoritarian regime which led to an enlargement of civil liberties and
an extension of the franchise was welcome as an interim measure. But
it was never thought to be anything more than a means to attain the
final goal of a socialist society. A more liberal atmosphere would have
provided the opportunity to build up progressive forces organisationally
and scope to widen and intensify the education of the people without fear
of arbitrary restraints on one's freedom of action. To this end socialists
were willing to tolerate the bourgeoise and even feudal elements in the
established opposition who were temporary allies in the common struggle
for a restoration of democratic liberties.

Today in the explosive bloodletting which is being witnessed daily in
our leading cities the character and the struggle is changing before our
very eyes and in a totally unanticipated manner. What was being viewed
as a middle class struggle for middle class goals under a bourgeoise
leadership has been transformed into a genuine popular uprising. Each
additional day of bloodletting is widening the social basis of participation
until today progressives must awaken to the fact that the proletarian
base of the cities are there in the streets with the students and other
middle class elements giving new vitality and durability to the struggle.
What is even more remarkable is that this struggle has spread from the
more politicised working class of East Pakistan to threaten the very
fountainhead of capitalist power in Karachi and Lahore.

This rather startling prognosis of the present struggle in Pakistan
merits examination. What submerged social forces have surfaced? What
has fuelled the fires to this rage? How did they remain submerged so long?
What is the relevance of this development to the social order of future?
In this paper we will try to provide a social perspective to the present

84

struggle. The fluidity of the present situation and the relative lack of focus on this aspect of the problem can make this no more than an aperitif for a more detailed analysis of this unique social phenomenon.

To begin with we will briefly examine the economic basis of popular discontent before we attempt to relate it to the social forces which are conditioning the present uprising.

Urban Discontent

For a full decade the highly efficient propaganda network of the regime has sold the economic achievements and the regime to the people. In this they have received sterling, if motivated assistance from a generation of U.S. advisors and academics who have pursued their own vested interest in promoting the image of capitalist successes in Pakistan and have used Pakistan as a shop window to peddle their ideology to the third world.

Whilst one can take more detailed and technical issue with the various upward pointing indices of progress we will accept the figures at their face value and question not their accuracy but their adequacy to serve as a measure of progress in the country.

The present popular explosion of unrealised expectations has irrevocably shattered the facade of stability of the attendant assumptions of a contented and quiet populace. A completely new perspective has today opened up on the problems of the country and people at home and abroad who had swallowed the fairy tales fabricated by our diligent spokesman must now take a new look at what has really been happening in this last decade in order to understand the forces who have been let loose on the streets today.

The widespread unrest in the country was initially urban and middle class in its composition and aspirations. Resentment was directed against the suppression of accepted freedoms and the opportunities for political participation. To this might be added the resentment of the petit bourgeoise against the manifest accentuation of social inequality in the urban areas. One such study of bourgeoise inequality showed that 34.5 per cent of urban income was earned in the top 10 per cent of the urban tax paying population whereas only 23.5 per cent of urban incomes were earned by 50 per cent of the urban population. This inequality was, however, much more acute for the whole urban population where the top 5 per cent earned 26 per cent of the income and the 50 per cent earned only 21 per cent of the income.

This stark evidence of inequality merely gives academic authority to what must be apparent to every clerk, shop assistant or student in any town or city in Pakistan. A feeling of resentment at the growing chasm between the few at the top and their own straitened circumstances must be a powerful propellant in drawing various segments of the urban population into the streets.

However, even this class constitutes a minority in the population. The real indices of progress are represented in the fate of the manual labourers and farm hands who constitute the bulk of the urban and rural population. Had they really improved their prospects the conditions and aspirations of an urban bourgeoise could have been contained by invoking the support of a much larger segment of the population. The real tragedy of the regime in the last decade has thus been not so much in the students who initiated the confrontations in the streets of the cities but in the conspicuous failure of workers and peasants to come out in favour of the regime and withstand this challenge. The erosion of liberty in this decade has bought no corresponding material gain beyond an acceleration in the affluence of a minority at the top. Both social justice and civil liberty have been casualties in this 'decade of progress'.

It is thus appropriate to look more closely at the predicament of Pakistan's forgotten millions to see exactly how they have fared. Having done this one can examine the social forces at work within East and West Pakistan which have contributed to their subjection over the years and the balance of forces in society which will tend to condition the struggle for a genuine social revolution.

Economic Basis of Working Class Discontent

We may begin by looking to the industrial labour force. Our manufacturing sector has indeed been the most dynamic in the whole economy and its performance has elicited the claim that Pakistani manufactures are one of the fastest growing in the world. It is thus appropriate to see how far the actual workers in these booming enterprises have been able to share in the affluence of their masters. A study carried out recently shows that in both wings of Pakistan, whilst money wages have risen between 1954 and 1964, they have risen less than the workers cost of living. This may be seen from the following table:

	Changes in Industrial Wages in Pakistan					
	Money Wages		Cost of living index		Real Wages	
1954	E.P.	W.P.	E.P.	W.P.	E.P.	W.P.
1962/63 for East Pakistan	Rs. 819.1	Rs. 980.9	101.2	96.8 (1955)	Rs. 794.5	Rs. 996.2
1963/64 for West Pakistan	Rs.1057.3	Rs.1109.2	138.0	127.4	Rs. 727.8	Rs. 870.6

The above figures serve to highlight the fact that whilst there is appreciable disparity in average wage levels in the two wings of Pakistan, in both wings workers have been faced with a visible decline in their levels of living over the decade examined. This decline must be seen in the context of the already low wages of the workers. The most recent figure ensures a monthly income of Rs.78 per working class family in East Pakistan which comes to an income per head of just under Rs.17 per month. In West Pakistan the position is barely an improvement on the East with a monthly income per head of Rs.17.4. These figures must be seen in contrast to the rise in business profits in both wings of Pakistan. This scissors movement of wages and profit has manifested itself in a declining share of wages as compared to profits in the total income of business enterprises which implies a redistribution of income from labour to capital. In East Pakistan the ratio of labour income to total factor fell from 0.37 in 1957 to 0.26 in 1962/63. In West Pakistan labour's share fell from 0.38 to 0.34. The spate of strikes throughout Pakistan today demanding higher wages may disturb the apologists of Pakistani capitalism. But it should have been apparent that once the dead hand of dictatorship was torn from the throats of the workers our modern Robber Barons would face a heavy reckoning.

Economic Basis of Rural Discontent

The growing impoverishment of the working class within the perspective of increasing inequalities in the urban areas is marked by a similar process in the villages. In West Pakistan the developed strategy, so actively promoted by the U.S. and World Bank advisers to the government, is committed to the promotion of the landlords and big farmers. This strategy is predicated on the need to channelise the fertilisers, insecticide and high yielding seeds to those farmers who can afford to invest in the tube wells, which provide the guaranteed water supply necessary to make this package work. In the last eight years about 45,000 tube wells have been privately installed. Given the high costs of investment and installation it follows that only the landlords or rich farms can afford to invest in them. Estimates reckon that 77 per cent of these tube wells have gone to holdings of 25 acres or more. Since only 8 per cent of farmers in West Pakistan have holdings of this dimension the class foundations of the tube well revolution are apparent. It should be no surprise to note that the poorest 50 per cent of the rural population in West Pakistan earn only 26 per cent of farm income whilst the top 10 per cent earn 28 per cent.

It is interesting to note that these same tube wells are giving a special dimension to the prevailing feudal relationship. By selling water supplies surplus to their needs to the smaller farmers they are forging special additional levels of social dependency on the poorer *kissan*s who now find that in an already feudal society the landlord has acquired an additional measure of control over the *kissan*'s life.

However, apart from its social implications the prevalent development strategy for rural West Pakistan is designed to accentuate existing inequalities in the rural areas. Thus those farmers who have the tube wells and can afford to use the development aids will prosper whilst the rest of the peasantry will remain committed to their traditional methods and in the face of rising numbers may even face a deterioration in their levels of living. It was no surprise that between 1959 and 1963–64 average family income in the rural areas stayed unchanged in real terms, which implies that at the base conditions more have deteriorated.

Whilst inequality between rich and poor will continue to be accentuated, that between the farmers of the central Punjab the others in NWFP, Baluchistan and Sind and even in the drier regions of Punjab will also increase. The tube well revolution can only apply to that part of the Indus plains which has a reservoir of sub-surface water. This is limited by nature to only a part of the Punjab. This has already been shown by the growth of farm output during the 2nd Plan. In the heart of the Indus Plain this was 6 per cent per annum; in the Frontier regions it was 1.8 per cent and in Sind/Baluchistan it was 3.5 per cent.

The growing influence of the National Awami Party in these regions may thus owe as much to the feeling of economic alienation felt by the farmers of Sind, NWFP and Baluchistan in comparison to the prospering Punjab peasant, as it does to dissatisfaction with the One Unit system.

In the East wing, even the facade of progress, however unequal, which has infected the West is not apparent. This may be seen from the following figures for per cent income of the agricultural population.

East Pakistan Per Capita Farm Income (In Rupees at constant prices of 1959/60)			
1949/50—53/54	54/55—58/59	59/60—63/64	64/65—67/68
228	201	202	198

These figures have been given added authority by evidence drawn from family budget studies. These show that between 1961 and 1963–64 when rice production was supposed to be booming and the works programme was at its peak, farm per capita real income in the rural areas declined from Rs.27.3 to Rs.24.7.

Within the framework of a stagnant agriculture, evidence points to growing impoverishment of the small farmers and land labourers and an increase in landlessness, which according to census reports increased by 66 per cent between 1951 and 1961. Farm budget studies in 1963–64 showed that 50 per cent of farmers controlled only 26 per cent of farm income whilst 10 per cent controlled as much as 27 per cent. A survey in 1963/64 pointed out that 62.2 per cent of farmers had less than 2 acres of land which marked a deterioration within the short time which has lapsed since the 1960 census when 51 per cent of farmers owned less than 2.5 acres.

As in the West wing, development strategy is designed to favour the rich farmer. He, however, has shown even less capacity to benefit from this compared to his counterpart in the West. Over the years he has grown idle through living off his income from leasing surplus land on 'barga' and money lending at 70/80 per cent per annum interest. As a result this strategy has failed even to promote its original objective of increasing overall output in agriculture as it did in West Pakistan, so that rural inequalities are increasing within the perspective of a stagnating farm sector.

The electoral compulsion of the regime made them even more committed to this strategy of promoting rich farmers. The bulk of the Basic Democrats come from this class of rich farmers. In the 1965 election for instance percentage of rural BDs in East Pakistan could be so classed. Since the system was based on securing the votes of the BDs, development strategy made the class interests of BD parallel to the political survival of the regime so that development strategy remained inflexibly committed to perpetrating these in these inequalities in the village.

The uprising had initially bypassed the countryside. But it was inconceivable that within a densely populated land area of only 55,000 sq. miles, where 95 per cent of the population are classified as rural, the flames would not spread to the village. The student demand for a resignation of BDs by 4th March was the occasion for accumulated peasant discontent to surface in a bout of arson and killing directed at BDs, corrupt local officials and village gangsters who acted as musclemen for the regime whilst battening on the villagers. The tensions of the village always carried the seeds of peasant revolution as was made explicit in my study of the development under the Basic Democracies. Its timing and intensity were thus the only occasion for surprise in the absence of effective political direction and organisation at the village level.

For the moment the opposition forces as much as the forces in the streets are as divorced from the social conflicts in the villages as is the regime. The essentially urban character of the movement as much as the middle class antecedents of the opposition has cut them off from the villages. Indeed had they any real roots there the present tensions created by the regimes development strategies could have been exploited to threaten the system from within. A movement of party workers into the villages with a view to make the peasant understand the social forces which condition his life could have educated the rural poor to their intrinsic power and could have, at least in East Pakistan, mobilised him to seize power within the union councils. This however was never on the cards. It was the awareness of this reality which has committed the regime to this system of indirect elections by the BDs in the full knowledge that in a politically insulated village the richer farmers will dominate the elections.

In West Pakistan of course the old feudal tradition adds a dimension of its own which makes the hold of the zamindar much more entrenched compared to the rich farmer in the East. However, even here the complete lack of political penetration by progressive forces into the villages in these twenty years has kept the peasant bound to the landlord and subject to his political dictation. The bogus land reform of the Ayub regime has, as was always intended, left the economic base and hence the political power of the landlords quite untouched.

At the time of the land reform there were, according to the Agricultural Census, 2 million farm households tilling land owned by zamindars. This came to 42 per cent of all farm households in West Pakistan. Another 17 per cent had to rent land in order to supplement their own holdings, so that three-fifths of all farm households in West Pakistan were under the control of zamindars. Twenty-four million acres or 49 per cent of the farm area of West Pakistan was thus owned by zamindars. Of these 24 million acres, only 7.75 million, or 31 per cent, was declared under the provisions of the land reform law, which applied only to holdings of 500 acres and above. Out of this 5.4 million acres were retained by the zamindars under one or other of the escape clauses provided by the law, so that in fact only 2.35 million acres or 9.8 per cent of the total area owned by zamindars was resumed by the state under the law. The resumed land was of the worst quality and in fact only 700,000 acres of marginal land were even under cultivation. The balance was waste land, virtually beyond reclamation. In consequence only 150,000 sitting tenants were given title to the 700,000 acres of cultivated land, which meant that only about 5 per cent of the households coming under zamindars control were fully emancipated. Given the trend towards inequalities in the last eight years it is likely that even this minor gain has been eroded as more small farmers are forced by poverty to sell their ancestral lands and become tenants of the rich farmers or zamindars.

The zamindar's economic domination of the village was reflected in his continued political control. In the 1962 election to the National Assembly 58 out of 78 members were zamindars. The class relations in the villages of West Pakistan were not just left under the Ayub Raj, but strengthened. In the absence of a peasant-based political movement the only hope for the peasant lies in the contradiction between the rising urban middle classes and the zamindars. A middle class movement aiming to capture the balance of power from the zamindars could aim for a genuine land reform which gave land to the tillers; a move which would at one stroke cut the economic base from under the landlord class by destroying the dependency of the tenant on the owner of his land. This in itself may not solve the problems of 90 per cent of the farm households who own under 12.5 acres of land. The experience of East Pakistan and even India has shown that the substitution of the feudal relationship by the emergence of a kulak or rich farmer class can still keep the small farmer and landless labourer in a state of subjugation. Unless zamindar's abolition is not accompanied by redistribution of land and a well developed system of co-operatives to enable economic utilisation of tube well and farm machinery where appropriate, land reforms can create a different order of problems. It may be too much to expect that reformers will learn from the lessons of East Pakistan and move from a feudal to a socialist and co-operative agriculture in one step. But certainly West Pakistan must get to the first stage of breaking the power of its landlords if even conventional bourgeoise democracy is to emerge out of this movement against the Ayub Raj. Till then the rural areas will continue to be outside the mainstream of West Pakistani politics and rural opposition to the regime will continue to be dominated by individual landlords in conflict with one-man rule.

East Pakistan having already eliminated its zamindar is ripe for graduation to the next step of the struggle, where political and economic power of the village kulak is broken and passes into the hands of the small peasant and landless labourer. The 20 years since the abolition of zamindari has merely heightened the frustration of this submerged class which has reached a highly explosive point as a result of the inequalities in development strategies under the Ayub regime. The fact that this growing discontent has found no political focus merely heightened the sense of frustration in the village and threatens any regime in the future with a convulsion which would make the present uprising seem mild in comparison.

Having spelt out the nature of the small forces in the village, the disparity in their development in the two wings of Pakistan and the potential for social change in the future we can understand why the villages remain uninvolved in the struggle at this moment. For an adequate understanding of the social basis of the present uprising we must turn to the social forces at work within the urban societies and East and West Pakistan that we must direct our attention in order to interpret the nature of the struggle and evaluate its possibility for social change. We will begin with East Pakistan.

East Pakistan

The tradition and ethos of East Pakistani politics has always been middle class. In the absence of a significant Muslim feudal class, political leadership in the course of the Pakistan Movement came to rest in the hands of the middle class, unlike the Punjab and Sind where it was the landlords who dominated pre-partition politics in the region. The growth and success of the Muslim League in the pre-independence Bengal was evidence of a nascent middle class Muslims aiming to arrest power from their Hindu counterparts.

Partition frustrated the basic assumptions on which the Bengali middle class fought for independence, when political power passed from the Hindus to the West Pakistani dominated central government. The reason for the paradox lay in the foundations of the present regime. The bureaucracy from the beginning exploited their technical and intellectual superiority over the politician. They used the personal divisions and lack of organisation among politicians to dominate the decision-making process. It was the possibility of restoration in the balance of power resulting from the impending general elections, in East Pakistan where the Awami League and NAP were likely to sweep the polls that persuaded General Mirza to call in the army. Under President Ayub Khan, the struggle for power between the bureaucracy and the politician ended in the unchallenged victory of the executive, who has ruled the country with the physical sanctions of the army for the last decade.

The fact that this central bureaucracy was West Pakistani and that the strength of the political forces lay in the Bengali middle class made, the autonomy issue particularly central to East Pakistan politics and in the Ayub years converted it into an over-riding concern. For Bengal the bourgeoise revolution, when middle class seizes power following the independence of a country, has never been realised to this day. The autonomy movement is generally an attempt to realise a stage in the country's development which has been achieved in West Pakistan, as with so many other countries, at the time of independence. Decision making by the West Pakistani dominated centre was made more objectionable by the much faster rate of government-sponsored development in the West wing. Thus disparities in levels of livings and economic opportunities which stemmed from this unequal development directly involved all segment of the middle class.

The alienation of this class of East Pakistani produced a traditional bourgeoise nationalist response. The demand for parity was a demand by the middle class for the jobs and economic opportunities they had been denied, as much the natural response of homogeneous cultural and social groups to rule itself with a minimum of interference from outside elements.

This traditional response however tended to involve a rather stereotyped response from progressives in both East and West Pakistan, who saw this as a distraction from the more fundamental struggle for social revolution. What made the East Pakistani situation unique was itself a legacy of the disparity problem. The earlier industrialisation in West Pakistan had built up a class of entrepreneurs there with considerable liquid resources, a network of working relationships with the West Pakistani civil servants who presided over the development process and some commercial experience. When in response to political pressures over-accelerating development in the East wing, commercial and industrial licences were being earmarked for use in there, it was this same class of entrepreneurs who surfaced in the East to underwrite these projects. Where they did not directly appropriate the bigger projects, it was their money which sustained the dummy Bengali entrepreneurs whose local connections were instrumental in getting the permits. Thus in a matter of time the leading industrial and commercial concerns in the region came to be owned or controlled by the same social groups who were dominating the economy of West Pakistan. In 1959, it was estimated that 2.5 per cent of industrial assets in the private sector were owned by Bengali Muslims.

The Bengali bourgeoise had been slow to manifest itself. Prior to independence it had been non-existent. All the commerce of the region rested either in British or Marwari hands. After independence the initial neglect of the region and the growth of a West Pakistan bourgeoise denied the local bourgeoise the opportunity to fill the entrepreneurial vacuum left by the departing Marwari and expanded by the spread of industrialisation. This phenomenon has affected both the character and prospects of capitalism in East Pakistan. The limited opportunities in the field of commerce tended in the first decade our history to drive the most able of the middle class Bengalis into government service. The academic and other professions remained the second options. It was only those who tried and failed in their pursuit of better options who tried their hand at business. This meant initially petty trade or low-grade jobs in the foreign or West Pakistani concerns that were based in the region. But when the flow of licences began to pick up under the Awami League regime and subsequently after the faster tempo of development in the country under the second plan in 1960 this rather pathetic collection of businessmen found themselves faced with unprecedented opportunities. Those who did not sell their licences to West Pakistanis for quick gain formed the basis of the new bourgeoise. Sustained by heavy loans from banks and institutional credit agencies and more recently by the EPIDC they began to enlarge their operations. This process has however still a long way to go before it approximates to the situation in the West. Indeed one of the reasons for the persistence of regional disparities today lies in the paucity of entrepreneurial skills and financial resources in East Pakistan to respond to a private enterprise-oriented development strategy. This same lack of resources and experience has fostered a sense of insecurity in the Bengali entrepreneur both as to this present position in society and their future prospects. In their background and thinking they are essentially petty bourgeoise and even today lack the confidence to defend their gains against a serious popular onslaught. In its absence they back East Pakistani nationalism to the hilt thereby hoping to pick up the additional loaves and fish which are thrown in the direction of

East Pakistan by the Centre with a view to forestall more fundamental demands from the people.

This has left the bastions of capitalism in East Pakistan still very much in West Pakistani hands. Any economic concessions to the region and even the threat of more political autonomy does not disturb the reality of their hold and even promises to extend the frontiers of their business empires. More growth in East Pakistan means bigger markets for enterprises situated in both regions. More business means more indigent Bengalis looking for West Pakistan's money to pay up the equity necessary to even qualify for a loan from the credit bodies. Thus within a continuing capitalist framework political autonomy and even the basic goals of parity stand to be frustrated by outside control over the commanding heights of the regional economy. The unique circumstances of East Pakistan have thus made it possible to merge the bourgeoise stage of its development with its socialist phase. True autonomy for the region must imply the seizing of the commanding heights from the West Pakistanis bourgeoise. As long as Pakistan remains one country this could only be done by extending public ownership into this domain, since it is not possible to expropriate West Pakistanis in order to hand their enterprises over to local capitalists. Even if this were to be done, pure conditions of efficiency may dictate against putting major industrial enterprises into their hands. The very fact that the ablest elements in the society are in public service since make them in the present context better custodians of the big industries than the newly elevated petty bourgeoise of East Pakistan.

Once the forces supporting regional autonomy could be harnessed to those wanting social revolution one has the basis of a unified political movement in the region. As it stands the autonomists need a socialist programme to realise their programme whilst socialists need the support of all those elements of the urban areas who have been educated in the idiom of parochial politics. Faced by a concerted front neither the West Pakistani capitalist nor their bureaucratic could hold out against the pressures generated by these combined forces. Once the notion of public ownership is established it would be much easier to widen the net of public ownership at successive stages. The capacity of the local capitalist to mount a resistance would be largely ineffective given his modest numbers and his immediate lack of self-assurance. Ten to twenty years from now he may have grown into a different animal but today he remains a pushover for progressive forces. All this makes the prospects of social revolution in East Pakistan a viable reality. If the contending political groups could be persuaded to re-organise the basic identity of their interests so that they could join hands in a struggle for a socialist and autonomous East Pakistan.

All this however remained a remote prospect as long as the iron hand of the regime restricted demands even for the more basic freedoms. In joining hands with West Pakistan political groups the local political leadership may have merely seen the present struggle as a means to an end and were thus willing to temporise in the more fundamental issues of autonomy. It is here that recent events have opened up entirely new dimension to the struggle which made it imperative for East Pakistan to re-define its relationship to the present movement. In order to understand this development one must attempt a brief social analysis of the present struggle.

As we know, the initial confrontations were led by the students. But anyone who has examined the anatomy of a demonstration or riot knows that whilst students may give the lead and slogans to such an assembly they rarely make up the body of the demonstrators. From the nooks and corners of the city emerge the urban poor. This as a group is distinct from the more easily identifiable urban factory workers. In any city or town there always remain an uncounted number of people who in the euphemisms of 'clubland' are dismissed as 'riff-raff' and 'hooligans'. They include the unemployed, casual day labourers, street urchins, news vendors, pick-pockets, professional beggars or anyone of an amorphous group who hang around cities waiting for something to turn up which will give them a more durable state in the life of the city. They live in hovels, pavements or wherever they find a nook. Within them resides all the pent up frustration and hatreds against a society which owes them no place and flaunts its wealth in their face.

It is not really possible to statistically distinguish this class but any quantitative analysis of urban power would equate those at the bottom of the poverty scale with this same group. The CSO the family budget studies of 1963–64 showed that in the urban areas of East Pakistan 65.3 per cent of the households had, on average, to live on a per capita income of less than one rupee a day. As a group this 65.3 per cent of the urban population received only 29 per cent of the total income of the urban areas. In contrast those earning Rs.900 and above per month covered only 3.3 per cent of the urban population but earned 23.1 per cent of its income. These figures of poverty however do not even include the very poorest of them who have no fixed abode to bring them within the disposition of the sample, so that one may reckon that rather more than

65 per cent are within Rs.1 per day and of those at the bottom of the scale live on under one-half of a rupee.

This class has for the first time in memory not run at the first sound of gunfire but has stayed by the side of the students in their pitched battles with the police and faced arrest and death as the price of their courageous resistance. They have at last made their presence felt and shown that they can no longer be ignored as a political element or lost in the maze of urban planning.

This element has of course been joined by the factory workers who have tended to mount their own assaults against the regime and the social order. In Chittagong and Khulna workers from the industrial areas have not only participated in the meetings called by students and opposition parties but have attacked industrial establishments at a heavy cost in lives. In Demra, an industrial suburb of Dacca, 50,000 workers participated in a frontal assault on the Adamjee Jute Mills the largest industrial enterprise in the country. From the industrial estates in and around Dacca at Tejgaon and Tengi workers have emerged to block railway lines, participate in demonstrations, fight alongside the students and other elements of the urban poor in the streets. Whilst their declining levels of living have underlined their lack of participation in the benefits of progress their explosion marks a militancy which is also directed against the class exploiters whose origins merely aggravates their alienation from the workers. The newly discovered use of the 'gherao' has given them an appropriate weapon with which to make long supressed demands. There is nothing to prevent them from extending these demands for the better wages to a complete expropriation of the enterprise. Public workers control of industry is no longer a fantasy and only requires the correct political direction.

This new pressure on the streets has been a unique and exhilarating experience for the students whose generally radical rhetoric has always included references to the sufferings of *krishak* (peasant) and *shramik* (worker) but who in practise had appeared as mere abstractions to the largely middle class students. Their common struggle has forged a bond sealed by the blood which both have shed in the streets. The more articulate student has at last found a reality in his radicalism, which can turn his slogans into realisable political objectives.

This is East Pakistan's moment of truth where correct political leadership could produce a radicalisation in East Pakistani society which in the normal course of events may take years to be realised. The authority of the regime is in shambles. Its political followers refugees from public wrath. Its class backers, the alien capitalist booking plane tickets to Karachi and beyond to sit out this conflagration. In this present mood and in the power vacuum which is widening daily in the province the long cherished goal of autonomy and social revolution are within the grasp of the people. If the Awami league and the NAP join hands and identify themselves with this mood and give it the political direction which is vital for it to acquire general acceptability they can draw upon the support of the entire population now involved in the struggle and many of those who are silent but not unsympathetic spectators. If this moment slips past not only will the pursuit of the twin goals of autonomy and social change be the more difficult to realise but the sense of disillusion fostered by the gap between the popular mood and leadership at the top will perpetuate a cycle of violence and anarchy which will promise darkness and uncertainty for the future.

West Pakistan

The radicalisation of the movement within East Pakistan need not involve a breach with the movement in the West wing. The move is dictated by the disparity in social development in the two wings which makes the available opportunities in the two regions widely different. The enemy is not the West Pakistani who as we have seen has his own grievances against the system and the majority of whose people remain as divorced from the benefits of faster development in the province as the East Pakistani. But different levels of social development are a reality and must be taken into account in assessing the political possibilities of the present situation. To elaborate this point it is necessary to look at the social forces which govern West Pakistan society. Such a survey is of less sensitive to the situation in the region than the earlier analysis of the East wing but will have to stand in order to round out the preceding analysis.

In West Pakistan political power had traditionally rested with the zamindars whose control of the land kept the peasantry subordinate to them. Their power was shared by the old ICS bureaucracy who themselves had links with the feudal class or belonged to a westernised urban elite which shared a common social ethos with the rulers. Some among the zamindar politicians, mainly from the Punjab, joined hands with the bureaucrats to frustrate the political goals of the Bengali middle class by pushing through the One Unit scheme. This inevitably bred tensions in the peripheral regions of the West wing not dissimilar to those witnessed in the Bengali middle classes. The basic traditions of the region had however always fostered between the zamindar and bureaucrat so that martial law rested less heavily on the former political leaders of West Pakistan.

Since independence two other ruling elements have emerged to share power. The industrialisation process sponsored a capitalist class in the urban areas, except perhaps for the Chiniotis from Punjab most of these were Muslim migrants born in Western India, the Memons, Khojas and Ismailis who settled in Karachi but expanded their empires throughout West Pakistan. By 1959 these particular communities controlled 41 per cent of all Muslim industrial assets and with another 9 per cent under Chinioti control were a dominant, inbred industrial group. Their control over commerce was even more pervasive and since 1959 their control over the economy has spread even further. Control gravitated to 20 families who today control 66 per cent of the industrial assets, 79 per cent of the insurance and 80 per cent of banking today. Whilst their lack of roots in the soil minimises their political representation, their power within the ruling class was considerable as they forged links with the traditional ruling groups by associating with landlords in their enterprises and employing bureaucrats. The feudal classes were themselves transferring some of their surplus wealth into industry just as some of these business houses began to buy land for commercial farming.

The fourth side of West Pakistani quadrilateral of power 'the army', has links with both land and business. An important part of the officer class came from landowning families and have in many cases added to this land by easy access to the barrage lands. Simultaneously links with the industries have been forged and the Boards of Directors of most companies is incomplete without the statutory retired general. Those with more enterprise such as Ayub's son have directly gone into business. This coalition of forces constitutes a homogeneous ruling class, which is willing to back any government that serves their interest. The fact that the present regime did this so admirably ensured a harmonious relationship founded on the vested interests of all concerned. To overthrow them would require a movement which can not only mobilise the mass of peasants and workers but can break the stranglehold of dependency which binds the peasant to his landlord by ties of dependency and tradition.

Till today there was no evidence that such a party existed. Those who proclaimed socialism were themselves dominated by the urban middle class and rural landlord, and lacked any roots either among the peasants or the industrial working class. What popular based organisations existed were thought to be no match for the massive deployment of class forces arraigned against them.

The present uprising as and when it surfaced was thus in its essence spontaneous, having its roots in the accumulated discontent of the urban middle classes rather than the efforts of any political party. Mr Bhutto was essentially the catalyst which ignited the hitherto neglected middle classes of West Pakistan. The students who initiated, fuelled and sustained the agitation, were themselves from middle class backgrounds and have not surprisingly drawn the whole spectrum of middle class into the struggle.

This development was a radical break with pre-1958 policies which, as we noted, was essentially feudal in its ethos. Though the One Unit scheme had certainly given impetus to middle class elements particularly in the Frontier. The demand for direct elections, a free press, and a more liberalised polity basically represented the frustrated urges of this class to participate in the political process. Its vehemence was however not just directed at the regime but against a social pre-dating the regime which had kept them outside the mainstream of politics. This factor makes the control of the present leaders from the old order much more reprehensive and therefore the struggle remains on the streets. As when it gets back to the polling booth they expect to reassert some of their authority by exploiting the traditional dominance in rural society. However, their authority is by no means unassailable compared to 1951 when 81 per cent of the population in West Pakistan lived in villages. The urban population in 1965 has risen to 24 per cent of the total population. This makes the concerns and motivations of the middle classes a highly relevant factor in the future direction of West Pakistani politics.

The growth of the urban middle class and its logical challenge to the older feudal leadership was so long in coming because of the 10-year interregnum in politics imposed by the Ayub Raj, where political forces were driven underground. The BD system was particularly inimical to the participation of this class so that when they exploded, the artificially bunded concerns of this class came out in a torrent to seek the natural political course from which it had been diverted. Mr Bhutto for all his feudal antecedents seems to have provided the focus for middle class political expression particularly in the Punjab, where the feudal leadership was entrenched on both sides of the fence.

In Karachi and Hyderabad, the refugee element had already established a middle class base which had grown very rapidly particularly in Karachi as a result of industrialisation. The resentments of the middle classes of

Karachi had been particularly apparent in the 1965 election when Karachi was the only district in West Pakistan to give Miss Jinnah a plurality.

The role in the Peoples Party of Mr Bhutto can expect to grow with urbanisation and industrialisation and to be particularly involved with the problems of democracy and liberalisation. However, its socialist rhetoric is likely to pose only marginal danger to the social order given the class base of the party. The feudal classes may hope that Mr Bhutto's own dependency on income from land tenancy will postpone the historic confrontation between the rising middle class and the feudal elements. In West Pakistan the touchstone for this remains the willingness of any party to invest ownership rights on the tenants actually tilling the land which would, as we have seen, break the political and economic power of the landlord and shift the balance of political power in the present context, to the middle classes. In the absence of any such fundamental commitment by the Peoples Party, political power would tend to remain with the present ruling elements, who would find no objection to coming to terms with Mr Bhutto by giving more expression to the concerns of middle class elements. Even the extension of some public sector acting as a genuflection to the socialism of the Peoples Party would not do violence to the social order and may even be welcomed by the ruling bureaucracy who would see this as an extension of their authority and an improvement of the power balance within the ruling classes in their favour. The sheer durability of the struggle has, however, begun to introduce its own dynamic into the situation. When so many people have been drawn into a struggle and in the face of the most brutal repression continue the fight, the aspirations of the participants tends to undergo qualitative changes. Thus what began as a demand for reforms has mostly resulted in the end of the entire regime. As the struggle goes on a mere change in the regime has itself seemed inadequate and more militant demands have surfaced. This possibility has been given currency by the eventual entry of the working class elements, whose demands and militancy threaten to bring the economy of West Pakistan to a standstill.

The militancy and widening base of the struggle must always carry the potential for Mr Bhutto and his Peoples Party to transcend their personal constraints and class differences and feudal character and widen their basis of support by genuinely committing themselves to a more progressive policy. However, the essentially fragmented and politically limited character of the working class movement must restrict their potential for resistance in the face of a ruling class backlash wielded by the army whose leaders appear to have no more taste for social revolution than the regime. Since the student movement itself is fragmented and localised in its influence, it cannot play the history role which the unity and organisational efficiency of the East wing students is playing today in giving a lead to the working class. In the absence of any organisational base it would not only be difficult but even risky for Mr Bhutto to seek a radicalisation in the movement which is so feasible in the completely different context of East Pakistan.

The imposition of martial law following the abdication of Ayub reflects the growing radicalisation of the struggle. Political settlement acceptable to the ruling classes was being challenged in the streets where more revolutionary pressures were building up. The complete standstill of the West wing urban economy may have been provoked by nothing more than the accumulated demands of every conceivable wage-earning group in the region coming to the boil after 10 years of imposed wage restraint under the regime's draconian labour laws. But this manifestation of labour militancy and a threat to the accumulated profits of the capitalists was enough to provoke the red herring of economic breakdown and the open invocation of military intervention in defense of the social order. The ruling groups in the armed forces have demonstrated their class character by responding to the pleas of the capitalist and have imposed martial law along with a 14-year penalty on strikers in order to contain the radicalisation process. It is possible they will get away with this because of the lack of unity and political organisation within the working class. But it can only be at the cost of bloodshed, bitterness, and distrust by all working men at the reactionary role played by the military high command.

In the East wing there is no such prospect of martial law containing the revolutionary potential inherent in the situation. Unlike West Pakistan the spread of the ferment to the countryside adds a numerical dimension to the struggle well beyond the scope of the limited forces available to enforce the writ of the Generals. More important, the West Pakistani character of the army can give martial law no other aspect than a naked attempt to curb the autonomy movement which now commands the whole province. It will appear as an attempt to frustrate a successful revolution by trying to reconquer East Pakistan for the ruling classes who see their power receding daily in the province. In this they will receive united and organised resistance. Thirty thousand students and workers have laid siege to Chittagong port for six days in an attempt to prevent recently despatched troops from West Pakistan from disembarking. This pattern of resistance can multiply a thousand-fold as students and their working class allies, blooded in earlier defiance of military curfews will join the peasants in turning East Pakistan into a battlefield for national liberation. In this situation if a bloodbath is to be avoided the Generals will have to come to terms with those commanding any semblance of popular support on the promise of regional autonomy.

How they will reconcile this with their traditional monopoly of revenue resources to finance their massive defense expenditures remains to be seen. But the movement for autonomy has gone too far to be curbed. The days ahead will determine whether this historic urge will be satisfied within the framework of one Pakistan.

On the Question of East Pakistan

Iqbal Khan

When the revolt spread to East Pakistan in February, it was primarily directed against Ayub Khan and his regime. As it gathered force, however, and especially after Ayub invited the opposition leaders for talks, East Pakistanis quickly realised that this was their chance to overthrow the hegemony of West Pakistan against which they had been protesting virtually ever since Partition. It is worth emphasising that their desire for autonomy, at this stage at least, is not motivated by any narrow, sectarian outlook. On the contrary it is the result of the avaricious policies of the politicians in whose hands the government of the country had unfortunately fallen, and who treated East Pakistan in nearly the same way as an imperialist power is known to treat a colony. East Pakistan was drained of its wealth and was discriminated against in almost all spheres of public life, and when the people of that province showed any sign of obstreperousness they were forcibly subjugated to the will of the central government in Karachi or Rawalpindi. The story of economic exploitation and political steamrollering of East Pakistan is by now too well known to need repetition; the point to bear in mind is that East Pakistan's present demand for autonomy is based on valid grounds and real fears.

That East Pakistan should have very considerable autonomy seems to be unquestionable also in view of its peculiar geographical position. It is clearly absurd to regulate the day-to-day administration of the province from a place over a thousand miles away; yet this is bound to happen if the political power is appropriated by the central government in West Pakistan. It seems obvious that for most political and administrative purposes East Pakistan should form an independent unit, just as it does geographically, ethnically, and culturally. For reasons noted above, and because it has the means of adequately supporting itself, it seems entirely right for the province to demand complete autonomy.

On the other hand it ought to be the effort of every Pakistani to maintain and strengthen the unity of his country—not merely in the symbolic way envisaged in the recent demands made by Mr Mujibur Rahman, but on a more real and meaningful way. But in so far as this entails a strong central government it directly contradicts the autonomy principle. This contradiction is, however, more apparent than real—or, rather, more contingent, i.e. a product of circumstances, than necessary. It is not impossible to conceive the conditions under which it will be possible to transcend this contradiction. Here is a brief indication of what these conditions will include:

(1) Politically the basic condition, already being demanded, for East Pakistan's accepting a strong national government is that is it should be given the weight in the National Assembly that belongs to it by virtue of its larger population. The principle of parity on which the Western politicians insist is quite arbitrary and the East Pakistanis are justified in rejecting it. The only virtue of democracy is that it allows for political power to be shared among various groups in proportion to their numerical strength in a country. Take away this fundamental principle and what is left of democracy?

(2) A 'strong national government' must not be conceived as a government who has power to bully the less powerful regional units. It should be envisaged as a means of achieving overall national unity and progress. The 'strength' of such a government will consist in: (a) ensuring minimum standards of life throughout the country; (b) guaranteeing basic democratic rights to all people; (c) ensuring that the political, commercial and economic activities of the various sections of the population and the regional governments do not infringe the above two principles; and (d) deploying and utilising all the country's physical and manpower resources in the most efficient and productive way possible. This will entail, among other things, the power to legislate on wages and prices, to lay down the policies and set targets for productive units within the regions, conduct foreign trade, obtain loans, determine priorities, and so on. Now the circumstance in which East Pakistan should be expected to hand over the control of these matters to a central government would be if guarantees were provided in the constitution that the national income will not be distributed among the regions arbitrarily but according to their need and, to some extent, proportionately to their contribution to the national income. East Pakistan may well demand also that for some time at least it should receive preferential treatment in order to make up for years of unfair exploitation neglect of its economy.

(3) The above condition cannot, however, be met in a private enterprise economy, since the principle on which such an economy operates is

'invest where you can get biggest profits' rather than 'invest where there is the greatest need'. It will be necessary, therefore, if East Pakistan's cooperation is to be secured, to do away with the private ownership of most of country's means of production and to regulate the economic and commercial activities of the country according to a national plan for development—in a word to socialise the country's economy.

(4) Finally, in view of the unhappy experience East Pakistan has had at the hands of the central government, the people may not be willing to delimit their autonomy unless they were satisfied that no central government would be in a position to force them to accept a policy or a law against their will. To some extent this can be ensured by means of appropriate constitutional safeguards. But East Pakistan's fears can be allayed only if it possesses its own army and air force and is generally responsible for its own defence.

The question inevitably arises: what are the chances of these conditions being acceptable to the West? On the face of it very little—for two reasons. Political life of Pakistan is still dominated by West Pakistanis who will not willingly accept the democratic principle of majority rule, since it will seriously diminish their power. Secondly, the reorganisation of economy on socialist lines which, as argued above, will have to be carried out to prevent the nation from splitting into two virtually independent halves can never be acceptable to the capitalists of the West who are now firmly entrenched there.

There may, however, be other, less unworthy, reasons for West Pakistan's reluctance to accept the above-mentioned conditions: viz. the fears minority areas usually have in a democratic system of their interests being ignored by the majority. The Western Unit's (or provinces', if the unit is divided into its components) interests can, however, be adequately safeguarded by the standard device of a bicameral legislature—advice proposed as early as 1954 by the Basic Principles Committee, and recently suggested again by A. K. Brohi in the Pakistan Times, though with different intentions.

It is probably necessary to make it clear that in this brief article my object is not to claim that East Pakistan will be willing to qualify its demands for autonomy if certain promises were made. It is rather to show that ways are open to our political leaders to preserve the unity of Pakistan by fair and democratic means. If the Western leaders do decide to take these ways (i.e. offer the guarantees, etc. discussed above), then East Pakistan should be prepared do delimit its autonomy, since by doing so it will lose little yet will make it possible for its own and other regions' resources to be utilised most efficiently by a government in which it will wield decisive power and influence. And it will have prevented the dismemberment of Pakistan in the bargain. On the other hand if the West's leader decided not to offer their Eastern brothers the guarantees that would enable them to accept a strong national government—i.e. did not accept East Pakistan's right to have a majority in the National Assembly, did not agree to socialise Pakistan's economy and did not allow East Pakistan to raise its own defense force, or, similarly, if East Pakistanis showed no willingness to delimit their autonomy whatever the guarantees, we would then be in no doubt that it is the destruction of Pakistan as a nation, rather than its presentation and development, that the leaders of our two wings really desire.

During the upheaval of the past few months various sections of the people of Pakistan have formulated certain demands. Contained in the next few pages are some of these demands available at this time.

People's Demands

Postal Workers of Lahore Demand

1. Enquiry against Chief Superintendent of the local Telegraph Office.
2. Restoration of right to strike.
3. Stoppage of the victimisation of office bearers of the Union.
4. Amendments to the labour laws and re-installment of the Gen. Sec. of the All Pak. Telegraph Workers Union.

Demands of Karachi College Teachers

1. Unconditional release of students, withdrawal of cases against them; acceptance of their demands and judicial inquiry into the atrocities perpetuated on them.
2. Re-instatement of the dismissed teachers of a college.
3. Immediate reopening of educational institutions.
4. Withdrawal of the University Bill and its replacement by new legislation drafted in consultation with all concerned.
5. Immediate payment of salaries to private college teachers by the Government.

Industrial Workers of Hyderabad Demand

1. Increase minimum wages.
2. Repeal the Black Laws.
3. Restore right to strike to Workers.

The Doctors in Karachi Demand

1. Formation of an Autonomous Health Service of Pakistan.
2. Class I status for all MBBS doctors.

The Demands of Dacca Medical College include

1. A medical university for East Pakistan.
2. Adequate scholarship facilities.
3. Better teaching for students, and allowances and accommodation for internee doctors.

Engineers Demand

The setting up of an Engineering Commission consisting of engineers and not CSP officers. They demand employment for unemployed engineers.

Radio T.V. and Cinema artistes of East Pakistan demand that art, literature, newspapers, music, cinema, radio and T.V. should be free from the unnecessary influence of the Government. They feel a strong movement for the establishment of the real cultural rights of the people must be launched in collaboration with the movements for political and economic rights.

Demands of Various Political Parties

Rawalpindi, February 18: Following are the demands of the country's various opposition parties and organisations.

Pakistan Democratic Movement: Federal Parliamentary Government directly elected under adult franchise; full regional autonomy; federal subjects to include defence, foreign affairs, currency and federal finance, inter-Wing communication and trade; removal of economic disparity within ten years; currency, foreign exchange, central banking, foreign trade and inter-wing communication and trade to be managed by a board elected by MNAs of both Wings; parity in services within ten years; parity in defence; incorporation of clauses two to seven of the 1956 Constitution.

Democratic Action Committee: Federal Parliamentary system of Government; direct adult franchise; withdrawal of State of Emergency; restoration of civil liberties and repeal of all black laws; release of all political prisoners; restoration of the right of labour to strike; withdrawal of all curbs on the Press; restoration of PPL to original owners.

Awami League (six-pointers): Federal form of Government on the basis of Lahore Resolution of 1940; Federal Government to deal only with defence and foreign affairs; separate fiscal and monetary policies; Federal Government to have no tax levying authority; separate external trade account for each federating State; States to have constitutional authority to maintain para-military or territorial forces.

Peoples Party: Constitutional structure to be of a republican pattern responsible to directly elected representatives of the people; universal adult suffrage; nationalisation of finance and key sectors of industry; amelioration of conditions of peasants and workers; people's right of participation in national defence.

National Awami Party (Bhashani Group): Provincial autonomy; dissolution of One Unit; amelioration of the lot of peasants and workers; nationalisation of banks, insurance companies and foreign trade; confiscation of foreign capital.

National Awami Party (Wali Khan Group): Parliamentary democracy; direct adult franchise; restoration of fundamental rights and unfettered civil liberties; complete regional autonomy for East Pakistan; restoration of all trade unions; neutral and non-aligned policy; dissolution of One Unit.

East Pakistan Students (All-Party Committee of Action): Restoration of provincialised colleges to their original status; extension in number of schools and colleges; night shift arrangements in provincial colleges; 50 per cent reduction in tuition fees; hostel charges to be subsidised by 50 per cent; Bengali as medium of instruction as well as work in all offices; increase in salaries of teachers; free and compulsory education up to Class VIII; medical university to be set up and medical council ordinance to be withdrawn; facilities of condensed course for polytechnic students; train and bus fare concessions; job opportunity guarantees; repeal of University Ordinance and full autonomy for universities; repeal of National Education Commission and Hamoodur Rahman reports; Parliamentary democracy on basis of universal adult franchise; federal form of Government and sovereign legislature; Federal Government's powers to be confined to defence, foreign policy and currency; Sub-Federation of Baluchistan, North-West Frontier and Sind with regional autonomy for each unit; nationalisation of banks, insurance companies and all big industries; reduction in rates of taxes and revenues on peasants; fair wages and bonus for workers; flood control measures for East Pakistan; withdrawal of all emergency laws, security acts and other prohibitive orders; withdrawal from SEATO, CENTO and Pakistan-US military pacts; release of all detenues and political prisoners including those of Agartala Conspiracy Case.—PPI.

The 1962 Constitution: A Critical Appraisal

Aziz Kurtha

'The days of constitutional struggle are over. The time has come to achieve democracy through violence.' It was in these terms that Maulana Bhashani is reported to have addressed a large gathering of students and workers on February 16. The immediate reason for that remark may have been the grand old man's desire to demonstrate to his rival opposition parties that his own cap is still in the ring, and that at this crucial hour no member of the opposition can afford to truckle to the Ayub regime and nor should he accept any last minute constitutional compromise as an easy way out of the existing upheaval. Although some liberals may regard his emphasis on violence as 'unfortunate', his statement usefully underlines the fact that any discussion today of the 1962 Constitution may be both an anachronism in the near future and also an irrelevant and ineffective channel of proposing fundamental changes. A hundred eminent constitutional lawyers deliberating for a year about changes in the constitutional framework of Pakistan could not achieve half as much as did the recent mass meetings, demonstrations and *hartal*s carried out by students and workers in Dacca, Karachi, Lahore, etc. in recent weeks. In any case it is worth noting that constitutional proposals always seem to follow and not precede disturbances on the streets. Nevertheless, it may be of some peripheral value to briefly look at the origins of the present Constitution and its most obvious shortcomings.

The point which must always be borne in mind and which will probably be found recurring in this journal is that politics in Pakistan has always been an essentially (upper) middle class *passe-temps* (or hobby). This has led to the promulgation and abrogation of Constitutions and laws by a small minority of the population who at best have been very remote from the needs and aspirations of the vast majority of industrial workers and peasants, and at worst have deliberately ignored their demands or repressed them. On October 7, 1958 shortly before the first general elections President Iskander Mirza was obliged to issue a proclamation abrogating the Constitution of 1956, and to place the country under martial law. The reasons given for this action were, paradoxically, that the struggle for power and corruption among the politicians, their exploitation of the ignorant masses and their prostitution of Islam had created a discreditable dictatorship in which adventurers and exploiters flourished. An identical censure could today be made against the very regime which for some eleven years claimed to have 'cleansed the nation'. This is not to suggest in any way that the constitutional position before 1956 or between 1956–58 was a model of democracy. A study[1] of that period has shown that between independence day and the suspension of the Constitution of 1956, notice was given of 56 adjournment motions; thirty-one of which were ruled out of order, thirteen were not moved or withdrawn after the government had given assurances, and ultimately only four were discussed. In 1951 a motion to discuss government's failure to support Egypt in the Suez crisis was ruled out of order on the ground that government had not failed to do anything it was obliged to do. Permission to introduce a motion to discuss the economic crisis resulting from a lack of planning was refused on the ground that it covered too wide a field. In 1954 a motion to discuss orders banning meetings in Karachi and the arrest of journalists and political workers failed to secure a hearing because there were remedies in the courts!

Origin of the 1962 Constitution

It must be recalled that after Ayub Khan had promulgated the Basic Democracies Order on October 27, 1959 and when the first BDs elected under the Order had obediently expressed a vote of confidence in him as President, a Constitutional Commission was set up on February 17, 1960. This Commission toured Pakistan extensively and prepared a questionnaire, which as publicly announced, was sent to everyone who applied for it. This facade of consulting public opinion about a new Constitution was unconvincing if only because some 80 per cent of the population was known to be illiterate and could hardly be expected to delve into the labyrinths of constitutional law. Moreover, those few who could and did wish to make comments were naturally limited by the questionnaires themselves. In fact, only 6,929 replies were received, that is from roughly 0.01 per cent of the population! Despite these short-comings it is worth looking at the sort of replies the Commission received

---

1. Mushtaq Ahmed, 'Government and Politics in Pakistan.'

and comparing these to the Commission's own proposals and the 1962 Constitution itself.

As to whether the new Constitution should be federal—65.6 per cent of the answers were in the affirmative and the Commission agreed. Regarding distribution of powers 54 per cent were in favour of the 1956 Constitution arrangement. This arrangement basically provided that the central Parliament could make laws with extra-territorial effect whilst the provincial legislatures could only make laws for the province. As regards executive powers the 1956 Constitution provided a list of Federal subjects, another of provincial subjects including railways, communications, and industries. However, the federal executive could give certain directions to the provincial government, e.g. to refrain from acting to the former's prejudice, or to construct railways or to take steps to prevent danger to the peace or economic life of the country.

Twelve per cent wanted the central power enhanced whilst 39 per cent wanted the central power limited to defence, foreign affairs and currency, all other powers being allotted to the provinces. Just over 50 per cent wanted a Parliamentary form of government, 8 per cent preferred a Presidential system and some 2 per cent were for a Khilafat system. What we have today, however, seems to include all the worst aspects of a one-man-band Presidential system and a feudal theocracy. The Commission recommend bicameral legislatures although 74 per cent of the answers desired unicameral legislature. It recommended that candidates for election to Parliament should be at least 30 years of age although only 12 per cent of the answers supported this view. The Constitution now fixes a minimum age of 25. It also suggested that the franchise should be restricted to those sufficiently educated or possessed of sufficient property to induce them to enquire into the qualifications of candidates. This is probably the most obnoxious part of the Commission's recommendations, resting as it did on the totally false premise that possession of property was somehow a magical gauge to assess a person's powers of rational discrimination and enquiry. The proviso regarding sufficient education was equably reprehensible as the regime was deliberately refusing to provide a minimum education and then using this handicap as a pretext for restricting the franchise. And of course the most startling commission in the 1962 Constitution was the absence of the well-known fundamental rights, e.g. freedom of speech and assembly, equality before the law etc. which could be enforceable by the individual in the Courts. This omission was all the more drastic in view of the fact that some 97 per cent of the answers to the Commission favoured their re-enactment as found in the 1956 Constitution. Instead of these fundamental rights, we found so-called 'principles of law-making' which could not be pleaded in any court. The fundamental rights had, therefore, to the government's dismay, to be enacted in the Constitution (First Amendment) Act of 1963.

Defects in the Present Constitution

1. Legislative Powers: Whereas under the 1956 Constitution the legislative powers were divided by subject matter into three lists—i.e. central, provincial and concurrent, the 1962 Constitution has only a rather long list of exclusive central powers which includes almost everything from defence, foreign affairs, currency and banking to weights and measures, mineral oil and gas, tourism, industries, and preventive detention. This means that the provincial legislatures cannot pass laws on any of these matters and if it does those laws will be invalid to the extent that they affect a central law. Moreover, the central legislature may make laws on matters not enumerated in the list of exclusive central subjects if the so-called security or economic or financial stability of the country requires it. It can also legislate on any subject for the capital territories in Islamabad and Dacca. The provincial legislature may legislate for the province only on those few matters which are not on the exclusive central list.

This extraordinary subordination of the provincial legislatures must be substantially amended to allow the East and West provinces as much autonomy as is consistent with the overall interest of Pakistan. Whilst this may appear vague, it is quite conceivable that if the central legislative power should be restricted to matters of defence and foreign policy. This would permit each province to develop in the way it thought best whilst it would retain a common link in those matters, defence and foreign policy, which it would be in the interest of both provinces to maintain. The smaller provinces within the two main provinces are not as diverse from each other, nor separated by as much territory as the two main ones but their exact position in any future Constitution must be considered independently in a separate paper.

Autonomy of East Pakistan: All the opposition parties are known to be agreed on the question of autonomy for East Pakistan. This problem must be clearly faced by all Pakistani socialists and we must not only recognise the demands for autonomy made over the last decade, but we must also welcome it. We must attempt only to ensure that the autonomy of the two wings is compatible with the development of a socialist system of government. It seems today that East Pakistan is, owing to its economic and political history and the relative absence of a strong class of industrial entrepreneurs, closer to achieving a socialist regime than is West Pakistan. If this is true then a Pakistani socialist, whichever province he may be from, must keep foremost in his mind the need to ensure that East Pakistan's march towards an egalitarian society, rid of an industrial or feudal ruling class, is unhampered by the machinations, military or otherwise, of those same classes who have for two decades plundered Pakistan's economy. Moreover, it would be naive to ignore that the two wings are at different levels of economic and social development and thus it is unlikely that there will be some synchronistic process of socialism in the two wings. As such the immediate need will be to ensure that the embryonic development of a social revolution, wherever it may be, is not throttled in its infancy. The call for autonomy must then be seen in this perspective. The example of a popularly elected Communist party and government in Kerala in India, which cannot however hope to nationalise major industries within its territory owing to the overriding powers of a capitalist central government should serve as a useful reminder of the political strait-jacket in which a socialist but subordinate provincial unit will inevitably find itself. Thus as an immediate measure the central government's power to dissolve provincial legislatures and to unilaterally declare an emergency in the region should be abolished. Moreover, under the present Constitution the courts are deprived of jurisdiction to determine whether a central law is *ultra vires* or goes beyond its constitutional authority. However, as a central law prevails over a provincial law to the extent of its inconsistency with the former it is conceivable that a court may be obliged to pronounce a provincial law invalid for repugnancy to a central law although the latter may itself be strictly *ultra vires*. These problems would be largely irrelevant if the demand for autonomy is accepted, but in any case it is desirable to give the courts jurisdiction in such matters regarding constitutional propriety. In a socialist regime the present structure of the legal profession and the courts would itself need radical change to rid it of the obvious middle-class bias it presently has. One does not need to labour the point that even a perfectly democratic Constitution could be an instrument of repression if its operation were left in the hands of those who either represented or displayed an undemocratic class bias.

2. Emergency Powers: Under the present Constitution only the President can issue a proclamation of emergency and only he can revoke it once promulgated. He may do so if subjectively satisfied that the country is threatened by war or if the security or economic life of the nation is threatened by internal disturbance beyond the power of the provincial government to control. Unlike the position in the 1956 Constitution, the elected National Assembly has no power of control in this matter. As is well known an emergency was declared during the 1965 Indo-Pakistan hostilities as a security measure, but it continued as a repressive police measure until very recently. The effect of a proclamation is that the President may completely by-pass the legislature and himself legislate by Ordinance, and most important of all enforcement of the fundamental rights can be suspended in this period. In the Indian Constitution a proclamation of emergency is automatically revoked after 60 days unless extended by Parliament and this is an obviously preferable situation. Until the important Jellani Case of 1966 it was held by the courts that a person could be detained under emergency regulations almost indefinitely if the detaining authority was subjectively satisfied about its necessity. The power to declare emergencies must clearly be subject to severe restraints and the power of detention should be proven to be justifiable on objective criteria of justice.

3. Fundamental Rights: So much has already been written about this subject elsewhere that to avoid repetition one need only make a few general remarks. Generally, the fundamental rights relating to security of the person, freedom of speech and movement, arrest, detention, religious instruction etc. prohibit 'the state' (i.e. the central and provincial government and legislatures and all local and public authorities) from doing certain things. The sorts of liberties paid lip service to in our Constitution have, with modifications, been recognised in many other countries. Peaslee's *Constitutions of the Nations* sets out the constitutions of some 89 countries where there is some similar recognition of these 'rights'. But the important question is not merely whether they exist on paper, but to what extent do they in practice limit the powers of a ruling class in favour of the individual. It is thus interesting to note that in the thirteen years since the fundamental rights were first copied out of the Indian Constitutions and introduced in Pakistan in 1956, they have only been in actual operation for about four years, i.e. between 1956–58 (martial law) and 1963–65 (Indo-Pak War). In other words there are fundamental rights, and there are fundamental rights. As one writer has said 'there are normative constitutions of...(some) countries...in which the Supreme Court interprets the constitution and the executive and legislature abide by the interpretation....And there are (other) constitutions devised to throw dust in the eyes of observers while the ruling clique or party does as it likes; here the Fundamental Rights, like bikinis, are important only for what they conceal!'[2] In the Pakistani context the 'fundamental rights' have been remarkable not so much for their protection of individual or collective liberties, but for the almost unique ease with which they have been jettisoned and emasculated in the interests of arbitrary and oppressive rule. The provision of an effective legal process for enforcing fundamental rights is obviously more important than their mere existence, and it is thus noteworthy that in Pakistan, unlike even in India, the right to effective judicial process is not a fundamental right in itself.

Similarly, fundamental right no. 7 provides that 'every citizen shall have the right to form associations or unions subject to any reasonable restriction imposed in the interest of morality or public order'. However, this has not prevented the Government from imposing crippling conditions on the right to form effective trade unions and to go on strike. For instance, each trade union must be registered in accordance with the Trade Union Act and a registrar can refuse registration with the consequence that the association of workers will not enjoy the limited immunity from legal process enjoyed by registered unions. Moreover, under the Labour Disputes Acts of 1965 no person can go on strike unless he complies with a number of conditions and gives the prescribed notice (49 days in the case of public utility services and 7 days in others). A labour dispute can be referred to a Conciliation Officer or a labour court by employer, employee or Government and no one may strike during or pending such proceedings. Representation by qualified counsel is not permitted before Conciliation Officers or the Labour Court. The East Pakistan Labour Disputes Act, 1965 provides a one-year penalty for going on so-called 'illegal' strike (i.e. one where the conditions for strike have not been complied with) and a maximum six-month sentence for instigating any 'go-slow' among workers, designed to improve their wages. So much then for the freedom of association and Principle of Policy No. 9 which lays down that 'Equitable adjustments of rights between employers

---

2. See, 'Changing Law in Developing Countries' (1963). Edited by J. N. D. Anderson. Incidentally, the above quotation is not cited out of any deference for the editor of this volume.

and workmen and between landlords and tenants must be ensured'. The above minor criticisms have not for the moment touched upon the most basic issue that the presupposition of worker-employer or landlord-tenant relationship is itself unjust. Fundamental Rights Nos. 11 and 12 provide that no person shall be compelled to pay any special tax for a religion other than his own nor required to receive instruction in a religion other than his own. In any other words he can be compelled to do these things providing only that it is through the medium of his own religion. It is also laid down that no citizen shall be denied admission to any educational institution receiving aid from public revenues on the ground only of race, religion, or place of birth. This is then a carte blanche for discrimination in private educational institutions.

Our Constitution has borrowed a device from the Constitution of Eire in that it contains a list of fundamental rights which are supposed to be justiciable by the Courts, and another list of Principles of Policy which can never be enforced in a court but which are supposed to bind the consciences of public authorities and who are required to act generally in accordance with them. The most classic demonstration of the uselessness of our constitutional guarantees is provided by the principles of policy which state that illiteracy must be eliminated (when over 80 per cent of the population still remains illiterate) and that 'the undue concentration of wealth and means of production in the hands of a few...must be prevented' (when as is well-known 66 per cent of all industrial assets, 80 per cent of banking and 69 per cent of insurance funds are in the hands of twenty families).

4. Presidential Powers: It is no exaggeration to say that under the present constitution the powers of the National and Provincial Assemblies are merely formal eunuch-like embellishments to a central omnipotent figure, the President. He is for all practical purposes the unimpeachable and unquestionable ruler of both wings of the country and he is not responsible to nor dependent on the support of a majority in the legislature. He does not have to follow ministerial advice and in fact the Constitution states only that he may have a Council of Ministers. He is the supreme commander of the defence services and may raise and maintain those services as he pleases. The conditions of services of members of the All-Pakistan services and appointments thereto are also made by or through him. There is thus nothing in law to prevent a President doubling their wages before an election, or at a critical hour.

The President appoints the provincial Governors, the Attorney-General, Comptroller and Auditor General, who must all perform such duties as he directs. Only he can proclaim an emergency and revoke it, and he can also legislate by Ordinance when the legislature is not in session if he is satisfied that circumstances make this necessary. His permission is required before any (financial) bill is presented before the National Assembly and he can veto any bill once passed. He appoints persons to the National Economic Council who hold office at his pleasure and help formulate the economic, financial and commercial policy of the central and provincial governments. He also appoints the National Finance Commission, consisting of the financial ministers of the centre and provinces and who make recommendations as to the distribution of the national revenue. Their recommendations can be rejected by the President.

These and other extraordinary powers bestowed on, or rather arrogated by, one man, which can be guaranteed to produce the worst Machiavellian characteristics even in a hypothetically honest politician, are explicable in the light of a steady development of absolutist power ever since the country's (myth of ?) Independence in 1947. The present culmination of a one-man-band political structure must also be seen in the context of developments immediately preceding the imposition of martial law in 1958. Unemployment was at a record level of eleven million and a number of strikes had erupted at the enterprises of foreign oil companies in West Pakistan in May and June 1958. The impending general elections threatened the domination of the Pakistani bureaucracy and particularly of their chief spokesman, General Iskander Mirza, who was increasingly worried about means of keeping a tight grip on political events in both wings of the country.

In the light of these factors it is not surprising that the then existing regime and its arch-supporters, viz. the big landlords and the growing numbers of industrial capitalists, should have wanted to take the trend of absolute power to its untrammelled conclusion. One historical work[3] has described this process as follows:

The big landlords of West Pakistan, who were represented in the leadership of the Republican Party, high-ranking army officers and close associates of President Iskander Mirza, demanded that bourgeois parliamentary democracy should be restricted, or even abolished, and replaced by strong-arm methods. They intended to put into practice the

---

3. 'History of Pakistan 1947–58' by Gankovsky.

scheme advanced by Iskander Mirza in his speech of March 23, 1957, to establish a Presidential government in Pakistan similar to the American system i.e. that the government should be responsible to the head of the state and not to the National Assembly ... The President's rights were to be considerably extended; in particular he was to be granted the right to dissolve the provincial legislative assemblies ...

Even a brief sketch of the development of an oppressive absolute power cannot fail to recall that as early as November 1955 Khan Sahib and other leaders of the Republican Party had proposed that all parties and other political organisations should be dissolved and demanded the establishment of an ironically-described Revolutionary Council consisting of the ten best men of the nation who were to wield absolute power in the country. The murder of Khan Sahib on May 9, 1958, did not unfortunately also kill his berserk ideas which were to be seen, implemented only a few months later in October 1958, and then introduced in modified form in the Constitution of 1962.

A democratic Constitution for Pakistan would have to be formulated completely outside, and not out of, the underlying assumptions of the Constitution of 1962. Hence the choice between a Westminster-style parliamentary system or a White House-like Presidential framework, which consumed so much wasted energy in 1961, becomes irrelevant. The need is not so much to plagiarise foreign constitutional models but to develop a truly democratic governmental structure best suited to our own requirements. In this direction not only must the present Basic Democracies system be utterly demolished, as seems now to be generally accepted, but that must be accompanied by a drastic reduction in the constitutional powers of any future head of government. General adult franchise must be complimented with a democratisation of the machinery of government without which the right to vote becomes a meaningless exercise in form-filling. Moreover, means must be devised to emasculate if not obliterate the present over-riding position of the armed forces and the civil service. Unless this is properly seen to any and every democratic step formed will always be jeopardised by the overt or covert blackmail of these two most entrenched elements of the ruling class. It is these elements, which, even more than the '20 families' have actually manipulated the real intricacies of oppressive government and which have, somehow, managed to scramble unscathed through every political upheaval.

Any future Premier cannot be permitted to treat a duly elected body of representatives as a nuisance to be avoided; he must be made answerable to it and the right to legitimately impeach and criticise him must not carry the risk of penalty. In the present Constitution those who wish to impeach him risk losing their seats if less than half the members of the Assembly support the resolution. The existing power to dissolve provincial Assemblies must be withdrawn as it could become a powerful and oppressive weapon in the foreseeable event of a socialist movement developing within a province.

Moreover, institutions must be developed which enable all adult members of the population to contest democratic elections on equal terms and ensure that elected persons always remain answerable to their electors. In this context, restrictions on amounts that candidates can spend on their election campaigns must be strictly enforced. Obviously in the absence of such provisions the proletariat and peasants can never hope to compete on equal terms with the middle-class elements who have traditionally made a toy out of the electoral system. All legal disputes concerning electoral laws are outside the purview of the courts under the present constitution and this is obviously in need of change. In fact, the entire legal machinery would need to be complimented with an elaborate scheme of free legal aid and advice. This must be a right in itself so that the aggrieved should not have to rely on the varying whims of charitable counsel. There will also need to be many procedural changes regarding the legislative process which cannot adequately be discussed here. But in a democratic constitution there can be no place for provisions requiring the consent of any person like the President before a resolution is presented; and the use of the entire financial resources of the country must be subject to the fullest debate both within the legislature and the smaller elected bodies in towns, villages and cities. Under the present Constitution the Assembly's powers over financial matters are very narrowly circumscribed and limited to discussion *without* voting except in connection with 'new expenditure', i.e. expenditure which exceeds by more than ten per cent, the amount previously approved for a given project. All other expenditure is discussed but after fourteen days the Assembly is *deemed* to have assented to the demand.

Conclusion

Even a cursory glance at our Constitution tends to show that it makes a mockery of the supposed philosophy underlying constitutional government, namely that it is a means of limiting government and of requiring those who govern to conform to law and rules. It may be argued that this is the inevitable result of the interaction and conflict of different class interests where law plays its traditional role as a weapon in the hands of those in the dominant class to preserve an oppressive status quo. Only a person blinded by the empty rhetoric and bombastic phraseology of constitutional provisions could seriously deny this, and yet one knows that even in socialist countries like the USSR and Cuba it has been found desirable to have Constitutional guarantees. Although it is a truism that even government *according* to a Constitution is no guarantee of social justice because the Constitution may simply establish the institutions of government and leave them free to act arbitrarily, one of the most crucial problems in Pakistan has been the ease with which even bourgeois legal rights have been discarded on a variety of civil and military pretexts. The position of the military in our political structure is something that needs analysis and radical alteration. For one thing the present requirement in the Constitution that the Minister of Defence must be a Lieutenant-General or officer of similar rank, is obnoxious in that it brings in military personnel into a civilian government and thus needs to be deleted. It may be conjectured that unless the present (upper and lower) middle class recruitment of the Pakistani professional forces is counter-balanced by the development of something like a grassroots, genuine People's Army, then the few advances painfully achieved on the road to socialism will be in constant danger of deliberate retrogression. As this may seem idealistic, although the proposal had been aired as early as the late 1950s, as an interim measure full-scale conscription for something like three years may be one method of reducing the power of the professional contingent in the forces. Some other means will also have to be devised to extirpate the entrenched interests of the professional and long-standing members of the Civil Service. A way out of this dilemma may be to subject the civil service in the urban districts or *thanas* to the control of elected representatives in those areas.

Note: This article was written before the imposition of martial law on March 25, 1969 and the abrogation of the 1962 constitution on the same date. However, it is obvious that a new constitution will have to be framed with reference to the provisions and failures of the 1956 and 1962 constitutions. Thus the above critic may still be of some value and the comments made on the position of the armed forces and the civil service are even more important in view of recent events.

Despatches from Pakistan

January 31,

There are demonstrations every day in Lahore, the assembly Chambers seem to be the terminating point. In Karachi the K.D.A. offices were attacked. In East Pakistan, doctors and students of the Medical College have called for blood donations for the victims of police firing. I believe Dacca was completely cut off on 25 January—no communications between Dacca and Karachi—papers announce wedding receptions of the sons and daughters of the bourgeoise every day! These events are both sombre and inspiring. One is amazed at the people will to rebel and react after years of oppression and continuing police brutality.

February 20,

Our school has been closed for two days again—there was terrible rioting the day Bhutto arrived—the procession went off very well—the largest ever here—but afterwards, as is usual, and was engineered—the local Pathans are paid to attack—and there was terrible bloodshed in Empress market where the Pathans attacked the UP butchers—you see the Prince of the ruling house imports them from Hazara—as was done when Miss Jinnah was fighting the election—also Karachi has about six lakhs of floating Pathan labour—uprooted urban and village with no ties here and nothing to lose but a day's work—made up for by the mercenaries pay—wherever the paid Pathans are in Karachi there is trouble—in warehouses, in cafes and so on—Dacca is a flame, a Reader of Rajshahi University shot by the police—in Lahore the police chase students into side-lanes and beat them up—terrible things happening—but the students are up to it—although in Lahore they are mainly Jamaat-i-Islami—I think I told you that girls from Lahore College and Kinnaird College scaled their walls to take part in the procession led by Daultana's daughter (!) and Hameed Nizami's daughter—anyway—they also walked barefoot in Rawalpindi, squatted down and defied Section 144 and the police—because some DSP was heard to say, 'We'll show them what we think of such women;' and the police had to apologise there and then. Somewhere else a women in a car stopped and beat up a police inspector with her handbag because she saw him manhandling a student. She said, 'Charge me, take me to jail,' but of course no one did—in our (women's) processions here hundreds of men and boys walked with us and no one even whistled.

There are threats of martial law unless the DAC comes to talks—there is deadlock now. Bhutto says no—Bhashani dare not and would not go to Pindi—and Mujibur Rahman is still in jail under the heinous Agartala conspiracy hoax.

Every conceivable professional group has marched—lawyers, engineers, doctors even women in white overalls.

We understand that Gauhar Ayub has sold his house to the sheikh of Abu Dhabi for 30 Lakhs (paid) in sterling and has joined the race to Sardinia where the Aga Khan is financing a huge building project, for the Ex's of the world! They are all collecting their millions for if and when their time comes—we'll let them go—take what they want people say—only GO.

It is amazing how the press has changed—craven swine that they were—the 'Morning News' wrote, 'although we hold no brief for Ayub's policies'…Christ since when—since the students opened the flood gates?

In East Pakistan it is the students who are the main political force— here it is partly so—but the students in large part support the right wing religious group—in Karachi the progressive student leaders are mostly in jail—and they too are divided of course into Peking and Moscow groups. Of course the working class in West Pakistan hasn't joined the Demos—because most of them are in essential services—but the Railway Demo in Lahore was fantastic—now Bakhtiar who is really the official (government backed) labour leader has also brought out his demo.

The main slogan everywhere, even with girl students, is 'Revolution and Socialism'. Ayub would be wise to resign—but naturally he is involved with capital and so on—and supported by the investors foreign and local.

February 26,
On the political front. Some college teachers are going on strike—no pay for so long—no fees since closure—the Governments has given Rs.5 lakhs I believe, but this isn't enough—they want Rs.40 lakhs to cover Karachi alone! Gordon College has closed down—no money so no staff salaries and so on—but now since Ayub's statement perhaps colleges will open—Mujeeb has attended the Round Table Conference [RTC]. It appears that he wants representation according to population, which means that the Capital would probably have to shift to Dacca—He was

asked by a journalist, 'But aren't you for secession?' He answered 'Me? No! Perhaps West Pakistan will want secession from us!' It seems that Ayub wasn't willing to let him out but was advised to do so, being told that once sparks would fly, maybe everyone would seek his protection again. Will the students agree? That remains to be seen! Meanwhile the Mullahs are mobilising—but the slogan of socialism is on people's lips and cannot be suppressed now. Anyway, the first RTC lasted 36 minutes and everyone came out smiling—rascals on both sides of the table—mostly old lags in the Opposition, Nasrullah Khan, Daultana, Sardar Shaukat, Mandoodin etc. Bhashani refused to join and so did Bhutto—who has mainly young peoples support, while quite obviously Mujeeb has also the support of the big interests in Pakistan ...

March 2,

Today Zakia Sarwar, Aliya Imam and two other college lecturers (male) went on hunger strike to press for the demands of the college teacher viz. a rise in salaries and so on—there was a big to do, garlands and so on. They were sitting on durries with 'gol takias', they will stay there for 48 hours—very brave of course and hats off to the two husbands of the two women. The Women's Democratic Federation is being re-organised, our Manifesto is being put into shape. The first All Pakistan Conference will be in Lahore in May.

March 8,

Lahore seems to have quietened down, compared with Karachi. In Karachi there is at the moment, so much freedom of both body and mind—it is wide and big though bare it is much more alive and vital—particularly the women—the teachers have proven themselves—Anita Ghulam Ali broke into the Jamia Millia yesterday where a Seminar was on with the Education Minister presiding—took over the platform—forced him to tender his resignation to the President and then grabbed the mic and gave the Millia what for, for daring to invite the Minister when the teachers are near death on their hunger strike—*Dawn* writes 'for the third time in a month we are constrained to bring to the public notice... the condition of our teachers.' Constrained indeed—I suppose they are still wondering whether the clock will turn back with vested interests so involved ...

Mrs Dawoodi is still on hunger strike—a widow with three children—we went and sat with her last night—what a fine woman—my goodness such stuff they are made of—the fasters all lie in the open. There is a rumour that students will be given degrees 'like that' to pacify them. What good will it do? There will be no room for them to take exams next year, will there?

On the 10th the RTC meets again—they are being watched by everyone—no one trusts them—they are out to compromise—by now with labour up in arms—they'll be murdered if they try.

Kohinoor was looted in Lyallpur they say. It reminds me of the 'Aziz Khan' novel—'What times we live in'—today every car is flying a black flag in support of the teachers.

Bid to Create Disturbances: Asghar's allegation against Government.

RAWALPINDI, March 11: Air Marshal Asghar Khan tonight made a scathing attack on the Government and accused it and its Party of hiring hooligans to create disturbances here in Karachi and elsewhere.

It is learnt that while speaking at the evening session of the RTC the Air Marshal referred to the transportation of large number of people from the rural areas to the cities for creating disturbances.

He is said to have stated that the ruling Muslim League Party with the support and connivance of the administration brought these toughs, paid them on daily basis, even gave them country liquor.

Karachi

In Karachi, the Air Marshal is said to have pointed out, people have been hired to create trouble in the industrial area. He accused the Government Party of collecting large funds through coercion from businessmen, industrialists and bankers for this purpose.

He alleged, it is said, in West Pakistan alone a sum of Rs. three crores had been collected in this manner for such purposes.

He is said to have given specific instances—one, for example, of a bank of Peshawar which was coerced to pay Rs. one lakh.

Replying, it is further learnt, President Ayub Khan characterised Air Marshal's allegations as 'sweeping remarks'. He, however, said that there may be some truth in them but then he is said to have added, political parties do have funds and there was no harm to make requests for funds.

From *Dawn*,
Karachi.

PAKISTAN LEFT REVIEW

Summer, 1969

Contents

Volcano Tranquilised

Editorial

If the first three months of 1969 will always be remembered for the heartening rejuvenation of political consciousness and action in Pakistan, the four months since March 25 will be noted for their uncanny silence and for turning back the clock a decade. Let us admit that the abrupt silence took both established political commentators and us by surprise. But to state that alone or to attempt to explain the subsequent political reticence as cowardice would be as insufficient as it would be silly and false. Students and workers who have braved police brutality and bullets on the streets do not retreat simply from the prospect of facing a soldier in arms. Part of the reason must surely lie in the fact that we have too often imagined a transient demonstration or a march to be a sufficient act of political protest and purgation. This is not in any sense to decry the value of demonstrations, let alone *hartals* and gheraos, but simply a plea that unless they are accompanied by a proper analysis of the problems and sufficient plans for the anticipated countermoves, the ephemeral gains will be misleading.

Moreover, we should now have learned the changes of over-emphasising the importance of personalities, and of protesting largely about them, as opposed to the particular and general issues facing the country. Ayub was anathema, and properly so, and we should welcome an inquiry into his assets and actions during his term of office. But for too many of us his removal was a sufficient victory in itself, and this again may partly explain the quiet after his departure. As we have seen only too clearly his departure, whether it was voluntarily or whether 'an Ayub' was done on Ayub, did not alter the oppressive situation and there certainly seems little prospect of even the most rudimentary development of socialism. Nevertheless, some very recent proposals have been aired in our Press and these include:

(1) Plans for a new educational policy involving the nationalisation of foreign missionary schools, the launching of a belated literacy programme

with a supposed literary target of 68 millions by 1980. There is to be a greater orientation of secondary education towards technical and professional studies. The madrasahs are envisaged as integrated into the normal school system with the introduction of Islamiyat as a compulsory subject in all schools up to Class X.

A minor reform, no doubt meant as a sop to the tremendous protests by students and teachers in recent months, is the promised autonomy of universities and a provision for greater student participation in their running.

(2) Plans for a proposed new Labour Policy include:

(a) The fixing of minimum wages from July 1 under the following terms: For unskilled labour in enterprises employing 50 or more workers.

Karachi Area	Rs. 140 per month
Other industrial areas	Rs. 125 per month
Other areas	Rs. 115 per month
In East Pakistan (tea garden industry)	Rs. 100–120 (for two-member family)

Needless to say, the proposed minimum wages provide an abysmal standard of living for a vast proportion of the population. The monthly profits of even the small industrialists and landlords will no doubt continue to run in the five-figure range per month.

(b) The right to strike and lock-out is to be restored, but ultimate decision lies with an industrial tribunal. It must be noted that before March 25 the principle of a right to strike was always recognised but it was now hedged with qualifications and restrictions as to render it meaningless. Some details of this were given in the article on the Constitution in our last issue.

(c) Unions will not need to be registered to benefit.

(d) There is to be a restriction of the class of public utility services where strikes are disallowed.

(e) The introduction of a system of boards of conciliation and voluntary arbitration. Again the details need to be seen first because if employers and government are given a right to refer a labour dispute to a board during which the right to strike is suspended then the network of conciliation boards will always work to the employees' disadvantage.

Details about the workers' right to institute a 'go-slow' (at present completely illegal) or the right to representation by legal counsel before a board (disallowed at present) are conspicuous by their absence.

Generally, our reaction to these new proposals should not be one of precipitate enthusiasm. What seems to be distributed as reforms and charitable largesse is no more than restoration of certain rights.

The promise of general elections seem always to be tied to a prerequisite condition that the various political parties should amalgamate, and settle their differences. This is a very meagre pretext particularly as several of the parties in West Pakistan have already coalesced. The latest announcement came on July 28 that a return to partial civilian rule and the holding of general elections would come 'probably next year'. It remains to be seen what this means in the present regime's vocabulary.

* * * *

Since 1966 the cost of income in Pakistan rose 12 times; but the industrial wages only ¼ of what they were three years ago.

A jail prisoner in Pakistan earns a higher per capita income than the industrial worker.

In 1965, when the East Pakistan railway union served strike notice, the government convicted 9,000 of its members, sent 4,000 to prison and dismissed another 4,000 from their jobs.

(*Dawn*)

Save Pakistan from Being Mortgaged!

The Economic policies espoused by the Ayub regime have caused enormous damage to our country. On one hand, they produced the bitter social injustices which at last exploded last Winter. On the other, they have dealt a terrible blow to our very independence. For the 'economic progress'—really a euphemism for the rapacity of a few powerful families—was made possible by taking inordinate loans from foreign countries. The series of Five-Year Plans which Ayub's economists produced rely exclusively on such loans.

It is estimated that the total outstanding debt at the end of the Perspective Plan period (i.e. 1985) will be no less than

Rs. 103,900,000,000!

According to some economists even this is an under-estimate. We, therefore, appeal to General Yahya Khan to scrap the existing Plans and replace them with new ones, relying, as far as possible, on Pakistan's own resources, as has been so successfully done by our neighbour and friend, China.

Our Enemies and How to Destroy Them: Literacy and Population Explosion

Considering that the two themes of this article are illiteracy and population explosion in Pakistan—subjects commonly discussed only in technical journals and rarely allowed to become soiled by the base vocabulary of popular politics—the above title might appear to be inexcusably sensational. And yet the threat to our future, and indeed to our independence, posed by the appalling illiteracy and the frightening rate at which the population of our country is growing, is far greater than that held out by any of our much publicised 'traditional' enemies. There can be little doubt that if today we are one of the poorest people of the world, if our agriculture still remains primitive and our industrial effort meagre, and if, with every year that passes we find ourselves more and more crippled by the mounting weight of foreign debt, one main reason for this is that our successive governments either totally ignored the two enemies I have mentioned above or have been too miserably incompetent to achieve any success against them.

The strength of these enemies is usually presented in percentages— of course understood only by those few lucky enough to have had an education—as 80–85 per cent (for illiteracy) and 3 per cent per year (for population growth). The public is hardly ever made aware of the implications of these figures in real, human terms. The ordinary citizen is seldom made to realise that 85 per cent illiteracy means that, for example, next year, when the population of our country is going to hit the 127 million mark, the number of illiterate people (i.e. those who, according to the official definition, cannot even 'read with understanding a short statement') will be at least 107 million—an outrageous state of affairs in human terms alone, quite apart from the damage it must cause to the country's economic and social development. Nor is the citizen ever awaken to the horror that if the rate of population growth at 3 per cent continues unchecked (and it is likely to accelerate further!)

there is a distinct possibility of our facing, despite the lucky discovery of 'Maxi-Pak', a major famine.[1] For, in ordinary language, what the population explosion amounts to is that in Pakistan a child is born every 10 seconds! In other words, every day in our country there are 10,000 more mouths to feed; 10,000 more bodies to protect from weather and disease; 10,000 new lives to bring up, to educate, and eventually to provide employment and shelter for.

No country in the world, not even one with the best institutions, could hope to make any real progress in the face of such powerful and intractable enemies. If Pakistan is to raise the standard of living of its millions of people, if it is to maintain itself as an independent and free country, it must first eliminate mass illiteracy and arrest the population explosion. To accomplish this is not an easy task by any means; but easy or not it has to be done, for the alternative is too bleak and frightening even to contemplate.

This is not, it must be stressed, to over-estimate the contribution widespread literacy and effective birth control can make to the task of national construction. There are indeed educationists, especially those with training in economics, who do not consider the achievement of literacy ought to be a priority task of the government in under-developed countries. These countries, they argue, have limited resources which should be invested only where they are likely to yield the highest dividends (in economic terms, of course). From this point of view, our primary concern should be to develop secondary education, rather than literacy or even primary education. Hence Dr Adam Curle could write:

> Primary education inevitably takes money from other more crucial forms of educational growth. Most authorities are agreed that the best way of reconciling economic expediency with the technical requirements of a country is a sound growth of secondary education, providing the army of trained but not excessively specialized persons who are greatly needed as technicians, clerks, nurses, agricultural assistants, supervisors, foremen, and business men, who also in all these capacities form the basis of solid citizenry.[2]

The argument appears reasonable until one asks: Is it really possible to make much headway in the sphere of secondary education without also

---

1. See note at the end of this article.
2. Adam Curle, *Educational Strategy for Developing Societies: A Study of Educational and Social Factors in Relation to Economic Growth* (Tavistock Publications, 1963).

developing the primary base at the same time? And, what is an even more important question, can real economic development of a nation be achieved merely on the strength of secondary school graduates, without requiring, for example, that people in the villages be able to learn for themselves the methods of improving their crops, keep a record of money transactions, read and understand instructions for the use and maintenance of farm machinery, etc.—indeed, without requiring that every person in every town and village should be able to participate in the political life of the country, for which literacy is an indispensable condition?

The truth is that, to those who hold that under-developed countries can ignore illiteracy and primary education, economic development means merely the betterment of a small section of the population: the educational policies they recommend do not make sense outside the context of a capitalist system.[3]

Similarly, there is a school of thought, also very influential, which denies the necessity of population control. This is the line generally taken by the communist countries. Taking their cue from Marx, the adherents of this view argue that the rapid rise in population is not so much a problem as a challenge—or, rather, it is a problem which can be adequately solved through economic development and the development of natural resources. Thus, a Soviet scientist, K. Malin, after examining 'mankind's potential means of subsistence—food and power—in the near and remote future', comes to the conclusion that 'mankind will never meet with the impossibility of providing itself with food if the more important food problems are tackled in good time and in an organised manner and solved according to a predetermined plan'.[4]

Another Soviet scientist, Vasily Nemchinov [1894–1964], declares:

Food shortages in many countries spring from defects in their social and economic systems. If the survivals of semi-feudal relationships in agriculture are eliminated, and if agriculture is freed from the insupportable burden of land rent, the situation will change ... The solution of the world's food problem lies not in reducing the growth of

3. Cf. Gunnar Myrdal, *Asian Drama: An Inquiry into the Poverty of Nations* (1968): 'In spite of its emphasis on development, this latter view (viz. that for under-developed countries expansion of secondary education is more important) which has a certain following among Western experts, conforms closely to the old colonial pattern of building up a highly educated elite with an attached lower rank of technical personnel functioning as subalterns, while leaving the population at large in a state of ignorance.'

4. K. Malin, *How Many the Earth Will Feed?* (Progress Publishers, 1963).

the population, but in the radical re-organisation of the economic and technical aspects of agricultural production.[5]

No doubt there is a grain of truth in all this. But when the population problem is looked at in the concrete context of under-developed countries, especially that of Pakistan, the unhelpful nature of these views soon becomes apparent. To begin with, the concerted and planned world action envisaged by Malin is simply not forthcoming; nor is there any likelihood of its materialising in the foreseeable future. Within any one country, there must obviously be a limit to what can be achieved through social and economic re-organisation and the development of natural resources. It is not without significance that the Chinese have been forced again and again to change their policy on this matter and now once more are trying to encourage population control. Moreover, in Pakistan there is little virgin land that can be reclaimed, though it is true that the country's mineral resources remain largely untapped. The direct relevance of these resources, however, is to industry. Now it seems highly unlikely that industrial development in Pakistan will make a great deal of difference to the unemployment situation in the country. For one of the country's worst economic features is the gross under-utilisation of labour. The emphasis on greater efficiency and part mechanisation which the agricultural and industrial re-organisation must entail is bound to limit the capacity of the economy to absorb surplus labour. In any case it is absurd to hope that any economy, however organised, can provide millions of new jobs every year indefinitely.

The moral to which this brief discussion points is unmistakably clear: the battle against literacy and population growth must be fought openly and directly; for it is our fate in this battle that is largely to decide whether we are to be an industrialised and civilised action, not vice versa. On the other hand, to hope that this battle can be won by the kind of feeble efforts so far made by our various governments—setting up of a couple of research projects, production of a few totally uninspiring and perhaps unintelligible posters, and some action here and there—is to be wishful to the point of being ludicrous. Not until a full-scale attack is mounted and the whole nation is mobilised will the battle for literacy and birth control be won in the short time we have at our disposal. For TIME is the essence of the problem. Already full twenty-one years have been squandered— thanks to the jabbers, humbugs and nincompoops who have until now

---

5. Quoted in Myrdal's *Asian Drama*.

held the reins of government and administration in our country. It will be the first and foremost task of a genuinely socialist government—whenever such a government is established in Pakistan—to declare a nationwide war on illiteracy and population growth. What follows is an outline of a possible campaign (strictly speaking two campaigns) against these evils. For want of space only the question of policy will be discussed here (that too summarily and without elegance), leaving other matters to be discussed in another article.

Outline for a Campaign to Eradicate Illiteracy and Control Population Growth

Let us assume a campaign (or campaigns) for wiping out illiteracy and to control population is to be launched next year, in 1970. It will be necessary to create a separate organisation to carry out this tremendous task. But before this organisation is set up some sort of a working committee must be established to take decisions on a number of policy matters and to undertake preparatory research. Some of the most important issues which must be decided before the campaign begins are as follows:

Issues Involved in the Literacy Campaign

1. The question of definition: At the very outset there will arise the question 'what is literacy?' In the last (1961) Census of Pakistan 'literacy' was taken to mean the ability to read a short statement with understanding. This clearly will not do. For one thing, this definition of literacy completely ignores writing and the ability to do simple arithmetic; for another, the only literacy worth striving for is the literacy which can be of use in everyday life. This kind of literacy is known as 'functional literacy' and is defined by the UNESCO in the following terms.

> A person is literate when he has acquired the essential knowledge and skills which enable him to engage in all those activities in which literacy is required for effective functioning in his group and community, and whose attainments in reading and arithmetic make it possible for him to continue to use skills towards his own and the community's development. In quantitative terms the standard of attainment in functional literacy may be equated to the skills of reading, writing and arithmetic achieved after a set number of years of primary or elementary schooling.

There is hardly any need to argue further in support of this view. Unless what is recommended in the above definition of literacy were agreed upon as the minimum goal to achieve, there would be little point in starting a literacy campaign.

2. The question of strategy: Another question that will occupy the attention of the policymakers is whether the campaign should aim at universal literacy from the very start, or whether it should try to achieve this in stages, concentrating first on the most promising group or areas (e.g. towns, factory workers, army etc.) then gradually widening its activities until the whole adult population is covered.

Experts recommend the latter method as both more economical and practical. The experience of some of the countries who have been most successful in abolishing illiteracy may also seem to point in the same direction. In Yugoslavia literacy work was first started by trade unions in industrial areas; in China the first efforts were directed at the youth (between 15 and 29 years of age) living in both the urban and rural areas; and in Russia the second all-Russian Congress for the elimination of illiteracy decided to concentrate their main efforts on populations between the ages of 18 and 35.

Nevertheless—and this is an important point—at least in Russia and China an attack was made both universally and selectively. For example, in China, although the major emphasis in the elimination of illiteracy was on the young people,[6] the campaign was not directed solely at them. Besides the 'anti-illiteracy' classes for the youth, there also exist thousands of spare-time and part-time primary, secondary and higher institutions for peasants and workers. Indeed, in the early years of this type of education was given emphasis and a high-powered spare-time Education Commission was created for this purpose. Most of the spare-time schools are run by individual enterprises.

In the USSR, where the fight against illiteracy achieved its greatest success, the campaign was, in fact, aimed at (virtually) universal literacy from the start. The 1919 decree on the subject, which was signed by Lenin, had stated that 'all illiterates between the ages of 18 and 50 were obliged to read and write in their native tongue', and it was only later that the age group 18–35 was selected as a special target for the literacy drive. However, throughout the period 1917–1940 the war against illiteracy

---

6. Leo A. Orleans, *Professional Manpower and Education in Communist China* (U.S. Government Printing Office, 1961).

was waged on all fronts and at all levels, though, as will be clear from the following sketch of the Russian strategy, extremely methodically.

In general the strategy adopted was that each year the education departments in the various districts, regions and republics constituting the USSR estimated the number of illiterate and semi-literate adults to be taught in their areas. These estimates took into consideration the size and composition of the population, the number of towns and villages and the distance between them, the cultural level and economic status of the population, and other factors. The regional departments also determined the specific numbers of illiterate and semi-literates to be taught by the various voluntary organisations within the area who offered to participate in the campaign. In this way, the literacy campaign was able to make a universal impact, albeit gradually and stage by stage.

It seems that real enthusiasm among people (without which progress is impossible) could not be created unless the effort to wipe out illiteracy were nation-wide and not merely confined to a particular area or group. That, however, should not prevent the authorities from working on a limited schedule—indeed, it will be necessary to do so in view of the considerable shortage of teachers there is likely to be in the beginning. The whole question of strategy is, however, bound up with the question of time in which the work of making the nation literate is to be completed and must be discussed in that context.

3. The question of time: Obviously, the aim of the campaign should be to achieve universal literacy in as short a period as possible, otherwise public enthusiasm is likely to flag, and in any case public energies will be needed in other tasks of national reconstruction. It is of course not easy to determine beforehand what period of time will be realistic for the kind of work involved (and it will only do harm to make unrealistic demands on workers engaged in the campaign), yet it is absolutely essential that a time limit is set for the whole programme and the campaign schedules are worked out on that basis.

Once again, it will help us to cast a critical glance at the experiences of Russia and China. In Russia, it is estimated, in the two years 1927 and 1928 (i.e. 8 years after the literacy campaign was launched) over 2 million illiterates received instruction; in the years 1930 and 1931 the figure was 11 million; the year 1932 represents the peak when the number reached 7.5 million.

This achievement was the result of a truly gigantic effort, and yet in our situation even this effort might take 60 to 70 years before full literacy was achieved (and that assigning that the birth rate was drastically cut down!) After the Communist revolution the Chinese people too found themselves confronted with the same bleak prospect. Faced with mass illiteracy the Ministry of Education had put out an ambitious plan aimed at eliminating illiteracy among over 3 million people in the course of one year (1955). Commenting on this, paper China Youth wrote: 'At this rate of progress, it will take nearly 60 years to wipe out illiteracy completely among 180 million youth in the country. That is to say, even in the generation of our grandsons there will still be illiterates.'[7] But what was to be done? The population, already enormous, was increasing at a fast rate, and China's resources, like ours, even given the best revolutionary zest among the people, were obviously limited. Yet China has already achieved a phenomenal success. It is reported that at one time, in the year 1958, 61 million people were attending literacy classes! Even if we regard this figure as exaggerated by as much as 50 per cent it still remains a remarkable achievement.

One of the main factors which made this possible (though one which also led to many excesses later condemned by the Ministry of Education) was precisely that the committee for the Elimination of Illiteracy of the State Council did not just launch their programme and hoped for the best, but set a time limit in accordance with what their national situation demanded and then proceeded to create the effort and other conditions required to fulfil their programme in that time. It was decided that 200 million persons were to be made literate within 7 years (starting from 1956). In accordance with this goal, schedules were worked out for specific projects: 2 to 3 years for eliminating illiteracy among the cadres in government departments; 3 to 5 years among workers in factories, mines, and enterprises; and 5 to 7 years among rural and urban areas generally.

However, in considering the Chinese example, an important fact must not be lost sight of: it is not possible to ensure standards in an operation of such magnitude. Indeed, the standards achieved by the majority of new literates in China are thought to be extremely low. This is inevitable; but to overcome this defect the Chinese diverted their best energies and resources into expanding and improving their elementary education, so that high standards could be ensured at least for their rising generation. Orleans, who studied the Chinese educational programmes for the National Science Foundation of America, wrote in 1960:

---

7. Leo A. Orleans, op. cit.

... the reports that scores of millions of adults in China have became literate during the past 9 or 10 years are undoubtedly either exaggerations or the result of such minimal requirements that virtually everyone who has attended literacy classes is now 'literate'. The area where the effort to reduce literacy has met with undoubted success is in the expansion of elementary education. With some 90 million children attending primary schools, it would seem safe to assume that the next generation will have a considerably higher proportion of literates.

Pakistan too, like China, cannot afford to wait even twenty years for the work of literacy to be completed. The need for eradicating illiteracy among the young is specially urgent. The strategy best suited in our circumstances will be to make a three-pronged attack in the following manner. The general aim of the campaign will be to cover the whole population between the ages of 5 and 50. But so far as the population group under 10 years of age is concerned the policy of the campaign will be to reinforce the efforts of the government to universalise primary education throughout the country, while the instruction of persons over 35 years will be left to voluntary effort and public enthusiasm. At the same time the campaign will spend its best efforts on the age group between 10 and 35. The campaign's time schedules will be planned so as to achieve complete literacy in 7 to 10 years' time (seven years being the time for people between 10 and 35 years of age).

If the population under 10 were discounted as not directly the concern of the campaign, the guess is that during the ten years of the campaign about 85–90 million people will be involved.[8] Considering that it was found possible in China to provide instruction for over 60 millions (or even half that number) in one year, the programme to educate 90 million in 10 years does not appear to be all that unrealistic.

Issues Involved in the Birth-control Campaign

1. The objective: Before the campaign is actually started, the policy makers will have to decide as to what extent the rate of population growth needs to be cut down to make it compatible with the country's economic progress. Now about one thing there can hardly be any doubt: the size of

---

8. This guess is based on a crude calculation: According to 1961 census persons between 1 and 40 years of age were about 70 million. In 1970 they will constitute the population between 10 and 50. To this another 17 million are added, being roughly the number of children born between 1961 and 1965.

the population even as it is at present is too great. In the words of the III Five-Year Plan (written in 1965):

> The population of Pakistan, estimated at over 110 million, exerts a heavy pressure on other productive resources. Unemployment and under-employment account for a full fifth of the labour force; yet, 45% of the population is below the age of fifteen, an indication of the potential increase in the labour force. In East Pakistan, where agriculture absorbs a high proportion of the labour force, the cultivator holds 3–5 acres on an average. In urban areas alone, dwelling units are about a million short of needs. Over four-fifths of the population is illiterate. Evidence enough that one of the major impediments to higher standards of living is the size of the population itself.

It is clear that our urgent population policy must be, if not to reduce the size of the population, at least to stop the population growing beyond what is necessary to keep it at its present level. To achieve this the birth rate will have to be drastically cut down—to more than 60 per cent of what it is now.[9]

It is estimated that at present, on the average, a woman in Pakistan gives birth to about eight children during her child bearing period. The rate of population growth could be reduced by 60 per cent if the size of the family could be limited to three children. This then is the goal the birth control campaign should set before itself—to persuade people not to expand their families beyond three children. But since no birth control campaign can do more than exhort people and therefore cannot guarantee that its objective will be realised, other methods will have to be adopted to make certain that at least some reduction in the size of families does take place. The whole subject will be taken up again when the question of strategy is discussed.

2. Time: The time factor is even more important here than it is in connection with literacy. Perhaps the best way to appreciate its importance is to consider the consequences of delay. The most obvious consequence will of course be the rise in the number of the unemployed. In this respect the situation is already critical when 45 per cent of the population have not yet joined the labour force. Any further delay in

---

9. M. R. Khan and L. L. Bean, *A Report on the Seminar on the Population Problems in the Development of Pakistan* (1967).

arresting the population explosion will mean adding to the rapidly expanding army of the unemployed.

But one year's delay in birth control means more than a simple addition of 3 per cent to the existing population, since about half of this additional number consists of girls, each of whom in turn will produce, on the average, eight children; so that the cumulative consequence of each year's delay over a period of time will add up to many times the initial increase. The whole problem is succinctly stated by Gunnar Myrdal:

> The sooner fertility is reduced, the sooner will the cumulative effects of the decrease in the dependency burden be felt. Moreover, each postponement of effective birth control measures increases the potential growth rates in later years because, as the larger cohorts of children grow up, it allows the continued rapid increase in the procreative age group—which is, after all, the basic determinant of the future size of population.
>
> ... we believe we can conclude that *a consideration of the economic effects of population trends should give the governments of the South Asian countries strong reasons for instituting as soon as and as vigorously as possible policy measures to get birth control practised among the masses of the people.*[10]

3. Strategy: There now remains the question of how to ensure that the size of an average family in Pakistan does not exceed three children, and that those couples who already have three or more children do not increase their families any further.

Let us not underestimate the seriousness of the problem this poses for a government interested in raising the standards of living of the people. On one hand is the absolute and urgent necessity for stopping the overall population of the country from expanding any further; on the other is the undesirability, indeed the impossibility, of controlling human behaviour in such a delicate and private sphere. And yet, the birth rate must be cut down to the minimum: there can be no two ways about it.

One thing is certain: family planning programmes, even if carried out with the utmost vigour, are not enough. They may take as long as twenty years to universalise the use of contraceptives and that is too long a time to wait. Moreover, family planning programmes can only rely on voluntary efforts; but in a country where there are so many powerful forces to inhibit the peoples' response to the call for birth control, it will be suicidal to depend exclusively upon individual initiative. The experience of a pilot

---

10. G. Myrdal, *Asian Drama* (emphasis author's).

project carried out in the Comilla *thana* of East Pakistan between 1961 and 1963 should give stark warning to anyone inclined to be optimistic about the effectiveness of family planning programmes.

The full story of the project will take too long to tell; what is worth noting here are 'achievements' of this project in the tiny sector of the population (about 10 or 11 villages) with which it concerned itself. Despite the 'intensive nature of the programme it is reported that the number of participants within the programme villages amounted to no more than 27 per cent of the target population of those villages, and it seems that these 27 per cent too consisted of those who had merely "registered to have purchased contraceptives"' (whether or not they used them, and if they did how regularly, is of course not known). Moreover, between March 1961 and May 1963, even from the 383 families that did register 172 dropped out! A further relevant fact that emerges from the report[11] from which the above information is quoted is that the majority of the women whom family planning appealed were between 25 and 36 years of age, i.e. those who had already passed their peak fertility period and were likely to have had five or more children before they started to plan their families.

The experience of the Comilla project may be taken to represent the prospects of a nation-wide family planning programme and should make it quite clear why it will be disastrous to rely exclusively on it for the purpose of achieving effective birth control.

But if family planning is not to be relied upon is there any other method of controlling the birth rate which might guarantee success better? Fortunately for us, there is; and even more fortunately, it itself involves a social reform which ought to be implemented for its own sake even if it did not have any bearing on the population problem. The reform in question concerns the age of marriage in Pakistan, especially that of girls.

The average age of marriage of women in our country at present is abnormally low. According to an official estimate the average marriage of males is 23 years, of females 15. In fact, the actual position with regard to females is more serious than appears from this estimate, for in rural areas, where the highest proportion of the population lives, the marriage age of women is between 11 and 15 years (in some cases it is as low as 7!).

Now if the age of marriage were raised it would have an immediate and significant effect on the population growth. In a very persuasive article in *Pakistan Development Review* two economists, Messrs. Khan and Bean,

---

11. A. Majeed Khan, *Pilot Project in Family Planning, Progress Report to May 1963.*

argue that if the average marriage age of women were to be raised by 5 years, it would bring about 30 per cent reduction in the birth rate, i.e. about half of the reduction needed to keep the population at a stationary level. Thus, the raising of the marriage age of women to twenty years will solve half of the population problem at a single stroke (and will produce many important social benefits into the bargain). The age of marriage of men at twenty-three or below is also low and needs to be raised by at least two years. Indeed, while these ages should be prescribed and enforced by law, efforts should be made to persuade the people to postpone marriages until even later.[12]

There is little need to dwell on the advantages of taking the step recommended above: it is obvious that it will be far less likely to encounter opposition from the people than is family planning (especially if some financial benefits are at the same time offered to the parents of girls between the ages of fifteen and twenty, say, for the first five years), and also easier to enforce throughout the country.

Even with this, it will be necessary to carry out a vigorous and sustained family planning programme. The aim of such a programme will be, as has been stated earlier, to persuade the people to limit the size of their families to three children and not to expand their families if they already have three or more children. To achieve this the methods that must be given the highest importance are sterilisation and the use of intra-uterine device (IUD); but the battle for family planning will really be won not through the use of any such method or 'gadget', but through publicity and education and ample provision of facilities.

No other country in the world (reminds Karol J. Krotki in his article, 'The feasibility of an effective population policy for Pakistan') has so far lowered its birth rate because of a 'gadget'. Withdrawal and abortions have been responsible for the decline in the French and Japanese birth rates and have had important effects in Great Britain and United States. Birth rates are lowered when people become aware that excessive children are a burden and that something can be done to avoid the burden. The key to the problem of family planning is information accompanied by service, the distribution of supplies and the availability of medical methods—not any one gadget.[13]

---

12. In China while the legal ages of marriage are 18, in the case of women, and 20 in the case of men, in practice men are urged not to marry before 28 and women before 22. D. Wilson, *A Quarter of Mankind: An Anatomy of China Today* (1966), p. 161.

13. Karol J. Krotki, *Pakistan Development Review*, 1964.

The decision whether any incentives should be offered to people to get them to practise birth control, and if so what these should be, is also a part of the 'strategy' and will be a matter of concern for the policymakers. Since it would prove too costly to give a material reward to everyone who offered to be sterilised or to use contraceptives, much more use will be made of 'dis-incentives'. This will entail withdrawing of any privilege, promotion, grant or loan to which a person might be entitled if, after the family planning campaign was launched in his area, he did not take steps to limit the size of his family. Certain special grants, loans, etc. may be offered on condition that they would be withdrawn if the recipient did not practise birth control. A socialist government will be in a particularly advantageous position in this respect, since by reorganising the land and industry it will seek to distribute profits more evenly among the population, and so will be able to withhold or reduce a person's share of the profits if he or his family did not cooperate in the national family planning effort.

Summary of Conclusions

It may be helpful to sum up briefly the main conclusions reached in the above discussion. With regard to the literacy campaign we have argued that the aim of the campaign should be to achieve at least 'functional literacy' (as it is defined by UNESCO experts) among population between the ages of 10 and 50, and that this should be accomplished within ten years. The general 'strategy' of the campaign should be to concentrate its best efforts on the age groups between 10 and 35, while the task of universalising education among children below ten years of age should be entrusted to the Ministry of Education of the state, and that of educating people above 35 to voluntary effort.

With regard to the campaign for population control, it is argued that the best way of ensuring that there is no further increase in the present size of the population is to lay down by law the minimum ages at which men and women may marry—and these should be considerably higher than they are at present, viz. 20 years for girls and 25 years for men. This law should be strictly enforced and in practice people should be encouraged to marry even later—e.g. by providing incentive to parents of girls. In addition, an energetic family planning campaign should be started whose main aim should be to persuade people not to increase their families beyond three children.

* * * *

When all the preparatory work is completed and sufficient stocks of the material to be used have been acquired, the campaigns will be ready to be launched. Their success, however, will largely depend on the Commission's ability to generate the people's enthusiasm—in other words, on the publicity campaign. This campaign will call for imagination and boldness, and will itself require the participation of a large number of people. What exactly will the publicity campaign be like? How will it, and the two main campaigns, be financed? What kind of social and political context is presupposed by a national effort of this kind? These are some of the questions with which the second part of this article will be concerned.

Note: In an article in *Pakistan Times* of May 18, Dr Z. A. Hashmi, Vice-Chancellor of the Agricultural University, Lyallpur, points out that: 'In 1878–79 food production in the Indo-Pakistan sub-continent, with a population of some 181 millions, amounted to 51.5 million tons and provided, on an average, 27.9 ozs of food per person per day … The per capita availability of food (in Pakistan at present) is only two-third of the amount consumed in 1878.' He goes on to point out: 'The shortage in terms of protective foods, particularly proteinaceous goods is even more pronounced. The current deficit of proteins in the country has been estimated to be the order of 100 million maunds annually of high-protein foodstuffs, such as milk, meat, fish and pulses.'

According to another report (P. Observer) East Pakistanis live on 'a near starvation diet of about 12 ounces per capita'. Moreover, the pressure on land has reduced the size of land holding in a very large part of East Pakistan to about ⅓ of an acre.

Book Review: *The Myth of Independence*

Aziz Kurtha

'The maintenance of law and order' is a protean political bogey, which can be invoked as much to dissolve the legislature and decree military rule in Pakistan as it has previously sanctioned the excesses of the CRS in the Paris Latin Quarter. But whereas *les evenements du Mai* 1968 may have shown that the spectre of political cataclysm haunts a highly-industrialised Europe, the inchoate uprising in Pakistan earlier this year has clearly demonstrated that workers and peasants even in a poverty-stricken and profoundly religious oriental society nurture under their skins a sulphurous fervour which awaits ignition. Mr Bhutto, the recalcitrant former Foreign Minister, who wooed the angry students of West Pakistan, was the essential catalyst in that makeshift experiment with insurrection. His incarceration in the midst of the disturbances turned out to be a godsend but for himself and the incredibly bold and perceptive students who precipitated the crisis. Mr Bhutto, who achieved meteoric success under Ayub's patronage, has always possessed that panache, that private élan combined with that hint of progressiveness which is the envy of his political rivals and which had a magnetic appeal to the students who were searching for someone to rally behind.

His present book is a relatively short but scholarly study of the trends in Pakistan's foreign relations from Partition in 1947 up to the present day. Unfortunately, it includes only a brief discussion of the 1965 Indo-Pakistan War and totally omits any consideration of the controversial Tashkent Declaration or the important Rann of Kutch arbitration. Apparently wishing to serialise his memoirs, a prefatorial remark notes that:

The truth of this chapter of history has yet to be told.

Mr Bhutto's essential thesis, developed at least more intelligently and lucidly than Ayub Khan's *Friends Not Masters*, is that Pakistan's legal independence, gained after a bitter struggle in the womb of British India, is increasingly circumscribed by Russia and America who are vying with each other to treat the subcontinent as a pawn in their different global strategies. His hostility towards the United States is unmitigated especially since it began to give military assistance to India in 1962, and even more since it halted the same assistance to Pakistan in April 1967. He bluntly describes how American 'aid' programmes are skilfully manipulated, first to procure a receiving state's economic dependence and later its political submission. The former trading posts of the East India Company have their modern counterpart in concessions to grant military bases, and he claims that the colonial policy of 'divide and rule' is now superseded by a neo-colonialist doctrine of 'unite and rule'. It may be a picturesque generalisation, but its core of truth will surely be acknowledged by many Afro-Asians.

Hence, in Bhutto's view, Pakistan must quit the Seat alliance which failed to come to its assistance in 1965, the Commonwealth must be 'decently and voluntarily' laid to rest in Westminster Abbey, and the country must pursue a policy of qualified neutrality in world affairs. One may understand his motives for proposing neutrality in that it may enable us, economically, to stretch our suppliant hands both ways and, politically, to remain unentangled in major East-West confrontations. But even his own account of the political price paid for Western 'assistance' demonstrates the folly of confusing 'aid' with charitable largesse. Thus, it may be preferable to endure the transient difficulties of absolute commitment than to hover indefinitely in a political limbo. He is rightly credited with pioneering the friendship with China, and he would strengthen those ties as the Republic has unequivocally supported Pakistan's position over Kashmir and they have a common enemy in India.

With India, however, he cannot even remotely envisage cooperation, which he feels would only benefit American attempts to form a bastion against China. Earlier this year Bhutto was reported to have told a meeting that 'Pakistan should be ready to fight a thousand-year war' with India, and the book confirms that he is happy to fan old prejudices and is apparently unable to think positively and unemotionally about Indo-Pakistan affairs. Hindu Indians did of course resist the creation of Pakistan, and India has undoubtedly flouted international opinion and its own undertaking about a plebiscite in Kashmir. But should Pakistan seriously develop nuclear weapons and can it really afford to spend more than the existing 60 per cent of its budget on defence expenditure, particularly when its immediate beneficiary would be a politically ambitious professional army? And this is the nub of the criticism—that Bhutto's relative militancy in foreign affairs contrasts sharply with his posture in domestic matters. Faced with what his book describes as 'predatory capitalism', and the extraordinary concentration of wealth in the hands of 20 infamous families, he is known, during his recent presidential campaign, to have favoured 'Scandinavian-type socialism' for Pakistan. In this context he could refer to a book by C. H. Hermansson, a Swedish socialist, who has shown, no doubt to Mr Bhutto's embarrassment, that behind the welfare services Sweden is economically 'run by 15 (named) families'. Or to put the matter in a different way, if Pakistan is to strengthen its ties with China, it needs something much more radical than social democracy at home.

One reputed British journalist has enthusiastically described Mr Bhutto as possibly Asia's Castro. Well, you never know; but he is probably better cast as Pakistan's potential Kerensky.

* * * * *

It is not difficult to be a revolutionary when the revolution has already flared up, when everybody joins the revolution simply because they are carried away by it, because it is the fashion and sometimes even because it might open a career ... It is much more difficult and much more useful—to be a revolutionary when the condition for direct, open, really mass and really revolutionary struggle have not yet matured, to be able to defend the interest of the revolution (by propaganda, agitation and organisation) in non-revolutionary bodies, in non-revolutionary circumstances, among the masses who are incapable of immediately appreciating the necessity for revolutionary methods of action.

(V. I. Lenin)

Living in Pakistan (A Sociological Report)*

N. H. Islam

Contents

Bureaucracy & Corruption; Cost of Living; Consumption of food, etc; Employment; Health & Hygiene; Mass Media; a day in a Beggars' life.

BUREAUCRACY, WASTE & CORRUPTION

The farmer (in the Campbellpur District) is perplexed. He is confronted with 20 agricultural organisations, all pretending to serve him, but many of them victims of corruption, intrigue, and red-tapism themselves. The Department of Agriculture alone has a dozen directorates ... all independent bodies militating more or less against each other.

There are then the Small Dams Organisation, the Agricultural Development Corporations (with its numerous agencies) the Agricultural Development Bank, and the Forest Department, hustling to reform the farmer. Depressed, uneducated, and poor, the farmer is required to take each one of them as a Solomon and be confounded by their sermons.

(P. T., 23 May)

Information issued by the Government of Pakistan shows that during

(1) the past decade (1958–69) 50,000 acres of land was allotted or sold cheaply to 444 government officials for rendering distinguished services.

(2) 10,009 acres in the Punjab were sold cheaply to 132 'retired and retiring government servants' (this was allotted on the basis of 25 to 150 acres per officer).

---

* Culled from Pakistani newspapers during the months of April–June 1969.

151

(3) In the Guddu Barrage area 28,023 acre were allotted to various people including members of Board of Revenue, judges of the High Court, higher officials of the WAPDA, army officers, civil servants and others.

(4) In the Ghulam Mohammad Barrage area 36 officers received a total of 6,192 acre.

(5) In D. I. Khan Division 2,245 acres were allotted among 11 officials each receiving from 75 to 240 acres.

Travelling allowance (T.A.) paid to government servants for official visits continues to maintain a gradual increase and it now constitutes 9 per cent of the total expenditure on the emoluments of gazetted as well as non-gazetted staff of the West Pakistan government (T.A. paid in 1961–62: Rs. 22,886,441; in 1968–69 Rs. 31,932,625).

According to a special committee set up last year to examine local administrative bodies 80% of the income of these bodies was spent on administration and only 20% on development projects.

(Dawn, 12 May)

The realisation of WAPDA's power supply revenue in West Pakistan is believed to be below 30%. The responsibility for the leakage of revenues in the power field is laid mainly on the staff responsible for the distribution of power supply.

(Dawn, 14 May)

In 1959 National Economic Planning approved a 'long-term multipurpose' project for remodelling old embankments, constructing new ones, and generally creating a system to check yearly flood and salination in East Pakistan. The scheme was entrusted to EPWAPDA and the estimated cost was Rs. 11,460 crores.

The first phase, begun in 1960–61, had a target of 2,600 miles of embankment and is due to be completed next year. But it has been reported that so far only 1,616 miles have been completed. However, different sources give different figures. About 4 years ago the Parliamentary Secretary of Planning Division claimed 1,600 miles had been completed; but a month later a Minister told the Provincial Assembly that no more than 1,211 miles had been completed. A government publication put the figure again at 1,600 miles, only to be refuted by a spokesman of East Pakistan government two years later (1967) who said no more than 1,250 miles or bunds had been constructed.

(Leader, Dawn, 9 June)

The Government of Pakistan had advanced about Rs. 12 crores in loans to small traders under credit scheme. It is reported that the government is finding it difficult to recover this loan. Many recipients are found to be neither traders nor shopkeepers and many come from Rawalpindi and Hazarah (Ayub Khan's native town). It is reported that among the recipients is a family which held very high position in the former government.

(*Jang*, 11 June)

At a recent session of the Divisional Council, Rawalpindi, various heads of provincial departments presented their reports. The claim made by an official responsible for animal husbandry that they had already distributed 300 leghorn poultry among the cultivators produced an uproar in the House, since no-one had even heard of such a project.

(*Jang*, 22 May)

The West Pakistan government has 10,000 cases relating to pensions pending for a decision.

(*Jang*, 22 May)

* * * *

... without a revolutionary mood among the masses, and without conditions favouring the growth of this mood, revolutionary tactics will never be converted into action; but we in Russia have been convinced by long, painful and bloody experience of the truth that revolutionary tactics cannot be built up on revolutionary mood alone. Tactics must be based on a sober and strictly objective estimation of all the class forces in a given State (in neighbouring states and in all states, i.e. on a world scale), as well as on an evaluation of the experience of revolutionary movements.

(Lenin)

COST OF LIVING

Prices in Pakistan

An objective study of the cost of living during the past few years shows that even in the wholesale market the prices have shot up by 25 to 35. The food price index, for instance, has risen from 125 in 1960 to 172 in December 1968. Likewise the index for clothing and footwear, housing and household operations and miscellaneous articles has now touched the level of 131, 128 and 121 as compared to 127, 101 and 99 in 1960.

(*Leader*, P. T., 11 June)

Coal: (Prices sharply risen recently—by 14%)
Official Price—Rs. 156.67 to 171.69 per ton
Being sold at—Rs. 191.48 per ton
Note: In 1966 when coal was imported only from China, price (ex Chittagong) was Rs. 96 per ton. In 1965 when it was imported from India it was Rs. 62.25.

Prices of drugs in Pakistan are higher than in any Western country. Some pharmaceutical firms are earning 300% profit. The druggists earn a poor income from the percentage fixed by the manufacturers and importers.

(Letter, M. N., 8 June)

There are 232 pharmaceutical manufacturers in Pakistan, but only 35 control 75% of total production of drugs and medicines.

(M. N., 24 May)

Books (foreign): Price varies from 65 paisa to 90 paisa per shilling, and Rs. 5 to 7 per dollar.

Children's books: novels in Urdu, soft cover, pages 150–250—prices from Rs. 1.50 to 3.50.

An original work in English—hard cover, pages over 600—Rs. 40.

A historical classic (tr. in Urdu)—hard cover, I class printing, pages over 200—Rs. 15.

Prices in West Pakistan

Prices in Khairpur (These are the prices fixed officially. Actual prices may be higher).

Wheat	Rs. 15 per maund
Buffalo milk	87 paisas per seer (at 'Waras')
Katcha milk	75 paisas per seer (at hotels)
All kind of milk sold otherwise then at waras or hotels	62 paisas per seer
Mixed sweet-meat	Rs. 3.75 per seer
Halwas	Rs. 4 per seer
Laddu, Jalebi, etc.	Rs. 3 per seer

Prices in Karachi (Not clear whether these apply nationally)

Bread No. 1 (retail)	Rs. 1.20 (recently reduced)
Bread No. 2 (retail)	62 paisa

Water rates are likely to be raised from Rs. 1.50 to Rs. 1.62 per 1000 galls (retail price), thus boosting the KDA revenue by more than Rs. 16 lakhs yearly.

(*Dawn*, 14 May)

The exporter members of Karachi Thread Spoolers and Mercerisers Group are facing great hardship because of the shortage of caustic soda, the price of which in local market has gone up to Rs. 160 cwt. But the imported cost of the soda comes only to Rs. 35 per cwt.

(Letter, *Dawn*, 7 June)

Prices in Bahawalpur (These are based on a personal report)

Beef	Rs. 6 per seer
Oranges	Rs. 1.50 per seer
Dalda	Rs. 7
Slippers (rubber)	Rs. 4.5 per pair

Rawalpindi: Good Quality Atta b. Rs. 22 and 25 per maund.

Hyderabad: The prices of the pulses have gone up by 150 per cent; and in Latifabad, 200 per cent. Milk has gone up by 13 paisa per seer. Reason for increase is not known.

Lahore: Ice, usually 12 paisa a seer, is being sold at 30 to 50 paisa a seer.

Prices in East Pakistan (From an article in *Pakistan Observer*)

Not only that prices are high and fluctuating, at any given day the price of an item varies from shop to shop and from area to area. Various milk products, mostly imported, are now very much a part of many a middle class family. The abnormal prices of these items is among the main irritants.

Prices in Dacca

Lactogen (baby food): varies from 6.75 to 8 per one pound tin (in February 1968 the price had gone up to Rs. 13.50).
Ostermilk (baby food): Up to Rs. 10.82 for 2 lb tin
Ovaltine: Rs. 4.50 or above (last year the price had gone up to Rs. 6). For the above, import policy is blamed. But Horlicks, now made in Pakistan, sells at 6.25 per bottle.

Saris: Imported from West Pakistan. The same sari in some shop sells at Rs. 22 at others Rs. 25. Even when the price is stamped at Rs. 16 per paid, was selling at Rs. 32 per pair.

Shoes: Impossible to be sure whether the shoe is worth the price being asked. A pair of leather sandals may cost Rs. 10 at one shop, Rs. 15 at another.

Toilet: These are these days a luxury. There has been a 40 to 70 per cent rise in prices in the past three years. Prices are still rising.

Indigenous soap—selling at Rs. 1.75 to Rs. 2 a bar a week ago. Now Rs. 2 to Rs. 2.25.
Toilet soaps—Rs. 1.12 per cake (a few weeks ago Rs. 1)
Toothpaste—Forhan's (medium size)—Rs. 2.87 a few weeks ago, now from Rs. 3 to Rs. 3.20.
Toothbrush (good quality)—at least Rs. 2.50

(Pak. Obs., 19 May)

CONSUMPTION OF FOOD & OTHER COMMODITIES

Per capita food consumption in Pakistan is 18.6 ozs per day; per capita consumption of proteins only 45.5 grams. In East Pakistan average per capita food consumption is only 12 ozs.

In Lahore—Daily consumption of poultry is reported to be 20,000 birds. Poultry farms in the city are able to produce only 2,000 daily.

(*Dawn*, April 30)

Non-cereal items (including edible oil, tobacco, tallo, and long staple cotton) worth $59 million are to be imported from U.S. during 1969–70.

(*Dawn*, 23 May)

Rs. 4 lakh worth of beverages are consumed daily in Pakistan. Most of them are of foreign origin.

(M. N., 24 May)

In East Pakistan the approximate coal consumption is 5 lakh tons yearly. This year coal is imported as follows: China—2 lakh 50,000 tons; Poland—27,000 tons; Australia—50,000 tons (Total: 4 lakhs & 27,000 tons).

Estimated maximum consumption of tea: 70 million pounds (production in 1968–69: 68 million) (contd.)

* * * *

The workers can acquire political consciousness only from without, that is, only outside of the economic struggle, outside of the sphere of relations between workers and employers. The sphere from which alone it is possible to obtain this and the state and the government—the sphere of inter-relations between all classes. For that reason, the reply to the question: What must be done in order that the workers may acquire political knowledge? Cannot be merely the one which ... the practical workers ... usually content themselves with, i.e. 'go among the workers'. To bring political knowledge to the workers the Social Democrats must go among all classes of the population, must despatch units of their army in all directions.

(Lenin)

EMPLOYMENT

There has been a lot of bitterness in the engineering profession over the fact that there is now acute unemployment among engineers, especially among those who have qualified over the last two years. Also, many of these young engineers hold the view that nobody can get employment without some special recommendation and that merit along does not count in recruitment.

(Letter, P. T., 11 June)

700 qualified electrical engineers are unemployed in West Pakistan.

(M. N., 21 March)

The Pharmacy graduates of Dacca University, except a few doing postgraduate work, are now roaming about the streets in search of jobs.

A good many of them are forced to work as representatives of medical firms which was only the job of Arts graduates and even Matriculates. Many have remained unemployed for as long as two years.

HEALTH & HYGIENE

According to an article in *Pakistan Times*, the current deficiency of proteins in this country is of the order of 100 million maunds annually of high-protein food stuffs (milk, meat, fish and pulses). The available protein is also of low quality—¾ of the protein supply being plants lacking in amino-acids. Protein foods are expensive and the well-to-do sections of society appropriate a large share of it. 'Deprived of proteins, children remain stunted and do not attain their genetical potential. The ill-health, pain and suffering caused to our people can be imagined from the fact that protein deficiencies and the infections and parasitic diseases to which they make the body more prone, result in the death of one out of four children before the age of 4 years...In adults, apart from direct ill-health, protein deficiency results in markedly reduced capacity for work and labour, seriously affecting our ability to undertake tasks of economic development and national defence. Recent studies have indicated that mental retardation is also caused by protein deficiency during infancy... we are raising a generation which is retarded ...'

> In Pakistan the per capita intake of oils and fats (necessary ingredients of human diet) is only 16 grams a day, while the minimum necessary for health is 50–60 grams.
>
> (*Dawn*, 15 May)

> A recent survey has revealed that the lower classes, i.e. those earning Rs. 100 or less, are in great distress. One of the most alarming things is that the occurrence of fatal diseases among them, especially that of T.B., is very widespread.
>
> (*Leader, Jang*, 22 May)

> The number of the sightless in West Pakistan is about 5 lakhs.
>
> (*Dawn*, 16 June)

> According to experts vision defects and various eye diseases are common in Pakistan, especially among the students.
>
> (*Dawn, Leader*, 26 May)
> (cf. prices of eye drops)

In Hyderabad over 35,000 T.B. victims i.e. 1/5 of the population of the city) have been reported. There is only one T.B. clinic, treating about 200 outdoor patients daily.

(Dawn, 24 May)

In Sylhet district cholera and smallpox have been raging in many parts and have killed 58 persons in 2 months. Local health authorities know only about 25 such deaths and seem 'to be ignorant of the outbreak of the diseases'. (In 1965 there were 114 deaths and in 1966, 161 deaths, from cholera. The Health Department has no statistics for '67 and '68).

Cholera has also broken out in 'epidemic form in Jessore (E.P.) and 14 people have been killed in a fortnight.

(Dawn, 12 May)

When contacted, one sanitary inspector of Jessore Municipality told newsmen that according to his records so far 10 persons died of strong diarrhoea. When asked how he distinguished strong diarrhoea from cholera he failed to reply satisfactorily. The sanitary conditions are extremely poor, drains and latrines are not regularly cleaned. There are a good number of unauthorised and kutch latrines. There is only one tube well in the locality of 2,000.

A great number of rural hospitals in East and West Pakistan have no qualified or experienced doctor and the hospitals are run by dispensers.

(Jang, 11 June)

Between February 26 and 6th June, 443 cases of gastro-enteritis were admitted to the Epidemic Diseases Hospital, Karachi. All were due to stale or contaminated food.

(Dawn, 7 June)

Karachi is hit by a mosquito explosion due to 'almost the entire Karachi sewerage being overflowed and exposed', 'and the bush growth, the grazing cattle and the hollowing of the Lyari river bed'.

Drug addiction among the young people in Karachi is increasing fast. There are a number of drugs on the market which are extremely dangerous and have already caused a number of deaths.

(Hurriyat, 6 June)

It is estimated that there are at least 10,000 pye-dogs in Karachi city, and 1 lakh in the outskirts of the city.

(Letter, *Dawn*, 15 May)

Dinajpur (E.P.), with population of ½ lakh, has no vegetable market. The existing small vegetable-cum-fish market has no drainage. The few drains, in Bahadur Bazar and Gundri Bazar, are in a 'menacing condition'. 'They are more stores of filth and garbage than outlets for dirty water. They are not cleaned for days, often for months'.

(Pak. Obs.)

Lahore littered with filth despite cleanliness drives: There are 8,000 sweepers in the city, out of which 6,000 are employed by Lahore Municipal Corporation and 2,000 are privately employed. No less than 15,000 more sweepers are required for 2 million residents. The city is reported to possess 100 bullock carts and 35 trucks for removing garbage which operate from Sanda Road, which is at a distance from the walled city where they are expected to operate. It is reported that due to the absence of underground sewage and defective disposal arrangements for refuse in walled city sanitary conditions are fast deteriorating. The sullage water flows out of each house to drains which are never more than a few yards long, with the result that it stagnates in depressions and pools and becomes a permanent breeding ground for mosquitoes and flies. The plans to keep sewers clean are like most paper plans, fictional.

(P. T., 19 May).

A recent analysis of food stuffs samples, made in Peshawar, revealed that confectionaries were the most adulterated food stuff, showing 100% adulteration. Beverages had 92.2%, milk and milk products 89.5%, sweetening agents 66.6% and edible oils and ghee up to 27.27% and 25% adulteration.

(*Dawn*, 14 May)

A recent analysis of beverages consumed in Pakistan reveals: '... not only that some of them contain saccharine in place of sugar and tartaric acid instead of citric acid, but also the water used is impure and unfit for human consumption .... Only a few of the aerated beverages are found to have the required quantity of the basic ingredients .... Not one drink in the market provides nourishment, and few contain protein.'

(M. N., 24 May)

Mass Media & Entertainment

Radio Pakistan (Karachi)			Broadcasting Time 15 hrs.		
Analysis of a Day's Programme (30 April)					
Music	hrs.	mins.		hrs.	mins.
Film Songs & Geets	2	35	For Universities	–	30
Ghazal	–	50	Feature (play ?)	–	30
Naghma (Bengali)	–	35	For Armed Forces	–	30
Western	–	30	Religion	–	25
Classical	–	15	Our Presentation (?)	–	25
Naat	–	10	Science	–	20
Commercial Services & Market Rates	4	25	Programme Summary	–	10
News (in 3 languages inc. 5 mts. commentary)	2	45	Story	–	5

Television			Broadcasting Time 5 hrs 5 min. app.		
Analysis of a Day's Programme (30 April)					
	hrs.	mins.		hrs.	mins.
Forsyte Saga	–	55	News & Weather	–	33
Music (Classical)	–	55	Children's	–	15
Film (Cartoon; Hollywood)	–	45	Religion	–	6
Quiz	–	37	Programme Summary, etc.	–	5
Comedy (Urdu)	–	33			

A Day in a Beggar's Life

Outside the Trinity Church in Karachi sits an old woman of 70 almost from sunrise to sunset. She begs. Behind her is the familiar story of poverty, the incapacity of old people to earn their living and the easy, care-free existence the begging profession offers.

Her story may well be the story of a majority of beggars roaming the streets of Karachi.

She came to Pakistan in the troubled days of Partition and now lives in one of the poor colonies with her son, her daughter-in law and their five children. She is too old to be of much use in the house, and the only way in which she can help the family is begging.

So, she has taken to begging. Her son works as a mason's assistant and finds work only intermittently. His meagre earnings on a working day barely suffice to feed and clothe his family.

The old woman's days are all alike. Early in the morning she is taken by her son to her usual place under the trees, with a small 'chapati' prepared by her daughter-in-law, wrapped up in her 'dupatta'. She sits for hours with her bowl in front of her.

Deserving

A modern person frowns at begging and perhaps rightly argues that unless charity is organised it is difficult to distinguish between a deserving case and an undeserving one, and that to give to an undeserving person is as great a crime as to withhold charity from a deserving one. Yet, somehow, this old woman's pathetic appearance and wails move a number of passers-by to throw a coin or two into her bowl. If she is lucky she may collect as much as a rupee a day. On an average her monthly collection amounts of 15 rupees.

Thus, she is very much an earning member of the family.

At the day's end her son comes to fetch her. She hands over her collection to him and is taken back to her corner of the hut. There she receives another small 'chapati' as her evening meal and is put to bed. The next day witnesses the same routine.

When the Vagrancy Act came into effect some years ago in Karachi, the old woman's family was in a dilemma. They did not want her to be kept in a beggars' home because they knew that the authorities, however kind, could never give her the same attention as her family did. Nor could they afford to keep her all the time at home. So they decided to get her a few boxes of matches to sell. This she would not do, having grown used to begging. The threat of a beggars' home, however, soon brought her round.

So, she found herself once again in her familiar place, this time imploring passers-by to buy her ware. Most of them passed her without a second glance, while a few found it easier to throw a coin in her direction rather than stop to buy her matches. There were others who collected more matches from her than the money they gave her warranted. She found all this most confusing.

Helplessness

At the end of the day, her son could not tally the money she had collected with the number of boxes sold. In spite of a few coins of charity, the money was much too short. Detecting annoyance in his face the old woman pleaded helplessness having never done this sort of work before.

This happened the next day and the day after next. Instead of helping the family she was thus becoming more and more of a liability and had, therefore, eventually to be kept at home. She was miserable but could do little to alter things.

A time soon came when the Vagrancy Act became non-effective. The beggars, both deserving and undeserving, who had disappeared from the streets of Karachi emerged again. This gave the old woman courage to restart her old profession. She had been waiting patiently for this opportunity and missed the feel of the money and the music of the coins as they fell into her bowl.

Marx's Concept of Man

Labour is, in the first place, a process in which both man and nature participate, and in which man of his own accord starts, regulates, and controls the material re-actions between, himself and Nature. He opposes himself to nature as one of her own forces, setting in motion arms and legs, head and hands, the natural forces of his body, in order to appropriate Nature's productions in a form adapted to his own wants. By thus acting on the external world and changing it, he at the same time changes his own nature. He develops his slumbering powers and compels them to act in obedience to his sway.

(Capital, 1.3)

Since, however, for socialist man the whole of what is called world history is nothing but the creation of man by human labour, and the emergence of nature for man, he therefore has the evident and irrefutable proof of his self-creation, of his own origins. Once the essence of man and of Nature, man as a natural being and nature as human reality, has become evident in practical life, in sense experience, the quest for an alien being, a being above man and Nature (a quest which is an avowal of the unreality of man and Nature) becomes impossible in practice. Atheism, as a denial of this unreality, is no longer meaningful, for atheism is a negation of God, and seeks to assert by this negation the existence of man. Socialism no longer requires such a roundabout method; it begins from the theoretical and practical sense perception of man and nature as essential beings. It is positive human self-consciousness, no longer a self-consciousness attained through the negation of religion, just as the real life of man is positive and no longer attained through the negation of private property, through Communism. Communism is the phase of negation of the negation and is, consequently, for the next stage of historical development, a real and necessary factor in the emancipation and rehabilitation of man. Communism is the necessary form and the dynamic principle of the immediate future, but communism is not itself the goal of human development—the form of human society.

(K. MARX. EPM. 1844)

164

مارکس کی نظر میں انسان کا تصور

("معاشیاتی اور فلسفیانہ مسودات" کے چند حصوں کا ترجمہ)

انسان ایک وجودِ صنفی ہے۔ صرف اسی اعتبار سے نہیں کہ وہ گروہ کو (دوسری چیزوں کے
گروہ اور اپنے گروہ دونوں کو) اپنا عملی اور علمی موضوع (object) بناتا ہے، بلکہ اس لیے
بھی (اور یہ دوسرے الفاظ میں وہی بات ہے) کہ وہ اپنی ذات کو اپنی صنف کی موجود
اور زندہ شکل سمجھتا ہے، یعنی ایسا وجود جو غیر مخصوص (universal) ہو، اور نتیجتاً آزاد۔ ۲

انسان اور حیوانات دونوں کے لیے زندگی کی مادی بنیاد یہ ہے کہ انسان (حیوان کی
مانند) خارجی قدرت کے سہارے زندہ رہتا ہے۔ اور چونکہ انسان کی ذات حیوان کی نسبت
زیادہ غیر مخصوص ہے اس لیے جس خارجی قدرت پر اس کا انحصار ہے وہ بھی نسبتاً غیر مخصوص
ہے۔ علمی نقطہ نظر سے پودے، حیوانات، دھاتیں، ہوا، روشنی وغیرہ سب انسانی ہوش کا جزو
ہیں کیونکہ یہ چیزیں علم طبعیات اور آرٹ کا موضوع ہیں۔ یہ ہیں انسان کی روحانی فطرتِ
خارجہ (spritual inorganic nature)، یعنی اس کی زندگی کی عقلی غذا جس کی تیاری

۲۔ حالانکہ اگلا سارا مضمون مندرجہ بالا خیال کی تشریح کرے گا، لیکن اگر یہاں اس خیال کی وضاحت کر دی جائے تو غالباً
مضمون سمجھنے میں آسانی ہو گی۔ "وجودِ صنفی" سے مراد یہ ہے کہ انسان ایک ایسی ہستی ہے جسے صرف اپنی انفرادی ذات کا ہی
احساس نہیں ہوتا، اسے یہ بھی احساس ہوتا ہے کہ اس کا تعلق نوع انسان، یعنی انسانی صنف سے ہے (جانوروں کو اپنی صنف کا
احساس نہیں ہوتا)۔ ہر چیز انفرادی اعتبار سے ایک مخصوص، یعنی محدود، ہستی رکھتی ہے (مثلاً شخص ایک خاص وقت اور مقام پر
پیدا ہوتا ہے، وغیرہ)۔ مارکس کے فلسفے کی سب سے بڑی خوبی یہ ہے کہ یہاں تاریخ فلسفہ میں پہلی بار انسان، سماج اور تاریخ کی
تشکیل میں کام یا محنت کو مرکزی حیثیت دی گئی ہے۔ چنانچہ انسان ہے وہ وجود جسے اپنے صنف کا احساس ہے، جس کا مطلب
یہ ہے کہ وہ محنت کے ذریعے باہوش طریقے پر قدرت کا استعمال کرتا ہے، محض اپنے وجود کو برقرار رکھنے کے لیے ہی نہیں بلکہ
انسانیت کو برقرار رکھنے کے لیے۔ اس بنیاد پر انسان کا دوسرے انسانوں سے رشتہ تشکیل پاتا ہے اور پھر سماج کی بنیاد پڑتی ہے۔
یہ خیال عام ہے کہ مارکسی فلسفے میں مادہ پرستی ہے۔ پاکستان میں اکثر لوگ اسلام کی فوقیت کے بارے میں یہ دلیل پیش کرتے
ہیں کہ اس میں روحانیت ہے جو کمیونزم میں نہیں۔ اس لیے اس بات کی ضرورت ہے کہ مارکس کی ان تحریرات کی اشاعت
کی جائے جس میں انسان کی انسانیت اور "روحانیت" پر زور دیا گیا ہے۔
سیدھے ہاتھ والے صفحے پر اور اس ترجمے کے آخر میں مارکس کی دوسری تحریروں سے دو اور اقتباسات شائع کیے جا رہے
ہیں جن سے امید ہے ان کے خیال کو سمجھنے میں مدد ملے گی۔ (مترجم)

شروع میں انسان کو اس لیے کرنا پڑتی ہے کہ یہ غذا دل خوش کرنے اور زندگی کو برقرار رکھنے کا ذریعہ ہے۔ اسی طرح عملی دائرے میں بھی یہ چیزیں انسانی زندگی اور محنت کا جزو ہیں۔ عملی دائرے میں انسان ان ہی قدرتی چیزوں کے سہارے زندہ رہتا ہے خواہ وہ خوراک کی شکل میں ہو یا گرمی، کپڑا، مکان وغیرہ کی شکل میں۔ عملی دائرے میں انسان کی غیر مخصوصیت اس غیر مخصوصیت کی شکل میں ظاہر ہوتی ہے جس کے ذریعے تمام قدرت اس کا خارجی جسم بن جاتی ہے (۱) اس کی زندگی کے براہِ راست وسیلے کی صورت میں، اور بعینہٖ (۲) اس کی سعیِ حیات (life activity) کے مادی موضوع اور آلے کی حیثیت سے۔ قدرت ۔۔۔۔۔ یعنی انسانی جسم کو چھوڑ کر ساری قدرت، انسان کا خارجی بدن ہے۔ یہ کہنے کا کہ انسان قدرت کے سہارے زندہ رہتا ہے مطلب یہ ہے کہ قدرت کی حیثیت انسان کے لیے اس کے جسم کی سی ہے جس کے ساتھ اسے مستقل ربط و ضبط رکھنا پڑتا ہے تا کہ وہ مرنے نہ پائے۔ اور یہ کہنے کا کہ انسان کی جسمی و ذہنی زندگی اور قدرت ایک دوسرے پر منحصر ہیں مطلب یہ ہے کہ قدرت خود اپنے آپ پر منحصر ہے، کیونکہ انسان قدرت ہی کا ایک حصہ ہے۔

جس طرح برگر داندہ (alienated) محنت (۱) قدرت کو انسان سے، اور (۲) انسان کو اپنے آپ سے، اپنے عملی منصب، اور اپنے زندگی کے مشغلے (life activity) سے اجنبی بنا دیتی ہے اسی طرح وہ انسان کو اپنی صنف سے بھی کشیدہ کر دیتی ہے، اور صنفی زندگی محض انفرادی زندگی کا ایک ذریعہ بن کر رہ جاتی ہے۔ اس کی وجہ یہ ہے کہ برگر داندہ محنت اول تو صنفی وجود کو انفرادی وجود سے جدا کر دیتی ہے اور پھر موخرالذکر کو بحیثیت ایک خیال کے مقصود بنا دیتی ہے اول الذکر کا، اور اسے بھی خیالی اور اجنبی شکل میں۔

وجہ یہ ہے کہ انسان کو اب [یعنی اس حالت میں جبکہ اس کی محنت اس سے اجنبی کر دی جاتی ہے] زندگی کا مشغلہ، یا حیاتِ بار آور [Productive life] ایسی نظر آتی ہے گویا وہ محض ایک ضرورت یعنی جسمانی وجود کو برقرار رکھنے کی ضرورت کو پورا کرنے کا ایک وسیلہ ہو۔ لیکن حیاتِ بار آور ہی حیاتِ صنفی ہے۔ یہ وہ زندگی ہے جس سے زندگی کی تخلیق ہوتی ہے۔ ایک صنف جس طرح کا مشغلہؑ حیات اختیار کرتی ہے اس میں بحیثیتِ

صنف اس کی ساری خصوصیت (یعنی اس کی صنفی خصوصیت) مضمر ہوتی ہے۔ اور انسان کی صنفی خصوصیت ہے آزادانہ اور باہوش طور پر سرگرمِ کار رہنا۔ [ایسی حالت میں] بذاتِ خود زندگی محض زندگی کا ایک وسیلہ بن کر ظاہر ہوتی ہے۔

حیوان تو اپنے مشغلہ ٔ حیات سے متصل ہوتا ہے۔ وہ اپنے آپ میں اور اپنے مشغلہ ٔ حیات میں کوئی امتیاز نہیں کرتا۔ اس کی ذات اور اس کا مشغلہ ایک ہی چیز ہیں۔ لیکن انسان اپنی زندگی کی سرگرمی کو اپنی قوتِ ارادی اور اپنے ہوش کا موضوع بناتا ہے۔ اس کی سعیٔ حیات باہوش سعیٔ حیات (conscious life activity) ہے۔ یہ ایسا پہلو نہیں ہے جس سے انسان خود کو مکمل طور پر ناقابلِ شناخت بنا لیتا ہو۔ باہوش سعیٔ حیات انسان کو حیوانات کی سعیٔ حیات سے ممتاز کرتی ہے۔ انسان وجودِ صنفی ہی اس وجہ سے ہے، بلکہ یہ کہنا زیادہ صحیح ہو گا کہ وجودِ صنفی ہونے کے باعث ہی وہ ایک خود آگاہ (self-conscious) ہستی ہے اور اس کی اپنی زندگی اس کے لیے ایک موضوع (object) کی حیثیت رکھتی ہے۔ اسی باعث انسان کا مشغلہ ٔ حیات آزاد مشغلہ ہے۔ وہ محنت جو اجنبی بن جاتی ہے اس رشتے کو الٹا کر دیتی ہے۔ وہ اس لیے کہ انسان، چونکہ وہ ایک خود آگاہ ہستی ہے، اپنے مشغلہ ٔ حیات کو، یعنی اپنے وجود کو، صرف اپنی زیست [جسمانی وجود] کا ذریعہ بنا لیتا ہے۔

خارجی دنیا (objective world) کی عملی تعمیر، یعنی خارجی قدرت کا جوڑنا بنانا (manipulation) اس بات کی تصدیق کرتا ہے کہ انسان ایک باہوش وجودِ صنفی ہے، یعنی ایسی ہستی جو اپنے صنف کو اپنا وجود اور اپنے وجود کو وجودِ صنفی شمار کرتی ہے۔ اس بات سے انکار نہیں کہ حیوانات بھی پیداواری کرتے ہیں۔ وہ گھونسلے اور رہائش کی جگہیں بناتے ہیں، جیسا شہد کی مکھیوں، سگہائے آبی، اور چونٹیوں کا طریق ہے۔ لیکن حیوانات صرف انھی چیزوں کی پیداواری کرتے ہیں جو اُن کے اور ان کے بچوں کے لیے قطعی ضروری ہوتی ہیں۔ ان کی پیداواری صرف ایک ہی سمت ہوتی ہے جبکہ انسان کی پیداواری کی کوئی سمت مخصوص نہیں۔ حیوانات، صرف، اسی وقت پیداواری کرتے ہیں جب انھیں جسمانی ضرورت براہِ راست مجبور کرتی ہے۔ اس کے برخلاف انسان جسمانی ضرورت سے آزاد ہو

کر پیداواری کرتا ہے، بلکہ اس کی پیداواری صحیح معنوں میں ہوتی ہی اس وقت ہے جب وہ جسمانی ضرورت سے آزاد ہو۔ حیوانات صرف اپنی ہی افزائش کرتے ہیں جبکہ انسان ساری قدرت کو دُھرا بناتا ہے (reproduces)۔ جانور جو کچھ پیدا کرتے ہیں اس کا ان کے جسموں سے براہِ راست واسطہ ہوتا ہے، لیکن انسان جو کچھ پیدا کرتا ہے وہ خود اس کی بندش سے آزاد ہوتا ہے۔ پھر حیوانات صرف اپنی صنف کے معیاروں اور ضروریات کے مطابق ہی بناتے ہیں، لیکن انسان ہر صنف کے معیاروں کے مطابق بنانا جانتا ہے اور یہ بھی جانتا ہے کس چیز پر کس معیار کا اطلاق ہوتا ہے اور کس طرح۔ چنانچہ انسان خوبصورتی کے اصولوں کے مطابق بھی تشکیل کرتا ہے۔

دراصل خارجی دنیا پر اپنی محنت استعمال کرنے میں ہی انسان خود کو وجودِ صنفی ثابت کرتا ہے۔ یہی محنت اس کی عملی صنفی زندگی (active species‹life) ہے۔ اس [محنت] کی بدولت قدرت انسان کی اپنی تخلیق اور اس کی اپنی حقیقت بن کر ظاہر ہوتی ہے۔ پس محنت کا مقصد ہے انسان کی صنفی زندگی کو خارجی حقیقت میں تبدیل کرنا۔ کیونکہ اس طرح انسان خود کو محض عقلی طور پر ہی نہیں دُھرا بناتا، جیسا کہ ہوش (شعور) میں ہوتا ہے، بلکہ عملی طور پر اور سچے معنوں میں۔ اس کو اپنی بنائی ہوئی دنیا میں اپنا عکس نظر آتا ہے۔ اب چونکہ برگردانده محنت انسان سے اس کی محنت کے پھل کو علیحدہ کر دیتی ہے اس لیے وہ اس سے اس کی صنفی زندگی بھی چھین لیتی ہے، یعنی اس کی سچی شیئیت (objectivity) جو اسے وجودِ صنفی ہونے کی حیثیت سے میسر ہے، اور انسان کو حیوانات پر جو فوقیت حاصل ہے اس طرح اس کی کمزوری میں بدل جاتی ہے کیونکہ انسان اپنے خارجی جسم، یعنی قدرت، سے جدا کر دیا جاتا ہے۔

جس طرح برگردانده محنت آزاد اور خود محرک (Self-directed) سعی کو محض ایک وسیلہ بنا دیتی ہے اسی طرح وہ انسان کی صنفی زندگی کو اس کے جسمانی وجود کا آلہ بنا کر رکھ دیتی ہے۔

ہوش، جو انسان کو اپنی صنف سے ملتا ہے، اس کی برگردانگی کے باعث ماہیت (nature) ہی بالکل بدل جاتی ہے اور صنفی زندگی انسان کے لیے محض ایک وسیلہ بن کر رہ جاتی ہے۔

Pakistan Left Review

Autumn, 1969

Contents

Shape of Things to Come

Editorial

It appears that the 'reformist' phase, which newly risen dictatorships sometimes go through in an attempt to make the public believe—and perhaps even to delude themselves—that it's in their power to solve the deep-rooted problems of the society, is now nearly over. But, as was to be expected, no sooner the 'reforms' were put on paper than it became evident how ludicrously incapable our new rules are of even understanding, let alone solving, those problems. Practically the first thing the new regime occupied itself with was an attempt, to quote the words of the Central Labour Secretary, 'to find out a lasting solution of the workers' problems for the betterment of their lot as well as of the whole country'. As usual, meetings, conferences, negotiations followed; but the net product of all that activity was a policy that was, to put it mildly, highly ambiguous on the question of the workers' rights, and which fixed the minimum wages of the workers at a level nowhere near commensurate with the steeply rising cost of living. Moreover, the proposed legislation applied only to 5 per cent of the entire labour force in the country. ('Will it be right,' asked a delegate at a Labour Conference, 'to keep industrial peace when 95 per cent of the workers have been excluded from the provision for minimum wages?'). Altogether, the proposed labour policy was so vague, complicated and unfair that the government could get it accepted only by 'restricting' the Conference in Dacca which was called to vote on it.

But the proposals on education, announced in a blaze of publicity, were in some ways quite alarming. It isn't so much the failure of these proposals to deal adequately with some of the basic problems of education in our country that gives one cause for concern; given the type of intellectual material available to the regime it would have been surprising had the Policy proposed anything of far reaching significance. What alarms one is the anti-progressive and anti-scientific spirit in which the Policy has been conceived. When 'Islamic values' and 'Pakistan's ideology' become the sole determinants of the content of education—the criteria of good

170

and bad teaching, the principles for the selection and organisation of syllabuses, the aims of intellectual and cultural activities—what kind of young men and women will our schools and colleges produce except philistines and narrow-minded bigots? This misguided revivalism (which has already been translated into legislation against printing or publishing any literature not in conformity with 'the ideology of Pakistan') could not but embolden all the backward and irrational elements in our society and discourage those who want to liberate us from the stifling hold of superstition and dogma. The identity of interests among the army, the mullahs and the capitalists (of which General Yahya's civilian cabinet is a most alarming embodiment) gives ample reason to fear for our nation's future. The dismissal of the Islamia College lecturers and the repeated violence in East Pakistan between the supporters of Jamaat-i-Islami and the progressive students are the result of the attempt, begun during the last days of Ayub's rule, to provoke religious controversy and then, in the name of Islam, to discredit and destroy the emerging socialist movement in the country. This 'pious' intention is all too obvious in the Proposals on Education the regime has put forward. It is not without significance that concepts like 'reason', 'truth', 'freedom', 'justice', 'scientific culture', 'enlightenment' do not even once find a mention in a document that pretends to be about the 'education' of our young generation.

As for the other big 'reform', viz. the 'Ordinance on Monopolies', proposed by the regime to show how sensitive it is to the people's demand to stop the concentration of wealth in a few hands, we quote here from an article by 'Economist' in the government's own *Pakistan Times* (Sep. 2, 1969):

In this country (says the writer) the concentration of economic power has taken place in certain family groups. The Ordinance does not take this fact into consideration. Its approach is segregated. Its scheme is based on the concept of an undertaking or an individual. Certain of its provisions intend to bring within its purview managing agencies but the powerful family groups have already more than one managing agency for their enterprises and may create many more and through this loophole they will manage to avoid the provisions of the Ordinance...

Incidentally, it may be pointed out that so far the (past) Government(s) had resisted pressure from industrial groups to permit them to promote investment trusts. The inclusion of investment houses in the provisions of the Monopoly Ordinance is ominous. Does it indicate a change in the thinking of the policy makers? Is it that the 22 families will soon be equipped with another powerful medium to finance their expansion?

After arguing that the Ordinance may not even achieve what similar legislations have done in other countries, 'Economist' continues:

> As for preventing concentration of economic power, the legislation will not even create an illusion. This objective, if at all it is an objective, can be achieved by reversing the policies regarding sanctions for industrial units, industrial trade (especially the export bonus scheme) institutional credit and taxation. Continuation of old policies will only bring about the results we are well acquainted with. Monopolies Ordinance is a very poor substitute for change in economic policies.

Thus, the various proposals for 'reforms'—hailed by the government's agents and lackeys as 'radical' and 'revolutionary'—serve merely to reveal the insincerity of our present rulers and the dark conspiracy in which powerful forces are united against the people. At the same time reports are coming that the country's economy is verging towards a traumatic crisis. A recent State Bank Report has revealed that by the end of last June the money supply in the economy (the factor which causes inflation) reached the phenomenal figure of Rs. 1098.59 cores, while the country's rate of growth dropped from 7.5 per cent (in 1967–8) to 5.1 per cent (1968–69). The situation is believed to be even grimmer in East Pakistan where the rate of growth was further arrested by exceptionally poor rice and jute crops. One writer, in a national newspaper, sardonically commented:

> The different pictures of economic performance in the two wings, for which not all the figures are readily available, may mean considerable difficulties during the current year 1969–70. While money incomes could not have risen fast in the western wing, the price trends in the former zone towards the latter parts of the year could only have meant more impoverishment in the countryside of East Pakistan, where the rise in prices does not usually benefit the peasants.

Indeed, within the last few months alone prices of food and other articles of everyday use have gone up by as much as 35 per cent. But this is not all. From a country where undernourishment and hunger was already chronic comes the news that during the last four years (Third plan period!) the consumption of food has declined instead of improving. The per capita food consumption in West Pakistan was estimated at 9 oz per day in 1960–1965 but was reduced to only 3 oz during 1965–1969! Similarly, rice consumption in East Pakistan declined from 16 oz to 15.2 oz per day. Mind you, these are not figures which the present writer has

cooked up to smear the fair face of his motherland; they are issued by
the Government of Pakistan itself. What glorious progress we have made
in twenty years!

Meanwhile, the poker game among political parties goes on. Currently
most of them are vying with each other in trying to pose as 'socialist'
and in trying to cash in on the growing regionalist movement. They
still fondly cherish the hope that it is only a matter of time before the
military government steps down and hands power over to them. They
haven't as yet become clearly aware of the trap in which the military
regime has cleverly caught them. The trap is the Constitutional Issue.
General Yahya Khan wants a consensus on that issue as a condition for
restoring democracy. Now the only body that may assume the right to
choose a constitution for the country—which in effect means deciding
whether the parliament should be constituted on the principle of parity
between the two wings or on the basis of population—is of course the
national Parliament itself. In other words, elections can't be held because
to do so will be to prejudge one way or the other the very issue the
elected Parliament is intended to settle! Result: indefinite stalemate and
a readymade excuse for the continuation of dictatorship.

Still, the military government might decide to relinquish power. If
it did so it wouldn't be on account of any preference for democracy (to
believe that is to live in a fool's paradise); it would be because the regime
may come to realise it cannot successfully tackle the grave economic
problems of the country (though, of course, the U.S.A. might step in to
save the situation for the regime!). But if General Yahya Khan waited
until the runaway inflation and decelerating growth had brought the
country near to disaster, the transfer of power might be attended by such
violence as the country has not yet witnessed. But if, on the other hand,
the regime decided to retain power in the face of a prolonged economic
crisis and social distress, either directly or through a new constitution
of its own (and one is reported to be under its active consideration), then
the regime might find terror the only way to prop and sustain its power.

This, then, is the shape of things to come. If the political parties in
the country allowed themselves to be beguiled by promises and cowed
down by threats at this stage, as they've been doing since last March, it
might soon be too late for them. The time for action is NOW! Instead
of pleading with the government for early elections, they ought to give
it an ultimatum. Instead of making and remaking political formations
among old leaders with outworn policies, they should organise the masses
in farms and factories, in offices, schools and *mohallahs*. But of course,

our old politicians neither know how to do this, nor would their vested interests allow them to be honest with the people. What the country is looking to is the younger generation: the new generation of trade union leaders, for example, the students, the educated unemployed. Surely, they have a common interest in bringing about an end to exploitations which cuts across old regional animosities and prejudices? Surely, they know that a radical transformation of the country's economy and democratic control both of the state and of means of production alone can relieve their hardships and bring them hope and justice? It is time these dispossessed and exploited, but socially aware, people stepped forward and wrenched the future of their country from the hands of the usurpers and power-greedy politicians alike!

Our New Educational Policy

Mahmood

The proposals for a new educational policy for Pakistan recently put
forward by the government aroused a countrywide debate which is
still going on despite the fact that the last date for the receipt of public
comment as fixed by the Ministry of Education has long since passed.
Apart from some 20,000 pages of comments which the Ministry is
reported to have received, most of the important national papers have
been carrying long articles almost daily for the past two months or so;
and this in addition to letters, speeches and conference on the subject.
It is significant that, despite the apparently liberal, even progressive,
character (reflected in such proposals as those for student participation
in the government of their institutions, the loosening of the bureaucratic
grip over schools, a literacy campaign, etc.) very few published articles
have wholeheartedly endorsed the policy. Indeed, in some of the best
articles ever written on education in Pakistan—e.g. the one by Manzoor
Ahmed in the *Pakistan Observer*—the proposed policy has been subjected
to sharp criticism.

The document on education reflects some of the weaknesses and
contradictions to be found in our people and society at large. There is
the same preoccupation with abstract, seemingly lofty (but indeed often
quite trite) sentiments, while at the same time, a lack of concern with
hard physical reality which bears directly and immediately on our lives;
the same inability to think logically and critically, or to produce original
and bold ideas; and, above all, the same deep conflict between traditional
and modern outlooks. Thus, while there is much talk about national
consensus, Pakistan's ideology, Islamic values, etc., there is little mention
of the actual physical suffering among our masses, and of the implications
this has for education. Particularly absent is any mention of some of the
well-known educational problems, such as the phenomenal wastage at the
primary level (more than 80 per cent) and the equally alarming failure
rates at other levels; while such a tremendously important matter as the
education of women (who constitute nearly half of our population) is

175

touched upon superficially, and the question of education in rural areas, where more than 80 per cent of our population lives, is not raised at all. Then there is no attempt to explain why of the total allocation made in the development programme so far only a small fraction (28 per cent) has been utilised, or why the targets so far attained in the polytechnic and vocational school education are respectively as much as 60 per cent and 80 per cent short of those set in the Third Plan. Similarly, there is to be found in the document not the slightest recognition of the fact that there exist a large number of schools in the country where such sub-human conditions prevail as those reported below:

> In Pabna (E.P.) there is one primary school to 10,000. The number of teachers is 29 i.e. one teacher to more than 250 students. Schools are run on double-shift basis, so that teachers have to attend school twice. The sanitary conditions in the schools are appalling because none of them has a latrine. Night soil is found in classrooms and here and there on the school premises. (*Pakistan Observer*, 18 June 1969).

How many more such schools are there in the country? What is the government doing about them?

But the most glaring shortcoming of the Proposed Policy is that there is in it no attempt to assess the country's manpower needs and to relate our education to those needs. We all know that in order to raise our abysmally low standard of life within not too long a period of time we must make a gigantic effort to industrialise, revolutionise our agriculture, raise productivity many many times, and so on. And since all this depends very largely on the right type of manpower, we expect an educational programme to spell out in quantitative terms exactly what is required and how the educational system is being geared to meet the requirements. For example, by exactly how much must the productivity in various sectors be raised? What type of skilled manpower will be needed to achieve that? What are the minimum levels of health and hygiene that ought to be ensured? How far short of the basic requirements in medical personnel are we and what should be done to make good our shortcomings?

But, alas, there is little attempt in this, as in earlier documents on education, to highlight these—surely the most crucial of all our educational problems?—in a scientific manner. In the absence of such quantitative frame of reference the public can have no means of judging whether a particular policy is or isn't on the right lines. When, for example, the present document says that by 1980 there will be 922 agriculture schools, etc. how can one evaluate the adequacy of such a project, even if we were to assume (a very big assumption, no doubt) that the project will be realised?

So, it might be instructive to look at some figures to see, by way of example, how barbarically short of basic manpower requirements we are and what urgent demands this situation makes on our education. According to the 'Twenty Years of Pakistan', produced by President Ayub and his associates, by the year 1970 there would be no more than one doctor to every 6,000 persons (incidentally, a most depressing fact is exposed, perhaps unwittingly, by the figures given in that book (p. 465). The ratio of doctors to population will be exactly the same in 1970 as it was in 1966!); one nurse to every 24,100 people; and only one Lady Health Visitor [LHV] to every 50,900! From this information it is possible to have some idea of the enormous problem posed for the country's education, if the 127 million people are to be provided anything like an adequate medical service. A population as ravaged by disease and malnutrition as is ours calls for at least 1 doctor for every 500 people, 1 nurse for every 300, and 1 LHV to every 250; but this, in our present situation is to ask for the moon. But certainly the ratio ought not to be lower than 1 doctor to every 1000 people, 1 nurse to every 600, and LHV to every 500.

On this basis the country will need, in 1970, some 100,000 more doctors than there will be according to present estimates (requiring about 50 times greater turn out from our existing 14 medical colleges); about 200,000 more nurses (or 17,000[1] nursing centres where at present there are only 26), and 250,000 more LHVs (more than 1,000 training centres where at present there are only 10). To this of course must be added the medical staff needed yearly to cope with the 4 million annual increases in population!

This is the kind of 'immediate reality' whose glimpse we should like to have in our educational policies. We expect our educational experts to devise methods and strategies for solving the kind of problems I have just given an example of. And this is where there is need for both ingenuity and boldness; for it is clear that in the face of problems of such magnitude and our existing meagre resources, nothing but a wholly new way of thinking can save us from disaster.

Take the problem of medical personnel again as an example. From the British we have inherited a class-mentality which informs our social as

---

1. i.e. on the basis of the present productive capacity which is about 13 nurses annually from each centre (!)

well as educational system. Thus, in the medical profession doctors are a class apart from the rest of the medical personnel, and this apartness is founded upon their having had a specialised and strenuous five years' course of medical education. The rest of the medical personnel, the LHVs, the nurses, even the LMFs are regarded somewhat in the same way as the menial servants are regarded in the well-to-do-households, or as the 'natives' were regarded in the days of the Raj. Consequently, our young men and women are deterred from choosing this type of work as a career—and of course the MBBS course is both too expensive and too demanding for most of them.

And yet it is the non-MBBS staff that the country needs most. While in India, J. K. Galbraith couldn't help remarking:

> As a layman I have sometimes wondered if medical education has really adapted to the situation of the poor county... The provision of such total training is the sine qua non of medical education. But in the developing country, with scarce resources, if we insist on... high standards for the few, may we not deny medical assistance to the many? Do we not get good doctors in the capitals at the price of having no one to set a broken leg or prescribe some morphine in the village?

Should our main effort therefore not be to train the non-MBBS staff? And since the hierarchical structure of the medical profession—together with poor salaries and conditions of work—discourages our people from taking these courses, should it not be replaced by a more uniform and democratic structure? Such a structure may entail giving all the non-MBBS staff the status of (junior) doctors; providing them with good medical training (2–3 years without long vacations after class X); abolishing private medical practice, and reducing income differences between doctors and junior doctors; restructuring medical education so that students for MBBS courses are drawn entirely from the ranks of junior doctors on the strength of service or experience, etc.

But of course this by itself won't take us very far. In order to meet the needs of the country—and indeed in the interest of education itself—we shall have to introduce even more fundamental changes. In a country like ours there is no justification whatever for confining medical education to colleges and hospitals. In the last few years we have heard a lot about 'preventive medicine'—but how can the doctor apply this, or learn about this, if his entire medical training is geared to hospital work? What we need in fact is a place in every doctor's course for what might be called 'field work', lasting from 6 months (in the case of junior doctors) to one year (in the case of doctors). For this work each medical school and college should be required to select a specific rural or urban area (a student may spend half of his field work period in a rural area and half in urban) and prepare a rough programme of work to be carried out. This programme may include draining or drying of stagnant pools and other breeding grounds of mosquitoes; disinfecting homes, shops, etc.; finding hygienic ways for rubbish disposal; waging anti-spitting campaigns; acting as food inspectors; killing of rats and other pests; inoculating the population against cholera, TB, etc.; spreading elementary knowledge of hygiene among the people—to name only a few types of work.

It should be an essential part of the students' training (who should be paid a salary while they are engaged in field work) to arouse public consciousness about hygiene and sanitation—by means of posters, slogans, public discussions, exhibitions, shows, etc.—and to organise the people themselves to carry out the tasks that need to be accomplished. The people should be encouraged to elect committees to whom various duties should be assigned, and the students should work with these committees. The local government authorities and the police should have special instructions to help the committees. The students may organise competitions with neighbouring areas in order to achieve maximum public participation in health projects.

These are some obvious ideas that come to one's mind. The point is that the Proposed Policy makes no attempt to discuss the country's education in these terms. Here the objection might be raised that what I am suggesting falls in the provenance of economic or state planning rather than that of an educational policy. But this indeed is the heart of the matter. It is impossible not to be amazed at the naivety of our educationalists, present or former, who talk of education as if it existed, or could exist, in a vacuum regardless of the social and economic conditions prevalent in the country. And not merely is it presumed that education can be meaningfully discussed in isolation from everything else in society, but that it can by itself effect fundamental and far-reaching changes in every sphere of life! This is yet another way in which the documents reflects the uncritical habit of mind of our people, in whose imagination education holds some kind of semi-divine status, capable of every kind of spiritual and material transformation. Consequently, when the country fails to make any headway, when poverty and disease go on increasing, when corruption grows more and more chronic every day, when politicians fight among themselves and prove irresponsible and incompetent, when people's wishes do not conform with the rulers' ambitions ... the blame for all these ills is laid at the door of education. Of course, every nation and every government has a right to have its scapegoats; what is sad is that in our country education is chosen as one. By doing so issues of vital importance for the country are confused, priorities distorted, and valuable resources wasted in implementing schemes which cannot possibly achieve the goals they are set because it's simply not in their power to do so.

Let's take a small example from the Proposed Policy to illustrate why it is really meaningless to talk about education without relating it to the economic and social conditions existing in the country. As everyone knows one of our greatest problems is the dearth of technicians and skilled people. According to the Proposed Policy 'at the secondary level of education, which should be the terminal stage for most people, no more than 4 per cent of the total enrolment is in vocation and technical classes, and even those enrolled in general classes prefer to enter college rather than active life!' The document rightly says that 'a massive shift' (60 per cent of the secondary students) is essential—if only to compensate for the failure to reach the Third Plan targets rather than as a further improvement of the situation.

But what are the measures recommended to bring about this shift?—

    i. Establishment of Directorates of Technical Education;
    ii. Introduction of vocational training in ordinary high schools;
    iii. Earmarking of 75 per cent of existing scholarships for technical students;
    iv. Making apprenticeships a compulsory part of training for technical college students, and
    v. Investigation of ways and means whereby it is ensured that employers give jobs only to certificate holders.

While one or two of these recommendations are certainly a step in the right direction, one is truly at a loss to know how these peripheral changes can bring about a massive orientation of our young people towards scientific and vocational education. Indeed, there is no attempt in the document to make a thorough analysis of the problem and to discover the causes that predispose the students towards general education rather than technical, and towards the university rather than 'active life'. Since this theme keeps recurring in the writings and reports of our educationists it might be worthwhile to look at the problem a little more closely.

The most obvious reason—i.e. 'obvious' but hardly even mentioned by our educationalists—is to be found in the miserably low salaries of the middle grade (and indeed even higher grade) technicians, particularly as compared to the semi- or un-skilled, but uneducated, workers. To gain a rough idea it is useful to compare the minimum wages for unskilled labour fixed recently, which range from Rs.115 per month to Rs.140, with the average wage of skilled labour as estimated in the Third Five-Year Plan, which is only Rs.75 in East Pakistan and Rs.135 in West. But the following figures, picked out from newspapers, will give an idea of the wage differentials between various groups a little more accurately. (In looking at these figures it is important to bear in mind the back-breaking cost of living, the presence of large numbers of none-earning members in every family, etc.)

Uneducated Semi-Skilled		Educated Skilled			Graduates		
		Min.	Max.		Min.	Max.	
Mason	Rs.126.80 pm	Electrician	Rs.150 pm		Executive Engineer	Rs.750	?
Painter	Rs.129.80	Tracer	110	135	Mechanical Engineer	900	1500
Carpenter	Rs.127.00	Draughtsman	175	450	Electrical Engineer	500	1500
Blacksmith	Rs.101.80	Overseer (with 3 yr. diploma from polytech.)	210	400	Metallurgist	800	?
Head Mason	Rs.169.80	Works Supervisor	120	400	District Surgical Of.	350	?
(In East Pakistan; a little higher in West Pakistan)		Municipal Medical Off.	160	–	Assist. Engineer	350	?
		Nurse	155	–	Lecturer (new scale)	500	
		Designer (polytech. Diploma & 5 yrs. experience)	350	925	Executive	375	1050

These figures show that while the wages of technically qualified people differ from those of the uneducated only marginally, a university degree promises at least more than twice as much, and, what is an extremely important consideration, an income that comes nearer to a living wage.

This of course doesn't explain why there is a general tendency among our young to prefer an Arts course to a Scientific one. To understand the reasons for that we'd have to look elsewhere. And the thing that leaps to one's eyes is the complete lack of those conditions which alone can bring about a general orientation towards science and the practical world. Here we may have been caught in a circle: in order to make technical education popular, the educationist says, technical and vocational subjects should be introduced in schools; but, on the other hand, students are attracted to such course only if there already exists a practically and scientifically orientated culture. Yet the circle can be broken, provided we reorganise our educational system on completely unconventional lines. For example, we will have to modify the traditional idea of education as something separate from life, given in special surroundings, by a special type of people. We will have to get used to the idea if every factory, workshop, and farm operating as a school as well as a place of work. In other words, the real breakthrough in education—in fact, the only breakthrough that matters in our situation—will come when children are, from the beginning, and as a normal part of their education, drawn into the process of production and the life of action. For science is nothing if not practical; and knowledge (as every educationist worth his salt ought to know by now) comes most easily and most fruitfully through direct and personal experience.

Finally, another factor that creates a built-in preference for university education, is the high esteem which such education enjoys in our society—another attitude we owe to our former masters. This esteem is not without a basis. Anyone who has knowledge of the English educational system knows that the English school has really no identity of its own: its syllabuses, its style of exams, indeed its whole ethos makes it merely a preparatory stage for the university. In Pakistan there is a further important reason why secondary education is not regarded by the students as a 'terminal stage' of their educational career. Usually, the school education is so thoroughly bad that the only hope of a 'real education' seems to rest at the degree level. What justifies the hope is the presence, in the universities, of the liberal Arts and Science courses ('liberal' because not geared to any profession), which gives the illusion that here at last one can find 'knowledge for its own sake'—some kind of pure wisdom not available in the engineering and agricultural colleges. And to a people as woolly minded as we are this is a big attraction. Add to all this the fact that the degree courses, particularly in the Arts subjects, are, and are known to be, very 'easy to pass', and who will be such a fool—especially if he remembers his intellectual limitations and aversion to hard work (the result of soft schooling)—to miss the chance of becoming a 'BA'?

But the 'undergraduate institution' (or the 'degree college') was the product of an age which had not developed the human and social concerns which alone mark the twentieth century as a higher stage in the history of civilisation. In today's socially conscious and highly purposeful world the traditional university courses which prepare one for nothing in particular, and which as an instrument of culture come too late in the educational process, is a dangerous luxury a poor struggling nation like ours can ill afford. The undergraduate institutions must go, and its place must be taken by professional institutions—medical colleges, teacher training colleges, engineering colleges, business administration colleges etc., while the universities must be reserved purely for high powered research.

Such a radical transformation of 'higher education' will inevitably have repercussions for the whole of the educational system; but here only rough contours of the new system that will emerge as a result can be drawn. From the hints already thrown in this article it should have been apparent that the barriers between practical life and education will have to be kept as few, and as low, as possible. To this we now add the idea that the schools must play the role traditionally reserved for the undergraduate institutions—that is, as centres of enlightenment and culture.

The system through which these ideas can be given practical shape is now possible to visualise. The basic education, involving children between, say, 5 to 13 or 14, will be given in primary or elementary schools, where the attempt will be made, by means of the modern 'direct experience', 'project', 'play', etc. techniques (a) to strengthen the children's personal qualities (self-confidence, discipline, initiative, adventurousness, love of family, country, etc.) and (b) to give them a sound scientific knowledge of their environment, beginning from their own locality and extending to the whole world.

The secondary stage will eventually consist of two types of schools: (i) the enterprise schools, for the 14–16 age group, and (ii) the academies, for young people between 16 to 18 or 19 years.

The students' first three years will be spent in gaining practical experience of productive processes in farms and factories. Here their studies will revolve round their work and will aim at giving them knowledge of the scientific and economic basis of the industry, its organisation, problems, etc. The teaching will be carried out by the workers as well as by specialists. During the last three years, however, the emphasis will be more on developing the intellectual and cultural side of the students. But here too, the students' own experience in the factories, etc. must provide the starting point for deeper studies; and science must play the central role.

On graduating from the academies the student will have completed his education. The higher professional institutions and colleges of technology will not draw their students from these graduates, but directly from the industry and professions, on the basis of desire, experience and performance. In this way the higher institutions will cease to exercise the pull on our young people which at present prevents them from treating Matriculation as the 'terminal stage' of their education, and will also become more useful and more economical than the present universities. In the transitional period, however, (i.e. while we are solving our manpower and other basic problems), a modified version of the above system may be introduced. This may take the form of lengthening the duration of the enterprise school (say to 3 years) and dropping the academies. But the programme of the enterprise school should be so devised as to include general education as well as education connected directly with the work the students might be doing. But the intake in the various types of enterprise school, or the number of students directed into various enterprises, in the transitional period as well as in the long run, must be in accordance with the manpower requirements of the country.

This then is the kind of educational system towards which the logic of our situation points. To those to whom it might appear too novel it needs only be said that in some from or other many advanced countries of the world have either already adopted this pattern or are in the process of doing so. But to introduce a particular system is one thing, to make it work efficiently quite another. The latter presupposes a strong national will, which in turn is a function of forces and institutions which lie outside the control of educational policymakers.

The Stranglehold of 'Aid'

S. Niaz

The acceptance of a rather crude form of capitalist growth philosophy for Pakistan has meant that our planners have had to rely more and more on foreign capital for attaining the objective of what the economists call 'self-sustaining growth' and for breaking loose from the so-called 'vicious circle of poverty'.

Apart from the crippling social and economic injustices which this system has perpetuated and imposed on the 120 million people of Pakistan (with the exception of the 'magic' twenty families,) there is no evidence to suggest that we are anywhere near attaining the objective. On the contrary, all the evidence seem to point in the other direction and what is even more alarming is that our planners are landing us straight into yet another kind of vicious circle, i.e. that of aid indebtedness without getting us out of the first one. If things are allowed to go as they are, very soon we will be mortgaging substantially large chunks of our national wealth to foreign capitalists and borrowing large sums from them not for promoting economic development but simply to pay back interest and amortisation on loans that we have incurred so far and propose to incur in the future. A number of our politicians talk glibly about the consequences of excessive reliance on foreign aid but none seems to appreciate fully the disastrous results which such a policy has already produced. Some of them, under pressure, have recently acknowledged the urgent need to nationalise basic industries, run both by indigenous and foreign nationals, which have plundered our economy for private gains. However, almost none of these proposals go far enough and absolutely none seems near materialisation. One of the beliefs underlying this article is that Pakistan must drastically reduce its dependence on foreign capital and find means to promote its own economic self-sufficiency. This aspect of the problem would require a separate study of its own, but suffice it here to say that our economic ills could only be cured by the adoption of a clearly socialist economic policy.

185

With this background it is time that an attempt be made to discuss and analyse the economic and political consequences of dependence on external assistance for the economic growth of Pakistan.

The Extent of Dependence on Foreign Assistance

In the first place, an attempt is made to try and give some quantitative measurement of Pakistan's increasing dependence on aid. This is done in the table below:

Table 1: Total Capital Imports		1955–60	1960–65	1965–70
1.	Total Capital Imports (in Rs. million)	5,070	10,100	16,500
	(a) grants	2,837	2,075	n.a.
	(b) loans	1,808	8,025	n.a.
	(c) private foreign investment	425	450	700
2.	Capital Imports as % of Development Expenditure	52.0	38.4	31.7
3.	External Assistance as % of Gross National Product	3.2	5.0	6.1

Source: Items 1 and 2 from Griffen: Financing Development Plans in Pakistan in *Pakistan Development Review*, Winter 1965. Item 3 from Mahbub ul Haq: *The Strategy of Economic Planning*.

From the table a number of facts stand out. These are discussed below.

1. Total inflow of foreign capital which was about Rs. 5,070 million in the First Plan period increased significantly by a 100 per cent in the next five years (Second Plan period) and is expected to increase by another 60 per cent to reach Rs. 16,500 million in the Third Plan period covering the years 1965 to 1970. This growing dependence on foreign assistance is also reflected when we look at the per cent share of external assistance in total gross domestic product which increased from only 3 per cent in the 1955–60 period to about 6 per cent in the years 1965–70. This doubling of the share of external assistance means that dependence on foreign aid has been increasing at a much faster rate than the immediate benefits we have been deriving from it in the form of higher rates of economic growth. Later on we will show that even the long-term benefits are of a highly dubious nature when we take into account the growing debt burden resulting from foreign borrowing.

2. Secondly, in order to know how vulnerable our economy is to the whims of our capitalist creditors we must try and ascertain the relationship of aid to the crucial variable in economic growth, i.e. development expenditure. Pakistan, as the figure in Table 1 shows, depends to the extent of about 32 per cent of its total developments expenditure on foreign aid. This percentage is uncomfortably large for Pakistan and provides aid donors with sufficient opportunity to determine or actively influence the social, political and economic objectives of the country as was amply evidenced during the Indo-Pakistan conflict in 1965.

3. Thirdly, in order to know whether the trend in foreign aid has been favourable or unfavourable to a country it is necessary to analyse further the concept of aid. Aid, as such, is rather a general term and does not tell us much about the various forms in which it is available. Here we will distinguish two major components of aid, i.e. grants and loans. Grants are the so-called interest free gifts which do not have to be repaid whereas loans are for a specific period of time and the debtor country has to pay back both the principal amount as well as the interest on it (at compound rates) over a certain fixed period. It follows that a country with a higher ratio of grants to loans is in a less favourable position than a country with a higher ratio of loans to grants. Not only is the real value of aid in the former case less but the burden of aid is also greater.

In the case of Pakistan (see items 1 [a], 1 [b] in Table 1) there is evidence to suggest that there is a strong trend for composition of aid to move in an adverse manner. During 1955–60 about 56 per cent of Pakistan's total capital imports were in the form of grants; the remainder 44 per cent was composed of loans and a small flow of private foreign investment. In the next Plan period, however, there was an abrupt reversal in the composition when the amount of aid doubled and the proportions of loans rose by about 444 per cent to form 80 of the total capital imports. Compare this with the share of loans in the First Plan period of only 44 per cent in the total.

Thus, not only Pakistan's dependence on aid is increasing but it is getting its aid on progressively more adverse terms. The situation is made even worse when we consider that there is an upward trend in rates of interest at which loans are advanced so that in future Pakistan can expect to get more aid only by getting itself deeper into indebtedness.

One can also detect certain political undertones in the apparent shift in the composition of aid that has taken place. Griffin states, 'it is perhaps … indelicate to suggest that grants decreased once Pakistan's alignment with the West, its acceptance of U.S. military aid, and its membership in SEATO and CENTO were assured ... but the suspicion remains nevertheless.'[1]

4. Fourthly, this de-emphasis of grants was associated with a dramatic increase in 'tied' loans. Tied loans compel the recipient country to purchase goods in the donor country. The long-run consequences of tied aid can be quite serious. It is a common belief that products purchased under tied loan agreements[2] usually cost 15 per cent–25 per cent more than world prices. It is quite likely that this is an under estimate since (a) foreign suppliers frequently raise their prices when loans are tied and world competition is eliminated and (b) there is evidence that German industrialists charge 40 per cent more than world prices under tied aid loan agreements. Briefly, we can summarise four main harmful effects of tied aid. These are:

i. It reduces the real value of aid substantially;
ii. Increases the real burden of debt per $ since the recipient country pays larger interest payments on relatively smaller volume of real aid.
iii. Makes domestic industries, which are financed out of tied loans, into high cost industries thereby adversely effecting their competitive position in world markets.

As item 1 in Table 2 shows, foreign debt servicing costs in absolute terms are expected to increase by about 17 times over the fifteen-year period 1955 to 1970. Over the Third Plan period alone (i.e. 1965–70) they are expected to rise at the rate of about 20 per cent per year; and will consume as much foreign exchange as the entire Indus Basin Project[3]— which as is well known is one of the biggest irrigation project, ever undertaken, in the world.

Also, debt service costs have been increasing at a much faster rate than the increase in our exports earnings, i.e. our ability to earn foreign exchange. They were only 2 per cent of our exports earnings in 1955–60, but since have risen dramatically and now stand at 16 per cent of our

1. Griffin: Financing Development Plans in Pakistan in *the Pakistan Review*, Winter 1965.
2. See the statement by Mr A. Jamad, President of the Karachi Chamber of Commerce, as reported in *Dawn* (Karachi) July 10, 1965.
3. See Glassburner: pp Balance of Payments and External Resources in *Pakistan Development Rev.* Autumn 1965.

earnings from exports. This means that of the total foreign exchange that Pakistan earns it has to part with 16 per cent of this just to meet its debt commitments and if they continue to increase at this rate they will eat up almost all our earnings of foreign exchange.

Future Projections of Debt Burden

At the present rate of increase of the debt burden a quarter of Pakistan's export earnings will be needed by 1974–75 to service the debt and nearly half by 1979–80. Even this projection is optimistic since it is based on the assumption that the average rate of interest on loans will remain constant at the present low level of 3 per cent (interest on loans from the World Bank is 7 per cent). All indications are that interest charged on loans will rise.

Prof. A. Rahman[4] has projected Pakistan's aid indebtedness into 1985 and has provided us with some interesting results. He tested the hypothesis advanced by the Planning Commission that Pakistan's net requirements of aid will be zero by the terminal date of the perspective Plan Period 1965–1985 (i.e. the country will be self-sufficient in 20 years' time) and found a major error of omission in Perspective Plan Projections. In their eagerness to show that their development policies were leading Pakistan towards economic independence our Planners only looked at the net aid requirements—a figure which does not take into account the burden of debt, i.e. the cost of servicing debt. Therefore, even if net aid requirements are zero by 1985, Pakistan will still require substantial and simply to finance a huge outstanding debt liability, which according to estimates would have increased from Rs. 3,985 million in 1965 to Rs. 103,900 million in 1985, an astronomical increase of about 25 times in 20 years.

Furthermore, even if Pakistan decided not to borrow any more after 1985 and repaid its outstanding debts in equal instalments of say Rs. 5,300 million per year (an amount which is almost double the debts outstanding in 1965) then it will take the country about 30 years to clear its outstanding debts. This means that we have no hope of being self-sufficient if the present policies are pursued, till the year 2015—a frightening prospect. Even this estimate may be somewhat optimistic since it is based on the naive assumption that terms of aid will remain unchanged.

---

4. A. Rahman: The Pakistan Perspective Plan and the Objective of elimination of Dependence on Foreign Assistance in PDR Autumn 1967.

What are the alternatives:

If we continued to follow our present strategy for economic growth then the following options will be open to us:

(a) do nothing about our dependence on aid and thereby accept the economic and political consequence that follow and the social and economic injustices that this system may perpetuate.

(b) try to do something to reduce the burden of aid but leave the present development strategy and the capitalist economic philosophy unscathed. If this assumption is accepted then the following sub-options will be available to us:

    i. Our exports will have to rise at a faster rate than the increase in the rate of debt service costs in order for us to be able to repay our debts without incurring any additional debts. This means that exports will have to increase by over 20 per cent per year, an almost impossible prospect given the world trading situation.

    ii. We can reduce our capital imports. But it will mean that we will have to cut our growth rates substantially.

    iii. Third method of meeting debt service charges is to default or repudiate our foreign debts. But this again, will give us relief for a short period only; as long as we continue to follow the present development strategy we will be constantly running into debt problems.

    iv. Introduces a discriminatory element in the transaction in that, whereas the borrowing country is tied to purchases from the donor country for the loan that it runs up, the latter is not obliged to do the same with the foreign exchange that it receives in interest payments from the debtor country. Thus, the country that is borrowing in fact exchanges free foreign exchange with tied foreign exchange—a highly one-sided state of affairs, which thus raises legitimate doubt as to the efficiency and logic of borrowing from abroad on discriminatory terms.

5. Finally, there has been an alarming increase in foreign private investment in recent years. As is shown under 1(c) in Table 1 this item almost doubled in the Third Plan period when compared with what it was in the earlier periods. Private investment is not strictly classified as aid but it has been included in the table simply to emphasise the extent

to which Pakistan's economy is becoming subject to the flow of foreign capital. Also, foreign investment is increasingly being regarded as a supplement, if not a substitute, for aid in our official circles. There is, in addition, a general trend in the main aid donors of Pakistan to pay more emphasis on increasing the flow of private capital as opposed to government aid. There has been ample evidence of this in recent years. Over the period 1967 to 1968, of the total increase in the flow of capital from developed to developing countries by 15 per cent, government aid increased by only 2 per cent whereas there was a 13 per cent increase in the flow of foreign private investment. If this trend continues, and there seems no reason to think otherwise, then Pakistan will find itself increasingly dependent on this kind of private capital and will have to adopt its political and economic climate to make it conducive for large international monopolies to reap the benefits of our labour.

This is not to say that it has not already happened as is clear from the following quote which is taken from an article in the *Financial Times* of October 7, 1968.

> ... Successive Five-Year Plans have consistently emphasised the importance of the role that foreign investment has to play in Pakistan's economic development. The Government offers a whole series of concessions and incentives to foreign capital, including guarantees providing for equality of treatment of foreign and Pakistani investors, provisions for the free remittance of profits, numerous tax and depreciation allowances, as well as arrangement for the repatriation of capital at any time .... Furthermore, there are no regulations making the participation of Pakistani capital in foreign controlled operations mandatory (except in few cases) ... Nationalisation of the private sector has also never been part of the Government's economic philosophy, but again guarantees are available to foreign capital against the risk of this eventuality'.

The above quotation conveys very lucidly the degree to which our political and economic options have been sacrificed and are determined by the profit-seeking investors rather than by our national interest.

Added to this is the fact that there is no evidence to suggest that Pakistan has been gaining on a net basis from inflows of private capital. Capital exports, in the form of repatriation of private capital, repayment of principal on foreign debts, and interest charges, have begun to rise at a substantial rate. In fact, private capital outflows appear to exceed the inflow, i.e. Pakistan is paying out more in profits, dividends and principal repayments than the total inflow of private capital into the country. 'It is estimated that in 1963–64 the level of such outflows was in the neighbourhood of Rs. 150 million exceeding the direct inflow of private capital by Rs. 50 million.'[5]

Debt Burden of Aid

Earlier on, we mentioned the strong possibility for Pakistan finding itself in a new kind of vicious circle, i.e. that of aid indebtedness. Since Pakistan is getting most of its aid in the form of loans, which are tied and whose terms (i.e. rate of interest) are becoming progressively less favourable to the country it seems that we may be entering the new vicious circle phase sooner rather than later.

Table 2: Debt Servicing Costs of Aid				
		1955–60	1960–65	1965–70
1.	Servicing of foreign debt (in Rs. million)	161	951	2,810
2.	Debt servicing as % of export earnings	2.0	7.0	16.0

(c) The Third major alternative is to meet the problem by completely restructuring our development strategy in a way which takes into account Pakistan's resource endowments and institutional rigidities. A detailed analysis of this is outside the limited scope of the present paper. But briefly we can say that so far Pakistani planners have been trying to generate growth by completely ignoring factors that are in excess supply in Pakistan, i.e. labour, and trying to concentrate on capital which is a scarce commodity and which can only be acquired by borrowing.

(d) And of course the fourth alternative would assume the adoption of a totally different economic policy geared to socialist principles. This matter cannot be discussed in a few lines and is best considered on a separate paper. Needless to say it would envisage reorganisation of the entire of our country.

The crucial role allocated to capital in growth theories is a by-product of the neo-classical growth models as expounded by Harrod and Domar, which, as Myrdal[6] has pointed out, although applicable (though not

---

5. S. S. Jafri, 'The Role of Private Foreign Investment,' a paper read at RCD Collogium at Karachi, June, 1965.
6. Myrdal: *Asian Drama*.

entirely) to conditions in developed countries where labour is scarce, cannot be applied blindly to under developed countries where labour is abundant and where institutional rigidities pre-dominate. This, however, does not mean that capital is unimportant, but at the same time its importance is often exaggerated. For instance, R. Solow[7] in his enlightening econometric study of growth in America found that capital contributed only a small amount to economic growth in the country; most of it (i.e. more than 70 per cent of the U.S. growth) was due to technical change and investment in human capital.

There are great possibilities if investment in human capital was increased in Pakistan; besides the capital import content of this kind of investment is also low. In addition, Myrdal has also pointed out that institutional changes, i.e. land reforms etc. will make a considerable difference to growth and development in Pakistan if these were undertaken. Such changes can be accomplished without borrowing from abroad.

It follows from the above analysis that there are alternative growth theories, to the simplistic neo-classical one that has been adopted by Pakistan, which offer us the possibility of achieving higher rates of economic growth without crippling debt burden and a disproportionate reliance on foreign assistance. But they demand a shift in the economic and political objectives of the country in favour of sweeping institutional changes.

---

7. R. Solow: *Technical Change and Economic Growth in Readings in Macro-Economics.* Edited by Mueller.

On Military Aid

Hamza Alavi & Amir Khusro

We reproduce here, as a supplement to the foregoing article, extract from a well-known article, 'Pakistan: the burden of US aid', written in 1962. The article (highly recommended to anyone interested in finding out the mischief US aid is doing in Pakistan) may be obtained by post from Libro Libre, 21 Theobalds Road, and W.C.I.

MILITARISATION AND SOCIETY

In the long run, the worst aspect of military aid is the complete change it produces in the balance of social and political forces in favor of conservatism and established vested interests. The dragon seed sown by military aid has produced a crop of military officers whose social roots are in the most conservative strata of our society. There is no countervailing force to hold them in check. Once in power they do not allow for easy and peaceful democratic political evolution. In Western societies the trade union movement is an effective countervailing force; the longer tradition of democracy, perhaps, also plays its part. In a country like India, where these two factors are to some extent operative, a military coup d'etat would not be all fair sailing. But in countries like Pakistan, where the trade union movements is relatively weak, the peasant movement non-existent and political evolution rudimentary, the picture is rather more grim. Perhaps there is no factor so inimical to the growth of democracy in underdeveloped countries as the militarisation of our societies.

In propping up dependent regimes in countries like Pakistan the US aims to safeguard American interests—the interests of the big corporations which have investments and business interests in our part of the world. In a Princeton University study of American military assistance, E. S. Furniss writes:

American concern with the internal stability of other countries covers economic, political, and military conditions. Under the heading of economic stability would come orderly development of the national economy, the creation of a climate favorable to American private investment ... As part of its objective of preserving internal order for political purposes, the U.S. finds itself in the military aid business in order to attract and preserve the cooperation of local ruling elites. In some countries, these leaders are found in the army itself; in others they are civilian politicians who control or are controlled by the local military establishment ... This distinctly non-military objective (of military aid programs) ... is more clearly discerned in countries whose political institutions are not wholly Western in type.

Furniss refers to:

the objective of attracting friendly power groups (as motivation for U.S. military aid to some Latin American countries) where the leaders of the national military establishment have been known to play a not inconsiderable role in juggling civilian heads of government until sympathetic civilian agents capable and willing to promulgate the military's policies were found. Latin American military officers have at times been known to despair of civilian leadership altogether and seize the reins of government in their own hands.

This, in a nutshell, is also the story of Pakistan. The military power group was already being strengthened and built up when the following remark appeared in a 'Summary Presentation of the Mutual Security Program' published in June, 1957 by the US Government. The document states:

From a political viewpoint, U.S. military aid has strengthened Pakistan's armed services, the greatest stabilizing force in the country, and has encouraged Pakistan to participate in collective defense agreements.

This is the force that now rules the country; not the 'armed forces' as such, but those who are in control of the armed forces ...

To return to our subject of military aid and US interests, we must note that military aid also brings considerable economic advantage for the US. In the words of former US Secretary of the Treasury Humphrey,

The military aid, and to what extent it may be continued as I see it, is just a matter of how much cheaper can we do it that way than we can do it another way. That is just a matter of figuring it out every time. As long as we can save some money by doing it, I am for it. As long as we can save some boys, I am for it.

As for the money saved, Congressman Jerry Voorhis stated at the House of Representatives Hearings on the Mutual Security Act (1956) that 'last year it cost $5,900 to have an American soldier overseas, without a gun in his hand. This program costs the $744 per each man in service with weapon in his hand, placed where our Joint Chiefs think he ought to be for our mutual security.'

Thus, during the ten years before 1959, the US provided $22 billion in military assistance to its allies who, in turn, spent $141 billion to provide 5 million men under arms and 30,000 aircraft. Thanks to the military pacts and alliances and also to the acceptance of joint training exercises and US military mission by some of the allies, these forces constitute an integral part of American military strategy. The US sees to it that the 'allies' maintain the level of armed forces it considers necessary. Thus, the Mutual Security Act asks the President to terminate aid when, in his judgment, the recipient ceases to 'make, consistent with its political and economic stability, the full contribution permitted by its manpower, resources, facilities, and general economic condition to the development and maintenance of its own defensive strength and the defensive strength of the free world'. Military aid thus succeeds in accomplishing the exact reverse of what some Pakistanis believe it does; it brings about for us an increase rather than a reduction in our military commitments and our military expenditures.

The type of 'hardware' that countries like Pakistan get under military aid is indicated by the statement of Otto E. Passman, Chairman of the US House Appropriations Sub-committee. Mr Passman, who was on tour of inspection in Europe said after visiting Norway, Denmark, and the Netherlands, that the US Defense Department was using the foreign aid program to dump its discarded weapons. He is reported to have made the accusation that the US armed forces had been hiding in the foreign aid program much of the billions of dollars worth of surplus material which they had needlessly and wastefully procured.

Underpinning Corporate Profits

One aspect of US military aid, which may well be the strongest driving force behind it, is the interest of the big corporations which supply the hardware. Not only the aid funds but also the increasing amounts which we in turn are forced to spend on defense equipment, are spent in the US. In Latin America, Dr Edwin Lieuwen (1923–1988) writes, 'The U.S. encourages the exclusive use of U.S. equipment, largely in order to simplify maintenance ... For this reason the U.S. opposes the sale of British as well as Soviet armaments to Latin America.'[1] Dr Lieuwen might have added that this pressure on the aid recipients to 'buy American' is not exerted solely for this reason; much of this pressure comes from US arms manufacturers. If Pakistan is not yet wholly restricted to US suppliers, the pressure is nevertheless in that direction.

How big is the stake? It is not just the amount that is received in aid from the US, in fact, we have steadily increased our defense expenditure ever since we started receiving military aid. Mr Sprague, Assistant Secretary of Defense in the Eisenhower Administration, in his testimony to the Senate Foreign Committee on March 28, 1958, said:

> The proportionate share spent by our allies has been increasing, and for 1957, countries receiving military assistance spent for defense the equivalent of $7 for every dollar of military assistance. This proportionate increase in their own defense efforts is also confirmed in the rising amount of sales of equipment under military assistance programs. For 1956 such sales totalled $79 million. For 1957 such sales increased to $312 million. There is reason to hope that an increasing proportion of military assistance can be shifted to military equipment sales.
>
> It is significant to note that again this year 85 per cent of the amounts spent on the program will be spent in the U.S. In fact we estimate that 92 per cent of the amounts spent on material purchases will be expended on orders from domestic U.S. industry. Thus a very substantial part of the cost is ploughed back into the U.S. economy.

Economically, still more is achieved. The fact is that some military aid is received in the form of surplus agricultural commodities! Against these commodities the Government of Pakistan credits equivalent amounts in rupees in special accounts with the State Bank of Pakistan. Out of these funds rupees are paid to the Pakistan government as aid to finance military expenditure. To the extent that any part of this money is used to purchase 'hardware' from the US (and much of it goes for that purpose), the foreign exchange has to come out of Pakistan's current dollar earning. This kind of military aid, therefore, not only imposes a heavy burden on badly needed semi-skilled manpower and in other ways indicated above,

---

1. *Arms and politics in Latin America* (New York: Frederick A. Praeger, Inc., 1960), p. 205.

but it also imposes a burden on our foreign exchange resources and thus diminishes the amount available to us for economic development.

US officials and others frequently reiterate that economic aid to Pakistan, rightly termed 'defense support,' is, in the words of the Mutual Security Act of 1954, 'designed to sustain and increase (the) military effort'. In view of this, it is not surprising to see that Pakistan's military expenditure, instead of diminishing with military aid, has increased steadily and has become an intolerable burden on our economy. The economic chaos in our country, for which 'politicians' are blamed so glibly, stems largely from this heavy burden. Thus Dr David Bell, Deputy Director of the Pakistan-Iran Advisory Group at Harvard, who has served on the staff of the Pakistan Planning Board, said in his testimony before the Senate Foreign Relations Committee: 'The inescapable conclusion would be that Pakistan, which was already spending too much of her resources on military purposes, was encouraged by the US military aid programs to spend even more for military purposes—obviously, this makes the problem of economic development much harder.' This, if anything, is an understatement; what we have witnessed in the last few years is a steady disintegration of our economy and impoverishment of our people. But well-meant criticism such as Dr Bell's is not enough to change the underlying forces behind US policy.

Reflections on Art

Salima Hashmi

In the sphere of art it is foolish to lay down laws as to the kind of works poets, novelists and painters ought to produce. This is specially true in the visual arts and music which, because they employ referentially 'opaque' media (as opposed to the 'transparent' medium of language which of necessity refers to the outside world), need have no connection with anything outside themselves. Hence the modern emphasis, by painters and critics alike, on form.

But the fact that colours and lines have no referential values doesn't mean that they are completely divorced from the world. After all, colours, etc. are themselves perceived as part of the world and can't exist apart from it. Thus Matisse:

> Those who work in an affected style, deliberately turning their backs on nature, are in error—as an artist must recognise that when he uses his reason his picture is an artifice and that when he paints he must feel that he is copying nature—and even when he consciously departs from nature he must do it with the conviction that it is better to interpret her.

Of course, there is such a thing as 'pure painting', but such painting is obviously limited in scope. Usually the achievements and discoveries of painters who aspire to a purist style become a stepping stone to a richer art in which they acquire a content and so cease to be 'pure'. E.g. the discoveries of Mondrian, Arp, Matisse, etc. paved the way to the richer art of Picasso, and that of the later periods of Matisse and Braque. Thus:

> The Fauves and Cubists (writes an art historian) were intent on achieving the 'pure' work of art, and tried to make it a living language. But at the same time an opposing current wanted the work of art to express the human passions, no longer—as in the past—by illustrating a 'subject', but in a modern manner, through the eloquence of form alone.

One must not forget that form in art, unlike form in nature, must be expressive. Once again, pure, i.e. abstract, art is possible, but even the most geometrical of art expresses some feeling—e.g. delight in balance, intricacy, tension, etc. Where such expressive quality is absent, the form is said to be 'dead' or 'mechanical'.

Finally, the notion of form in art is intelligible only within a tradition. Or, rather, the form of a particular work consists in its particular style, and is a historical phenomenon. Hence it is that one can trace the development of style from say neo-classicism, to Impressionism, to abstract art, and so on. One style is connected with another, be it in the form of a rejection or continuation. It is only because a particular style occupies a particular place in history that it has meaning. It is difficult to conceive of a style occurring outside history—except of course as the original source of a later development, in which case it must appear as 'simple' or 'primitive'. What you cannot have is a complex or sophisticated mode of painting without first having 'simpler' modes to prepare the way for it. This is because genuine art is very much tied to a people's ways of seeing, feeling, in short, their consciousness, which is intimately related to their social milieu. In other words, consciousness, and therefore artistic styles, develop and become more complex as society develops and grows more complex. For this reason, only in special circumstances can the cultures of societies at greatly different stages of development exercise a genuine, fructifying influence upon each other. More usually, any borrowing of ideas, styles, etc. from another society remains a kind of 'curiosity', an unnatural graft upon the culture of the borrowing society. (Is this more true of artistic styles than of ideas?).

But apart from being determined by its own tradition ('art history') and the existing social reality, a style may also be influenced by the geographical, climatic and other physical conditions of the environments in which it originates. In this way it becomes the expression of a very concrete experience of a particular group of human beings, even though it may well contain elements that may be 'universal'. Thus Impressionism, although it rested on new discoveries about appearances that are universally valid, nevertheless couldn't find home in other countries, especially not in the northern countries, because it was so closely related to French and Mediterranean conditions—the abundance of soft, but bright, light (for example) which throws up colours of objects into full relief, and indeed makes them transparent in a way the sombre light never can in the colder countries of the north (hence the dark, sombre tones of many a German painting). (But this 'bondage' with regional, etc. conditions shouldn't be over-emphasised).

It would seem therefore that although a style of painting may be found in more than one country and painters belonging to different cultures may be adept in painting in a manner that doesn't 'belong' to them, there is a fundamental relationship between a particular style of painting and the experience of people among whom it originates.

Now it is precisely such a distinctive style that one finds lacking when one looks at the works of Pakistani painters. One finds there talented abstractionists, gifted cubists, even 'primitives', but searches largely in vain for a painter who may be trying to express our people's basic experiences.

The painters who seem to come closest to doing so are Chughtai and Zainul Abedin. Chughtai's merit lies in that he draws upon our own traditions rather than those of the West. His geometrical forms resemble the abstract forms in Islamic buildings rather than the forms in the paintings of the abstract school of the West; his colours more sensitively evoke the evening half-light colours close to our experience than the gay, reverberating colours of a Mediterranean city; his stylised and yet sweeping, enclosing, sensual line is immediately recognisable as related to both the miniature and the classical Hindu art, and is obviously close to our own culture. Moreover, the languidness and repose, the wistfulness, and the mood of vague longing that permeates the atmosphere in Chughtai's paintings are more definitely a part of our temperament than are the fleeting experiences of an impressionistic painting, or the disintegration, frenzy, violence, etc. of a cubist-expressionist painting.

But if one reflected on what is *lacking* in Chughtai's paintings, or on what one rebels against in them, one could begin to form an idea of what a really Pakistani art—i.e. the art that would reflect our own social and emotional worlds—would be like.

Now, for all its closeness to our experience, Chughtai's art is essentially aristocratic and romantic, and in both ways removed from the normal experiences of an adult Pakistani. Even more than the vague yearnings it evokes, our daily experience is made up of an acute sense of frustration and oppression; even more than the half-tones of evening light, our normal experience, both in the cities and in the country, consists of dazzling, relentless light, of bleached colours, and of stark contrasts between light and shadows. Our experience of space comes mainly from sun-baked planes rather than from cool, dreamy landscapes. And our normal life is lived almost stiflingly surrounded by half-nourished and diseased humanity, or by emaciated cattle, against a background of dirty, narrow streets, government quarters, or mud houses, rather than among elegant objects against a background of marble screens and exquisite canopies. Even Chughtai's men and women bear no resemblance to us.

A distinguished historian of Art noted that an important difference between the western art and the eastern art is that the former is always addressed to an audience. The western audience which is sensitive to art possesses a rich knowledge of art and its history. Can the Pakistani artist who paints in western style assume a similar audience in Pakistan? Since, in fact, there exists no tradition of painting in Pakistan (and therefore no audience) is it not more appropriate for the artist to begin where the ancient Egyptians and the ancient Greeks began—i.e. with a folk art?

Not surprisingly, it is to folk arts and crafts that the younger artists and designers in Pakistan are turning. An institution which has taken small but valuable steps in this direction is the National College of Arts (once the Mayo School) in Lahore, which has persisted in its attempts to create a distinctly Pakistani tradition despite the displeasure of the official art pundits and educational bureaucrats. The College has collected a large number of works of folk art, which may well one day become part of a National Folk Museum. There were plans for compiling an index of folk design, but this idea proved to be too novel for those who hold the purse strings of the College and so it still awaits fruition.

However, some of the young artists and designers the College has produced seem to be imbued with a new outlook. They are no longer satisfied with mere copying the west; instead, they are beginning to show a genuine willingness to create forms out of their own visual experience. In this they have been greatly helped by the rise of the national industry—especially textile industry—with its consequent demand for designs of all kinds. It is in fact in the field of design, where the function of his work becomes of primary importance, that the Pakistani artist is able to resolve his problems to some extent; and it is here that the students of the NCA have been able to make a real contribution to the concept of 'a Pakistani from'. By going back to the roots of folk symbols and forms, and by re-moulding and recreating them in a modern idiom, the young designers have at last forced the textile, advertising and public relations set ups to break away from second-hand Japanese and American stereotypes.

It is, however, necessary to stress that this understanding of our folk heritage is still fairly superficial. For one thing, no real research has gone into it, for reasons that apply to almost every other field in Pakistan; for another, mere revival of folk forms, however ingeniously assimilated to the 'modern idioms' cannot by itself lay the foundation of a genuinely profound art. For example, some of the established artists, like Safdar, Hanif Ramay, have in the past few years tried to experiment with calligraphy forms, the Pakistani landscape, etc. But these explorations have resulted in painting which, though it has an obviously 'Pakistani' line, colour and form, is as far removed from the day-to-day experience of an average Pakistani as were the works of their Cubist or Symlist period.

The truth is that there has been a drought of 'radical' painters in Pakistan. Occasionally of course there do emerge such painters, but they are not allowed to survive. Example, Novera Ahmed—a highly original and radically inclined sculptress whose frustration at the hands of the establishment and society eventually drove out of the country. Some of her pieces are in private hands, since no public body could be persuaded to offer its patronage. Other promising painters, like the talented and sensitive Murtaza Bashir, have either given up painting or have settled back to producing the cubist, Op or Pop images now so popular with the Pakistani new-rich. Similarly, Sadequain, one of the more accomplished young painters, has produced some works which come close to the Pakistani experience, but here too one is beginning to detect the demands of the new philistine class without whose patronage the artist can't survive.

Shakir Ali has, within the last few years, started painting again and has startled his students and friends. Though by no means detaching himself from the sophisticated art forms of the West, he has produced a large volume of work which has been the basis for discussion and departure by younger painters such as Zahoor ul Akhlaq.

But these are isolated examples. On the whole one cannot avoid the conclusion that the Pakistani painters, like other educated people in our country, are completely alienated from their own people and culture. This, however, is not the main criticism of them, since this alienation is the result of a complex historical process. The main criticism is that our painters do not make any attempt to overcome their alienation; indeed, most of them seem to take some kind of pride in it. True, their hands are tied by economic necessity, and by the nature of their society they live in. But they are not the first to find themselves in such a predicament. Throughout history the artist has been victimised and persecuted by his society, but that did not stop him from giving expression to the truth, however unpalatable that truth might have been to the established order. Wherever there has been injustice, the artist has been the first to protest; wherever there has been oppression, the artist has been among the first to raise the banner of revolt. The history of art is also the history of the artist's ceaseless struggle against tyranny, hypocrisy, and vulgarity. More than anything else, it is this moral quality, this human concern, this spirit of challenge expressed in visual form that one finds sadly absent in Pakistani art.

Pakistan Left Review

Spring, 1970 (Farewell Issue)

Contents

A Farewell to Our Readers

Editorial

For various reasons, including financial ones, we have decided to close this review. We would like to thank all those who helped us either by writing for the *Review*, administratively and/or financially. Let us hope the journal served a useful purpose—and judging at least from its increasing sales, it seems to have been appreciated by many Pakistanis both in Europe and those who have been able to read it in Pakistan itself.

We shall be watching the promised forthcoming elections in October 1970 with great interest—in the full knowledge of the ridiculous vetoing power which will be held above the elections, and the fact that it is at least the third time in our history that elections have been *promised*. Recent events in Cambodia tend to show, however, that elections, political parties and meetings will be tolerated by the ruling class only as long as it suits its own ends.

The very real possibility of foreign imperialist intervention in our country, at the instance of a client indigenous regime, will have been brought home even more clearly to Pakistanis.

In a different context the successes of the Palestine Liberation movement, and particularly Al-Fatah, will have taught more of us that ultimately the only way forward is through a socialist alliance between peasants, workers and intellectuals to build up a genuinely revolutionary movement in Pakistan. The closure of our journal by no means implies the end of our activities—these shall continue until Pakistan becomes a socialist state.

Has the Revolution Arrived in Pakistan?

Iqbal Khan

Something extraordinary is happening in Pakistan. Cutting across old and established political traditions, personal rivalries and provincial hatreds there is emerging a mass movement in Pakistan. What is more, it draws its inspiration not from some doubtful ideology, but from concrete demands from social justice. First at Toba Tek Singh, then only a few weeks ago at Mahipur in East Pakistan the cries went up.

گھر گھر ٹوبہ ٹیک ہے   پورب پچھم ایک ہے

شور بو ہارا، شور بو ہارا!   لوڑ بے کارا، لوڑ بے کارا؛

شور بو ہارا، شور بو ہارا!   جیت بے کارا، جیت بے کارا؟

The one was a powerful endorsement—more powerful than any constitution can ever provide—of the essential unity of Pakistan; the other an expression of the determination of the oppressed people of Pakistan to fight and to win.

This mood is not confined to the peasants alone. Throughout the length and breadth of Pakistan people—factory workers, government employees, teachers, students, journalists—are engaged in a momentous fight for the rights they have been denied for years. There must be between one and two of workers currently out on strike in the various cities. Here too the provincial barriers have broken down, and, what is more, the strikers are fully aware that their fight is not just between them and their employers, but between them and a whole system of economic and political robbery that wears the sanctimonious mask of religion, but ultimately rests on brute force and on CIA money and machinations.

Of course, no one need pretend that the movement that is making its appearance in Pakistan will, or can, bring about a socialist revolution in the country. That, despite the talk about guerrilla war and workers' rule, this is a something the leaders of the movement, most of all

Maulana Bhashani, are fully aware of is written large in the very goals the movement has set before itself. These goals are of course confined to the demands picked up and publicised by the Pakistani press. Demands for provincial autonomy on the basis of the Lahore Resolution of 1940, for making the elected Constituent Assembly fully sovereign, and for class representation in the National and Provincial Assemblies are not only highly problematical, they have, as such, nothing to do with socialism. For example, the Lahore Resolution demanded: 'The area in which the Muslims are numerically in a majority as in the North-Western and Eastern zones of India, should be grouped to constitute Independent States, in which the constituent units shall be autonomous and sovereign'. Even if there were some sense in splitting Pakistan into two 'Independent States' of East and West Pakistan, it is very doubtful if the provinces of West Pakistan could, *in the present circumstances*, make any economic or social progress as fully independent and sovereign units. Of course, they could, given the supersession of the present deep antagonisms between one Pakistani people against another by a socialist consciousness and a fully socialist socio-economic organisation. In that event the development of regional resources and the setting up of heavy industry could be carried out by the mutual cooperation of the various provincial governments. In the present circumstances, however, mutual rivalries and short-sighted interests could not but paralyse the country's growth. In any case, the shortages of resources and of skilled manpower require some kind of centralised planning and centralised utilisation of these resources, not a dispersal of them into uneconomic and inefficient smaller units. What is, however, more serious is that by advocating a return to the Lahore Resolution, the NAP is simply playing into the hands of the very enemies of the people against whom it is launching its attack—for it is obvious that it is the jagirdars and zamindars, the tribal chiefs, and the bourgeoisie in the provinces who would be the direct beneficiaries of provincial autonomy!

Similarly, the sovereignty of a parliament which in any case is going to be dominated by the capitalist and feudal classes can hardly be of any value to the people. The most puzzling of all, however, is the demand for class representation in the Assemblies. If the demand is for representation according to the strength of the various classes, then apart from the very real difficulty or demarcation of one class from another—do skilled labourers belong to the same class as the unskilled labourers? To which 'class' belong the dependents in every family, whose number is far greater than that of those who work? Do the landless peasants constitute a class of their own, or do they share the class of the propertyless workers in the towns?, etc.—apart from all these difficulties, it is the height of naivety to suppose that a demand of this kind can either be accepted by the ruling classes (for it would mean voluntary renunciation of power) or can amount to very much in an illiterate society where people have been conditioned by centuries of suppression and exploitation. At the very best it could attain a semblance of democracy; but that in any case is being 'granted' through universal franchise! It's hard to imagine anyone going to launch a 'guerrilla war', stake the lives of thousands of people, and indeed risk the nascent social consciousness among the masses for such objectives as these!

No doubt these objectives were taken by the Press out of context of the whole 18-point list of demands put forward by the NAP, but the other demands reflect as great vacuity of vision as those already mentioned. Take, for instance, those that are more pronouncedly socialistic in character: the distribution of government land among the poor and the landless peasants; exemption from revenue of peasant holdings of less than 5 ½ acres in East Pakistan or 12 ½ acres in West Pakistan; greater facilities for work; and the abolition of private ownership. Is it to attain these goals that a 'guerrilla war' or 'mass action' (the inability to draw a clear distinction between these alone betrays an utter lack of realism and maturity) is going to be launched on the 1st of June? In a country where the population is growing at the rate of 3 per cent yearly and is already nearing 130 million, what far reaching or permanent benefits can be secured by redistributing a limited amount of government land? Or, again, in a country where the main problem is not merely to see that *social justice* is done but to lay the foundations of a scientifically progressive society, where, indeed, real social justice cannot be achieved without modernising the society, and in the first place agriculture, what fundamental social problems can be solved by securing tax exemptions for a limited number of peasant properties? As for the demand for the abolition of private ownership, it is admittedly a social demand, and if met can bring about tremendous changes in society. But one may be excused for suspecting that demand is being used by our Pakistani 'Naxalites' of NAP more as a slogan than as a meaningful demand for the transformation of our society. For try as you may you will never find in the many speeches, statements, or interviews of our leftist politicians any deep or consistent analysis of our conditions, or even the slightest attempt to elaborate what exactly the 'abolition of private property' means in the specific circumstances obtaining in our country. Hardly ever has there been a revolution, at any rate a socialist revolution, whose leaders have been so indifferent to questions of this kind and who have so completely substituted emotion and rhetoric for knowledge and reason.

But the NAP's demand for the abolition of property, their decision to launch 'mass action' if this demand is not met and *at the same time their assurance that this action would not be aimed to unseat any officer or government* raises an even more fundamental problem—raises indeed a doubt as to whether the NAP leaders are serious at all. Considering that the property relations are the backbone of the entire power structure in our, as it is in any, society, does it make sense to talk of destroying those relations but not aiming to 'unseat any office or government'? Are the NAP leaders under the illusion that our President and generals, administrators and the guardians of 'law and order', in short, our ruling classes will remain untouched while NAP's guerrillas accomplish their social revolution? How could a seasoned and serious party like NAP become a prey to such childish illusions? How, above all, can one explain what led a sincere and shrewd leader Maulana Bhashani to support so vacuous a programme by an ultimate weapon of guerrilla war?

For an explanation we must look not so much at the forces and factions at work within the Party as at the peculiar conditions in which it has to operate today: at the dialectic of its present situation. The contradictions which the National Awami Party's posture reflect are the direct result of this historical reality. Conceived as a party of dissent, as a people's party, it allowed itself to remain virtually dormant for ten long years. It dug no deep and extensive roots among the masses; it gave no proof to them that it was capable of realising for them a better order of existence. In short, if opted out of history. Then, history surprised it in the shape of the last winter's revolt. What the Party ought to have brought about through deliberate actions and conscious leadership was accomplished by history through its own inherent logic. Instead of directing the events, the NAP, like other parties, found itself being directed by the events.

On the other hand, once awoken, it was faced with the task of leading the masses—the masses whose revolt against Ayub was based palpably on social and democratic issues. Here once again NAP's opportunity. Could the emerging social consciousness of the people be deepened at the moment and their energies directed on correct lines, it would have been possible to turn the revolt against Ayub into a socialist revolution. But the NAP—the only party that could be expected to do this—had no instruments which could bring about such a transformation. Had NAP spent the years of its political inactivity in its own political-tactical-ideological education, it would have now given the much-needed theoretical lead to the mass upsurge. Had it utilised those years in underground organisational and propagandist activity, it would have now given the people practical leadership. Above all, had the NAP used the dark decade to form a body of dedicated, theoretically and practically sound revolutionaries, it would have provided a new set of *leaders* of the mass movement, whose failure to emerge was one of the main reasons why the movement was eventually frustrated. Had the NAP at its disposal these, or at least some of these, means to direct and transform the Revolt instead of the gheraos last winter we would have had complete occupation of the means of production; instead of forcing the industrialists to meet the workers' demands for wages, we would have seen industrialist owners replaced by workers' councils; instead of the rumoured beginnings of a Naxalbari type of movement in the countryside, we would have witnessed the end of feudalism and the establishment of the Soviets in the countryside ...

But the truth is that the National Awami Party was formed as a political not as a revolutionary party. Its organisations, its technique, its mode of thinking is therefore geared to the task of fighting elections, of working in the context of a parliamentary democracy. At the same time it is genuinely concerned about the welfare of the people and is convinced that only socialism can solve their problems. Hence the split-consciousness which the NAP manifests. On the one hand it finds it necessary to behave as the other political parties do—by adopting their political techniques (e.g. speeches, mass meetings, instead of patient organisational work); by adopting their language (e.g. Islam, provincial autonomy, etc.); by adopting their strategy (e.g. alliances with other parties), etc. On the other hand, as a socialist party, it knows that the capitalist and the jagirdar can never be made to share their wealth with the workers and the peasants through peaceful means, so it finds it necessary to adopt a revolutionary posture.

What the National Awami Party hasn't realised is that the path of revolutionary party does not run parallel to the path of the conventional political party, however *popular* the latter might be. The revolutionary party never forgets that its task is complete overthrow of the existing order, i.e. not only the abolition of one class by another, but the abolition of a whole lot of institutions and organisations, customs and ideologies that hinder the development of society. The revolutionary party is also quite aware that the accomplishment of such a task depends on its capacity to seize political power and *lead the masses*. How it can seize political power depends of course on the circumstances existing in a particular country; but in repressive regimes it precedes the leading of the masses, in bourgeois 'democracies' of one sort or another it is the latter that must precede the former. Now in Pakistan at the moment it is quite unclear what shape the government is going to take in a few months' time and for this reason alone the talk about a guerrilla war or revolution would appear to be premature. *For in a 'democratic' situation, through which our country is passing, the loyalty of the masses is divided among a large number of claimants to leadership, the issues to not appear to them as being fundamentally related to their own class interests, and consequently a revolutionary initiative on the part of one party alienates one section of the masses from another, instead of forging solidarity among them.* The revolutionary action is thus either paralysed, or destroyed by the enemy. Reflecting on the lessons of the Cuban experiences, Regis Debray writes:

> Thus, in order for the small motor i.e. the guerrilla army really to set the big motor of the masses into motion, without which its activity will remain limited, it must first be recognised by the masses as their only interpreter and guide, under penalty of dividing and weakening the people's strength.
> (Revolution in the Revolution? p. 108)

If it is important for the revolutionary army fighting against a colonial regime or a dictatorship to first win the people's unambiguous loyalty before embarking upon a revolutionary war, how much more important must it be for the revolutionary party in a democratic situation! Before it resorts to the Naxalite type of insurrection, the revolutionary party must carry out an intensive campaign of political organisation and education. It is precisely in this context that lies the value of peasant rallies and conferences. But this work of propaganda cannot be confined to any particular form or level: it needs to be carried out in a variety of forms on a variety of levels—among students, intellectuals, workers, non-workers, peasants, and women.

'In a variety of forms' does not mean any doctrine will do so long as the word 'socialism' is attached to it. This is precisely where the revolutionary party must begin—by laying down a clear and comprehensive definition of what it understands by socialism, i.e. by educating itself. Of two things there seems to be no doubt—one, that there is no such thing as 'Islamic Socialism'; and two, that socialism, if it is to mean anything must be 'concretised' by reference to Pakistan. Why there can be no such thing as 'Islamic Socialism' is not difficult to see. Socialism in its scientific form is

Marxism; and Marxism rests on the belief that man can change his 'fate' because this fate is not something preordained by a supernatural being, but is the result of historical forces which man can bring under his own control and turn to his own advantage. For this reason socialism relies on knowledge and revolutionary action for improving man's situation, whereas religion relies on prayer and submission to God's will. Even more fundamentally, the religious conception of 'truth' is something eternal, laid down once and for all, while for socialism 'truth' is never absolute, but something that changes and develops. Hence, far from being related to each other, religion and socialism are diametrically opposed to each other, as dogma is to science. As for the moral concern which socialism shares with Islam, that no more provides a basis for 'Islamic Socialism' than does the common moral concern of Christianity or Buddhism and Islam provide a basis for 'Islamic Christianity' or 'Islamic Buddhism'.

But, it might be argued, does the "'concretisation' of socialism by reference to Pakistan' not mean that we modify our stand in accordance with the very deeply rooted religious feelings and prejudices in our country—especially if we are ourselves clear that we are doing this only for *tactical* reasons? But surely, the pitiful conditions of the masses, their poverty, their inhuman exploitation is just as palpably real, as 'deeply rooted', as their religious sentiments? If a revolutionary movement cannot be built on these realities, there is something wrong with that movement. The truth is that, 'Islamic Socialism' is the programme of those who are less interested in socialism and more in their immediate electoral success: it's the creed of the opportunist not that of the revolutionary.

And yet, let no one imagine that because Islam as a religion is opposed to socialism, therefore socialists in Pakistan should have nothing to do with it. For Islam has been, and still is, an important *cultural* force, especially in our country. It is this cultural heritage of Islam that Pakistani Socialism must try to assimilate. But a pre-condition of this assimilation is a detailed and critical understanding of Islam's nature and achievements. Only in the process of such a reassessment, and as a result of it, can we evolve a rich *Pakistani-socialist culture*.

And now, what is meant by 'concretising socialism by reference to Pakistan'? Simply this, that it is not enough to learn about the theory of socialism. The revolutionary movement in Pakistan must be based on an understanding of Pakistan's particular social, economic and cultural problems, and on the solution of these problems in the light of the experience of other socialist countries. Since we are obviously not so lucky as to possess revolutionary intellectuals of the stature of Lenin or

Mao, a Pakistani revolutionary party will do well to establish a centre for such studies, whose function it should be to publish and popularise its findings among the masses. Only through such means can we lay a scientific basis for revolutionary action and raise the consciousness of the people.

But only *theoretical* consciousness; not that *active* social consciousness which comes about only through struggle, through political involvement. It is precisely as a pre-condition of this that the existence of a revolutionary vanguard is essential. For only such a vanguard can, almost by definition, unify the discontent of the oppressed sections of society—which otherwise tends to be expressed in an incoherent form: workers' strikes, student revolts, etc.—and turn it into revolution. Whether or not the time is ripe for a revolution in Pakistan, it is undoubtedly ripe for the emergence of a revolutionary party. Such a party may either emerge from among the more committed socialists in the various leftist parties and trade unions, or it may—though it is unlikely at this stage—result through a radicalisation of one of those parties.

But is it not exactly what the 'Naxalites' of the NAP are? Have they not radicalised Bhashani's party in exactly the way I am suggesting? Unfortunately, not. The 'Naxalites', as is apparent from the name given to them, rely on spontaneous uprising of the masses to carry out the revolution. But it is quite clear that spontaneous uprisings can never achieve this, since they must either degenerate through lack of organisation or direction, into indiscriminate destruction and anarchy; or, if they are able to transcend their own spontaneity and become vaguely conscious of their destiny, they must call for a leadership that could clarify their aims and guide them. 'The greater the spontaneous upsurge of the masses and the more widespread the movement,' says Lenin, 'the more rapid, incomparably so, the demand for greater consciousness in the theoretical, political and organizational work ...'

Secondly, instead of boycotting the forthcoming elections (as the 'Naxalites' wish to do) a revolutionary movement will seize the opportunity either to come to power itself, or, since it might find it cannot yet hope to win the election, to help get other leftist parties elected, *so that those parties could exercise effective checks and controls over the repressive tendencies of reactionary, rightist regimes.* For genuine revolutionaries are nothing if not realists. They know that in order to carry out their work successfully some freedom must be allowed in the country. It is therefore in their interest if the parties sympathetic to their cause hold a strong position in the National Assemblies. But of course the 'Naxalites' do not see the necessity of this, since they do not see the necessity of 'carrying out their work', which of course becomes superfluous if one relies, as they do, on the spontaneous upsurge of masses.

It is clear, then, that the 'Naxalites' are not the party of the socialist revolution in Pakistan, which is merely another way to saying that there is a need for one.

Leftist Debate in West Pakistan

Feroz Ahmed

In the absence of a legal Marxist party in Pakistan or a journal providing a medium of expression for Marxists in Pakistan, it is very difficult to ascertain the views of Pakistani Marxists on the issues facing the people Pakistan and at this critical juncture in the country's history. Yet, for those Socialists who are living abroad and are trying to make their modest contribution to the people's struggle against neo-colonialism and capitalism, a knowledge of currents of Marxist opinion in Pakistan is both useful and essential.

This writer had the good fortune of recently receiving a few publications of the Marxist left in West Pakistan, intended primarily for restricted circulation among the membership. What appears below is an elementary analysis of the leftist debate on the nature of the present struggle and the events of the recent past that shook the ruling classes of Pakistan, based on these publications[1] and personal communications with leftist elements working in the different political parties in West Pakistan.

Leftists in the Legal Parties

Subsequent to the banning of the Communist Party of Pakistan in 1954 Marxists had to take the recourse of either going underground or of working in a number of 'legal' parties, such as Ganatantri Dal, Azad Pakistan Party, and the Awami League. Since its formation in 1957 till the schism that developed in the National Awami Party shortly before the downfall of Ayub regime, the unified NAP had been the main political party of participation for Pakistani leftists. So much so that many rank

---

1. 'The Revolutionary Upsurge and Its Lessons,' a document of the leftists aligned with NAP (Wali Khan), April 25th, 1969; 'Maujuda Surat-e-Hal Aur Rahe Amal,' a document of the C.R. Aslam faction of NAP, June 1968; 'Martial Law Aur Hamare Faraez,' a document of C.R. Aslam group, April 1969; Quoted by Ferozuddin Mansoor in 'Maulana Maududi ke Tasawarat', Karachi: Maktabe Shams, 1969.

and file socialists and sympathisers came to regard NAP as the 'Marxist' or 'Communist' party of Pakistan.

The fact that the NAP was not a Marxist party but a hotchpotch of regionalists, nationalists, and socialists was appreciated by many a class-conscious Marxist working in the ranks of the NAP. Such individuals regarded the NAP as a representative of the 'national bourgeoisie' and, therefore, an essential ally in the anti-imperialist struggle. From the sketchy information available, it can be inferred that solidarity was lacking among the leftist elements, and dissentions and discords were quite common. These differences, however, tended to be more personal than ideological. The challenge to the unqualified leftist support for NAP did not become serious for some time.

While, on the one hand there was a growing disaffection with the NAP among the more ideologically oriented leftists, a group of leftists, who had moved up into the higher echelons of the NAP's hierarchy, came to be identified more closely with the NAP's programme as advocated from the public platform. In a way an establishment and an anti-establishment of the left was developed. The Sino-Soviet friction, the Chinese support of Pakistan during the 1965 war with India, and the Soviet efforts to dilute Chinese influence in Pakistan with the help of established channels, further widened the gulf, and finally proved to be divisive for both the leftists as well as their 'national bourgeois' allies in the NAP.

Whether the centrifugal tendencies among the leftists in the NAP were primarily responsible for the splintering of the NAP or the fragmentation of the NAP provided accommodation for the feuding leftists is difficult to ascertain. But the division of the NAP into the various factions and the emergence of Bhutto's Peoples Party gave a wider choice to those Marxists wanting to participate in the 'legal' parties. At the present moment, there are at least three major political parties or factions into which leftist elements of West Pakistan are divided. These leftist groups and the parties they are aligned with are as follows:

Group A	Pakistan Peoples Party: especially in Sind, Karachi, and Lahore areas.
Group B	NAP (Wali Khan-Usmani group)—confined to N.W.F.P and Karachi.
Group C	NAP (C.R. Aslam group)—primarily in Lahore area with some adherents in Karachi.

Documents representing the viewpoints of the various Marxist factions in East Pakistan and of the leftists working with Peoples Party in West Pakistan are not available for analysis. But the fact is that on the major national and international issues the leftists belonging to Bhashani NAP in East Pakistan and to PPP and Aslam NAP in West Pakistan have minor differences. The availability of the documents of at least one of these groups, in addition to that of Group B, enables us to have a general idea about the two antagonistic positions on the various issues. As will be seen later, the views of Group C are not always in consonance with those of Group A and the East Pakistani leftists in Bhashani NAP. We could have conveniently categorised the two major viewpoints as pro-Peking and pro-Moscow or militant and moderate or revolutionary and revisionist etc. But since such a classification would be arbitrary and unrealistic, we will avoid such a usage. However, while treating the differences among Pakistani leftists as more or less dichotomous, we must make this observation that this is being done because of the lack of sufficient literature rather than due to a conviction that the differences among the non-Wali Khan NAP leftists are not significant.

Nature of Contradiction and the Line of Action for the Leftists

According to both Group B and Group C, the principal contradiction of the present moment in Pakistan is that between the imperialists (especially US), and their stooges (monopoly capitalists, feudalists, and bureaucrats) on the one hand and workers, peasants, petty bourgeoisie, and national bourgeoisie on the other hand (1:10, 2:1). Both groups are of the opinion that the accomplishment of 'National Democracy' and not Socialism should be the immediate objective of the progressive movement in Pakistan (1:10, 2:3). However, there are significant differences between the two groups insofar as the assessment of the relative importance of the various classes, identification of the enemy, question of alliances, and the attitudes towards the other leftists are concerned. Some of the salient aspects on which the various leftist groups differ will be discussed in the text that follows.

Feudalism

According to the theorists of Group B, feudalism (referred to both as zamindari and jagirdari) is historically outdated, and 'in our country as a whole, only remnants of feudalism are found'.[2] Jamaat-i-Islami, according

---

2. 'The Revolutionary Upsurge and its Lessons' (NAP-Wali Khan Publication), April 25th, 1969, p. 4.

to this Group, 'represents the feudal ideology in as pristine a form as possible in the conditions of to-day'. Since, feudalism is not a strong factor in the interplay of political forces in the country, its representative body presents no special threat to the people's struggle in Pakistan. Leftist elements who are engaged in controversy with the Jamaat are, therefore, 'cranks' and 'fools' who are trying to substitute feudalism for monopoly and bureaucratic capitalism as the main ally of imperialism. In the same breath however the document of Group B calls Jamaat as the 'most faithful ally of imperialism'.[3]

The document of Group C, entitled 'The Present Situation and the Line of Action', contains a detailed discussion of the class contradictions in Pakistani society and analyses the position of landlords in the power structure of the country. The paper points out that during the early years of Pakistan, landlords were the most powerful force in the ruling arrangement and, therefore, held sway in politics. Due to the reasons of history and the prevailing situation in the subcontinent, it was not possible for the feudalists to go back to a political system that ideally associated with feudalism, i.e. monarchy. Parliamentary democracy, which was the form chosen by India and which is logically a political institution of industrial capitalism, was ironically accepted by the landlords of Pakistan. Since the capitalist class was negligible in strength and the lack of political consciousness in the peasantry could allow the landlord to manipulate their numbers, parliamentary democracy was not found unsatisfactory by this class. Right from the inception of Pakistan till the military coup d'état of 1958, landlords were the senior partners in the ruling alliance with the capitalists and the bureaucrats. During the martial law of 1958 and Ayub's land reforms, according to Group C did not destroy the landlords as a political force. The rising bourgeoisie, which had an inherent contradiction with this class, did in fact get better off economically by closer collaboration with the imperialists and did succeed in pushing the landlords in a secondary position in the power structure. The triumvirate of political power remained the same, only the positions were changed. The Basic Democracy system was one of the devices to curtail the political power of landlords by creating a patronage system in the countryside which had to be loyal to the bourgeoisie and the bureaucrats for its own survival.

Also, during the Ayub era, a new class of landlords emerged that is, pensioned officers who were allotted land in the interior of West

---

3. Ibid.

Pakistan and were provided with American farm machinery, chemical fertilisers, better seeds, and agricultural loans. These so-called pioneers of the 'Green Revolution' were an element who owned their prosperity to the collaboration with imperialism, and were, therefore, ever grateful to their masters.

According to the analysis of Group C, a large number of old landlords did not accept their secondary position and were waiting for an opportunity to raise their heads. Adult franchise and parliamentary democracy were familiar tools with which they had enslaved the masses before, and these were not only essential for the restoration of their hegemony but constituted appealing slogans to mobilise public support behind themselves. This class manifested itself in the form of the PDM ('Pakistan Democratic Movement')[4] and Jamaat-i-Islami was the better organised component of it. According to the theoreticians of Group C, collaboration with the PDM would amount to helping the ascendency to power of the landlords and hence undesirable. The same document also predicted in June 1968 that elements of the PDM will 'compromise with the Ayub Government because that is their class character and historic fate'. This prognosis was upheld by the subsequent events.

The PDM will be discussed later but a few remarks concerning the character of Jamaat-i-Islami will be made here.

As one could judge from the above, both Group B and C of Pakistani leftists consider Jamaat-i-Islami as the core of feudal political structure, but according to Group B, Jamaat is a political force of no importance. However, in Group C's view, if the landlords lose the battle for political ascendency, then Jamaat may degenerate as a political force in time.

Since, theocracy and clericalism were historically associated with a feudal order, and in the classical Marxist sense a parochial party would be a natural component of the feudal system, there is a temptation on the part of many leftists to identify parties such as Jamaat with feudalism. Such a tendency is reinforced by the Jamaat's record on the question of zamindari and jagirdari. Maulana Maududi once remarked, 'People who declare Jagirdari as illegitimate and insist on its abolition are going beyond the limits of Islamic law.'[5]

Jamaat's opposition to interest and a number of other tools and institutions of modern capitalism, including change in inheritance laws

---

4. This has now, of course, become 'Pakistan Democratic Party'.
5. See Ferozuddin Mansoor's 'Maulana Mundidi Ke Tasawarat' (Karachi: Maktabe Shams, 1969)—original source of the quote is *Tasneem*.

and fertility control, lend support to the idea that Jamaat is basically a feudal political party.

However, not every historical phenomenon and development is amenable to classical Marxist analysis. Although the essential feudal character of Jamaat is undeniable, there are anomalies that must be taken into account.

1. The relationship of Jamaat-i-Islami to the feudal system is not identical to the theocratic structure of European feudalism, where the rise of bourgeoisie and the separation of church and the state resulted in the withering away of church as a political force.

2. Jamaat, with all its yearnings for the restoration of the Kingdom of God return to the 'golden rule' of Islamic era, remains basically an urban party and does not have any appeal in the countryside, with or without the help of landlords. Whereas the landlords chose to stick with the Unionist Party, Muslim League, and the Republican Party, the petty bourgeois trader class in Punjab and Karachi has formed the backbone of Jamaat.

What appears to be a more consistent feature of parties like Jamaat-i-Islami is their parasitic nature. The mullahs in general, either live on the doles of the wealthy men or suck the blood of the poor. Their parasitic existence could only be tolerated in a class society. If a capitalist, rather than a feudal society, is the order of the day, mullahs will have little problem in adjusting themselves to the new system.

Also, under the present international circumstances, Jamaat and its sister organisations elsewhere are close allies with imperialism and receive large sums of money from US imperialists. Even after the demise of feudalism, it is most unlikely that such parties will become defunct. The natural course open to them would be to drop off their feudal trimmings and align themselves with the comprador class. There is nothing in Jamaat that makes it intrinsically inseparable from feudalism. The recent directive of Maududi to 'pull out the tongues of those who speak of socialism' may well be an indication of Jamaat's efforts to win the support of the big capitalists.

The importance of Jamaat as a reactionary force cannot be belittled. This organisation has now come down to a position of physical violence, and has made itself available as stormtroopers of imperialism and the local bourgeoisie. Whatever be the fate of feudalism, Jamaat will continue to operate in the *urban* areas at the instigation of imperialism and its *capitalist* agents to poison the minds of the *proletariat* in the name of religion, divert them from class struggle, and if need be to perform open sabotage.

Allies in the Present Struggle

All the groups of Pakistani leftists recognise that the objective conditions in Pakistan are not ripe for a full-scale class struggle, and subjectively, the level of class consciousness in workers and peasants and the degree of revolutionary organisation are not adequate for a direct class confrontation. All recognise the need for a broad-based front, and single out national bourgeoisie and petty bourgeoisie as the potential allies at this stage of the struggle. However, on the practical level they all seem to have different ideas about who is an ally and who is an enemy.

Leftists of Group A consider Pakistan Peoples Party [PPP] as a genuine representative of the national bourgeoisie, having a strong anti-imperialist plank. Group C also sees PPP as a national bourgeois phenomenon but points out the opportunistic character of this class and does not advocate an alliance with the PPP. Group B views the so-called Pakistan Democratic Movement (now Party) consisting of Jamaat-i-Islami, Nizam-i-Islam, and the old guard Muslim League as the logical allies in the present struggle (as has been pointed out earlier, Group C regards PDM as essentially a resurgence of the old feudal lords) and consequently entered their alliance to form the Democratic Action Committee (DAC). Group B heralded its own entry into the alliance by asserting 'minus N.A.P., there was the lifeless P.D.M.; with N.A.P. was born the historic D.A.C'.[6]

The Wali Khan group of the NAP and the leftists elements in it participated actively in the DAC and were the only 'left leaning' faction to be present at the round table conferences called by Ayub Khan. This group's closeness with the PDM was accompanied by its strong aversion to the groups claiming to be leftist. Thus, in their document, Bhutto, Bhashani, and C. R. Aslam are characterised as 'national chauvinists'. The document goes further in calling Maulana Bhashani a 'bearded crook' and 'father Gapon' (who allegedly led Russian workers to massacre during the Revolution), and Bhutto as an 'imperialist agent' and the 'bureaucracy projected left leader' etc.

---

6. Revolution Upsurge, p. 5.

Group B's enthusiasm for PDM and antipathy towards Bhutto, Bhashani and their leftist accomplices could be traced to the following *apparent* reasons:

1. Analysis of the situation: According to the theoreticians of this group, 'the only issue that had crystalised in the minds of the people' during the events of late 1968 and early 1969 was the struggle against the tyrannical autocratic regime. Therefore, the eight-point 'anti-autocratic programme' which made no reference to One Unit and the economic demands of the people was sufficient. And for the attainment of the limited goal, the alliance should have been as broad as possible and should not have excluded even Jamaat-i-Islami.

2. Analysis of the character of the PDM: Group B does not view people like Daultana, Chowdhury Mohammad Ali, Nawabzada Nasrullah etc. as representatives of feudalism, and does not, therefore, consider their movement as the resurgence of feudal political power. In other words, according to the logic of Group B, there could be a true democratic movement without underlying vested economic interests. This group looks at Jamaat as a feudal party but since feudalism is dying anyway, why bother with Jamaat.

Both these premises could be contested very seriously. First of all, in the class analysis of a society—with its economic infrastructure and political superstructure—there is no such thing as autocracy. It is foolhardy to suppose that Ayub's was a one-man rule and that it did not represent class interests. It is also highly irresponsible to assert that the people themselves were not prepared to put forth their economic demands. It is difficult to imagine that the working classes of Pakistan (who knew that the doors of even the most participatory bourgeois democracy will be closed on them) would consider the abolition of 'autocracy' as their primary aim rather than the fulfilment of their economic demands—and this, too, after experiencing a decade of severe exploitation and worsening economic conditions!

But there seem to be at least two other plausible reasons why Group B virulently attacks other leftist elements.

1. Character of Wali Khan NAP: The West Pakistan NAP, even in the heydays of NAP's unity, never appeared like a progressive party. Hassan Nasir and G. M. Syed were indeed strange bedfellows. The recent splits in NAP were not only based on provincial lines but also on class and ideological lines. It is not surprising to see the champions of regional nationalism such as G. M. Syed who belongs to the most reactionary type of Sindhi landlords, and Wali Khan and Abdul Majeed Sindhi cannot identify themselves with the working classes and have no concern about imperialism that is threatening the people of Pakistan. The spectre of 'Punjabi Imperialism' is haunting their minds and they do not think beyond their provinces. While regionalism of East Pakistan has a petty bourgeois accent, that in the NWFP, Baluchistan, and Sindh is tribal or feudal. The 'Jeeye Sindh' (May Sindh Live) Movement of G. M. Syed and Co. is essentially an attempt to distract the attention of the masses from the class issues and get them involved in the emotional regional appeal, and use them in the power struggle to re-establish hegemony of the *Waderas* in Sindh. Excesses done to Sindhi culture and literature during the One Unit period have provided fertile ground for the *Waderas* to exploit the frustrations of the intelligentsia. Deteriorating conditions of Haris, likewise, have been attributed to Punjabi domination rather the feudalism.

Similarly, Wali Khan, whose entire appeal is based on Pakhtoon nationalism, and Achakzai, who would like to carve out a Pushto-speaking entity from Baluchistan are willing to go to Kabul for support.

It is clear that the leadership of Wali Khan NAP by itself can hardly provide a progressive platform for the Party. The leftists aligned with this party have either no influence on its policies or have degenerated to such an extent that they feel most irritated when class issues are raised. This still seems true of Wali Khan NAP.

2. Soviet Influence: Prior to its banning in 1954, the Communist Party of Pakistan took its orders from Moscow and the Communist Party of India. And since India was the occupying power in Kashmir and the USSR supported such occupation, the Pakistani Communists consider it their 'proletarian international' duty to oppose the right of self-determination for Kashmiri people. The 'leftists' of Wali Khan NAP are descendants of the adventurist Communists of the early days and they continue to be tied to the apron strings of Moscow and have a soft corner for India.

The Soviet Union according to this writer has found it opportunate to use this group in the attainment of its goal in the region and in its conflict with China. The subservience to Moscow goes to the extent that this group has come out in favour of the Soviet-proposed and American-backed idea of regional security pact against China. Such an alliance, to say the least, is not in the interest of any class in Pakistan, except possibly the segment of the comprador class that is most intimately linked with US imperialism.

Imperialism

All the groups of Pakistani leftists acknowledge the overwhelming presence of imperialism—especially US imperialism—in the country and consider it their first task to drive it out. However, their assessment of the form, motivation, tactics and allies of imperialism varies greatly. According to the analysis of Group C, imperialism makes its presence felt neither by direct political domination nor in the form of large capital investment in industry, but in the form of loans. The imperialists must safeguard their investments, and the elements most appropriate to play this watchdog role are the classes which have benefitted the most from these loans, i.e. the monopoly capitalists, feudal lords and the bureaucracy. The feudal lords who have a vested interest in the maintenance of neo-colonial economy are best represented by the opposition parties of Ayub era, principally PDM.

There is no systematic analysis of imperialism in the document of Group B discussed in this article. However, it does admit that there were 'well entrenched' imperialist agents in DAC and that Air Marshal Asghar Khan was a new addition to it. It is at least gratifying to note that Group B could recognise the true colour of Asghar Khan who was most enthusiastically welcomed in the columns of *New York Times* and the *Christian Science Monitor* if not in the streets of Pakistani cities.

Group B leftists also include the Military in the pro-imperialist alliance, 'this army having intimate connections with the imperialists, especially due to CENTO and SEATO and bi-lateral pacts, is a willing tool in their hands and in those of internal reactionaries'. This assessment is true of at least the top brass of armed forces but, as has been pointed out by Group C that many petty officers and soldiers do not subscribe to the political role of the military and cannot remain unaffected by the anti-imperialist movement in the country.

While we have no clues to Group B's assessment of the motives of imperialism, we find the analysis of Group C less than satisfactory. Imperialism exerts itself in a given region not necessarily for the *direct* economic exploitation of that region. In the global confrontation of imperialism and anti-imperialist forces, the US imperialism wants to weaken the forces of anti-imperialism wherever it can by military, economic and political means. The country in question may not afford any significant economic advantage to the imperialist. Thus, we see the most brutal war of the modern imperialism being waged in Vietnam, not for the direct economic exploitation of Vietnam but for the global defeat of the national liberation movements. The US interest in Pakistan may not lie as much in its concern for its loans as for the strategic importance of Pakistan in imperialism's present confrontation with China and a possible future collision with Soviet Union (at present, though, there is only a collusion between the two super powers).

Events of October 1968–March 1969

There is a lot of bitter exchange among the rival leftist groups with regards to who should be credited with the leadership of the upsurge, what the slogans should have been, who prepared the ground for martial law, and what would have happened if blunders were not made.

All the leftist groups agree that the peasantry was unorganised, especially in West Pakistan, organisations of the proletariat were weak and ideologically disoriented, and the trade unions were controlled by the government or management agents. In short, the level of political consciousness of the working classes was very low prior to the beginning of mass upsurge. There was also no political party of the working classes or the revolutionary left—a fact admitted by Group C but not by Group B.

The upsurge was initially spontaneous and petty bourgeois in character, but joined at later stages of the working classes. It was a broad national democratic movement the direction of the evolution of which was towards People's Democracy. Slogans of socialism in this context, according to Group B and C, were premature and divisive. (Note here the difference between the followers of Bhashani and Bhutto and Group C.)

As has been stated earlier, in general all the leftist groups agree that the present phase of struggle should be anti-imperialist, anti-monopolist, and anti-feudal. But when it came to the specifics of the real situation, Group A leftists thought it necessary to raise socialist slogans and to accelerate class struggle, while Group B consider 'anti-autocracy' to be the sole role of the 'class conscious' elements in the upsurge. Group C does not mention the specific role a revolutionary leftist should have played during the upsurge, but contends that unless the working classes have been organised into a political party of their own, the proletariat cannot lead the anti-imperialist struggle.

We shall attempt to evaluate all the charges and counter charges of the rival factors of Group B against the leftist workers with Bhashani and

Bhutto that they were responsible for creating the 'anarchic' conditions and paving the way for military coup needs to be verified. This charge corroborates the then government's apparent reason for proclaiming martial law, and supports the Right wing position with regards to the responsibility for the coup.

So far as the extent of 'anarchic' conditions is concerned, reports of Pakistani as sell as foreign newspapers agree that there were only a few pockets in the country where violence and looting had taken place (and most of it for justifiable reasons). And, if the statement of the then Governor of East Pakistan, Mr Huda,[7] and the accounts of British and American newspapers—which were not sympathetic to our working classes—are to be believed, violence had indeed ebbed before the proclamation of martial law. There is also evidence that the government has deliberately provoked and abandoned all the measures to restore and maintain order. It is, therefore, clear that the 'anarchic' condition was only a false pretext for the coup.

Violence or not violence, slogans of socialism or no slogans at all, the declaration of martial law was prompted by the disturbed homeostasis of the propertied classes. There is no basis to Group B's allegations against Bhashani, Bhutto, and their leftist allies. If these gentlemen had behaved like nice little boys, it is not certain that martial law would not have been re-imposed. Their inaction might have resulted in a peaceful situation in which Ayub, Mujib, and PDM could have divided the pie among themselves rather than allowing Ayub to have it all, but the working people would have hardly had a chance to assert their strength. It is either a height of optimism or extreme naivete to believe that the upsurge in Pakistan would have resulted in the defeat of imperialism had X behaved in one way or the Y had gone the other way. Neither is it prudent to assume that it would have brought about a significant shift in the class composition of the ruling elite. It was clear to those who were raising the slogans of socialism that socialism could not be brought about by the six-month-long upsurge. There is no document of such leftists available for the present analysis but it seems unlikely that anyone seriously envisioned socialism as the outcome of the agitation. However, this situation was an unprecedented one so far as the mass participation is concerned and it was the most opportune time to raise the short-term

---

7. Mirza Nurul Huda (1919–1991) was appointed Governor of East Pakistan on 23 March 1969 when Abdul Monem Khan was removed under the pressure of the Mass Upsurge, 1969. But he was governor just for a day and had to resign when Yahya Khan promulgated martial law in Pakistan.

economic demands of the workers and educate them with regard to the necessity of socialism.   ✳

To this author what seems to be the greatest lesson of the upsurge is that without an organisation of the working classes, without the unity of revolutionary leftists, and without a serious attempt to understand the dynamics of the class structure of Pakistani society, the energies of the masses will continue to be exploited by the propertied classes and the opportunistic petty-bourgeois leadership (especially in East Pakistan), and the leftist will remain in their position of sweeping the floors for G. M. Syed and Z. H. Lari.

It is neither the purpose of this article nor is it possible from the present fragmentary analysis to take sides in the leftist debate in Pakistan. But one thing that seems very obvious from the documents and the public utterances of Group B, is that this group, tied to G. M. Syed, Usmani, Wali Khan and the like, is playing the most reckless game any leftist could play.

Two Important Weeklies from Pakistan

Lail-o-Nahar (Urdu)	*Forum* (English)
Published from Karachi	Published from Dacca
Available from:	Available from:
Iqbal Company Ltd.	41 Hatkhola Road
Chalamar House	Dacca 2, East Pakistan
Hessel Street	
London, E.1	

Two Poems

Faiz Ahmed Faiz and Mao Tse-Tung

THE HARVEST OF HOPES
Faiz Ahmed Faiz

Cut them all down,
Those crippled plants —
Bring water to ease their last distress!
Tear off from the spray
Those twisted blooms —
Don't leave them to hand in wretchedness!

This harvest of smiling hopes, my friend,
Is doomed to be blighted once again:
Those labours that fill your days and nights
Are doomed to be this time too in vain.

But once more feed with your blood dry clods
In crannies and corners about the field,
Moisten them with your tears afresh;
Then think of coming season's yield —

Yes, think of the coming season's yield
When ruins will once more strike these lands!
… One day a ripe harvest shall be reaped;
Till that day dawns, we mush plough these sands.

REPLY TO COMRADE KUO MO-JO
Mao Tse-Tung

On this tiny globe
A few flies dash themselves against the wall,
Humming without cease,
Sometimes shrilling,
Sometimes moaning.
Ants on the locust tree assume a great nation swagger
And mayflies lightly plot to topple the giant tree.
The west wind scatters leaves over Changan,
And the arrows are flying, twanging.

So many deeds cry out to be done,
And always urgently;
The world rolls on,
Time presses.
Ten thousand years are too long,
Seize the day, seize the hour!
The Four seas are rising, clouds and water raging,
The Five continents are rocking, wind and thunder roaring;
Away with all pests!
Our force is irresistible.

The Life and Thoughts of Bhashani

Interviewed by Tariq Ali

This is the first part of an extract from an interview Tariq Ali had with Maulana Bhashani last year. We are grateful to him for his permission to print this extremely interesting—and historically valuable—document in the PLR.

Bhashani: ... But there's such an urge in the people that you'll find full scope for doing work among them. The smallest shopkeeper, labourers, peasants ... all will work with you—95% of them. But if you say one thing when you meet the capitalist, another when you make contact with the jagirdar, another ... who will trust you? If you want to do some work you must do it with one class, one organisation. Which is that class?—The one that is the most oppressed. If a jagirdar comes, or a capitalist comes, we'll say to him, these are our demands. If you accept them we are with you. But on one hand you[1] accept socialism, then you talk of the 1956 Constitution, is there any room for socialism? This is a blatant contradiction. Who made the 1956 Constitution? Chowdhury Mohammad Ali, Daultana; all the big landlords. Not a single problem of the poor has been solved in it. Neither is there anything in it about the labourers, nor about the peasants, nor about the *mazarai*. Not a word. Leave aside socialism—which would mean the end of private ownership. We asked for 12½ acres here, 5 acres there—as a first step. If even on this there's no support, can they help you bring about socialism? Now we are against imperialism, and that Constitution favours imperialism. SEATO, CENTO, these pacts, the whole Pak-American friendship are in this Constitution. How can we accept it? While that Constitution was under discussion, the Pak-American pact came about; first, informally in the [foreign] ministry—on a verbal level. But in the days of Chowdhury Mohammad Ali and Shaheed it was confirmed. How can we accept it?

---

1. Maulana is here referring to the liberal minded leaders and people, generally.

Tariq Ali: True. But until we organise among the peasants and labourers in West Pakistan we'll hardly get anywhere.

Bhashani: That's right. But this struggle that has been going on continuously for the past four months, this is without any organisation. The suffering had become so acute, and feelings against the capitalists and the landlords have become so great that however you call them they will come. And if we go after the capitalists or the jagirdars, why should the labourers join us? They must have some faith in those who want to organise them—whether they [the organisers] are the friends of the capitalists or of the people, of the oppressor or the oppressed. Until there is this trust, this confidence, that whatever people do there's in it no deceit—until then there can't be any organisation. Take the students. Although a large number of them come from rich families, still there is some consciousness among them. Make use of it; join a party—say, Bhutto's party—seize it. Bhutto is one man; the party is not his [personal property].

Tariq Ali: But the money is his.

Bhashani: Money, maybe. But seize the party somehow. Bhutto can't dare go back on his word—he has signed for socialism. Wherever you go make known the Bhashani-Bhutto pact. Nor can Bhashani deny it. The formula for socialism is known the world over, you can't chop and change it. It is that socialism is incompatible with private ownership. No socialism without nationalisation. So by getting him to sign the pact we've secured at least one thing …

Tariq Ali: But, Maulana, after signing Bhutto issued a statement saying that the kind of socialism he wants is the British type. There's no socialism *there*.

Bhashani: Doesn't matter what he says in an interview. You must ask: the joint statement which you signed with the Maulana, for which socialism did you sign? He ought first to have made up his mind, compared his socialism with the socialism of the Maulana, and then signed it. The majority of the people will be for our type of socialism; his socialism won't be supported by anyone except Daultana and Gurmani. He hasn't a way out; his political life will be finished if he says he only wants the British type of socialism, because he will then have to say he doesn't want the Bhashani type ... If he really is of that view, he should work with those who sympathise with them; why is he with us?

Tariq Ali: Many of his statements indicate the he wants only one thing—the presidentship of Pakistan.

Bhashani: But there must be the support of the people to gain the presidentship. Not a single person in East Pakistan will vote for him. How is he going to become the president? In West Pakistan he's not alone: there are five people who are contesting for it. Here, in East Pakistan, in spite of all this lack of unity and rivalry (among the leaders), if one stands for an office, no other Bengali will stand against him. Not so in West Pakistan. But becoming a president won't solve any problems. It's the system that needs changing. What will he do if 2 lakh people gheraoed his president house?

Tariq Ali: Isn't it possible to unite the NAP in West Pakistan?

Bhashani: After all this is the class character. Whether it's socialism or communism, it's the leadership that lets it down. These people don't represent the common man. They have a very narrow idea of politics. There's no world view.

Tariq Ali: They have destroyed the movement in interminable quarrels and recriminations ...

Bhashani: Our movement will go on getting stronger. Because the problems aren't going to get solved; they will go on increasing. The more the people go naked, the more they are deprived of medical care ... the more our movement will spread. The conditions are in our favour; for bribery will go on increasing, and black-marketing. Until these disappear, our agitation is not going to stop. Now if this military government continues, oppression will continue. It will be to commit suicide if I start fighting it. I'll be killed at once; or will be given 14 years. Still, I believe things will progress. The international position is very tricky. They can't suppress us entirely. We'll move forward, with that organisation—You see, I'm only one person: I've to be everywhere and do everything. Still they can't suppress our movement, neither America, nor Russia, nor India ...

Tariq Ali: When you visited China, Maulana, what did Mao say to you?

Bhashani: He said: The relationship China has with Pakistan at this time is very weak, America, Russia and India, they will all try to break it up. You are our friend. If you will fight against this government, it'll give those people an excuse—i.e. to America and India. Better do your work more quietly. We don't want to create any differences among you—this is not our policy. But let us make a little more headway. Let our relations with your government get a little stronger; not easily broken.

Now that has come about. For one thing, the border treaty has been made. On the more important part of the border an agreement has been reached with China. Then, the plane route has been established and people can visit each other's country easily and see both sides. The third is the one relating to the route via Gilgit; the business by means of the mule, camel, etc. has been opened. The fourth is armament. Forty-eight per cent of the arms in Pakistan is Chinese. Their spare parts have to be sent for from China … So, they (Pakistan government) can't back out of it (i.e. relationship with China). The fifth is that the Chinese market these days isn't less than that of America, Russia or India. The goods of everyday use we import, Chinese goods form a very important part of them, although the government has caused a great increase in their prices by means of bonus vouchers—Had there been no bonus voucher, the prices of Chinese goods were so low that they would have captured the whole market. The bonus voucher has caused a tax of Rs. 125 on every article worth Rs. 100! … Moreover, at the present time, China is the biggest buyer of jute. So, the relationship is not so weak that Pakistan can back out at the first sign from America or Russia. But what should China do: Yahya Sahib courts her friendship more than we do! The long-range rifles India has got, Pakistan didn't have them. Now China has given us. Not many—but some. So it'll develop gradually. We have also got 100 tanks from Russia … and also money from the Consortium. Now if the struggle begin, whatever they have given they can't take back. The point is, if Pakistan goes too far with China, all the imperialist powers will break off their relations. Then there's another reason. Then there's another reason: the people in power are a little frightened, too, that if India attacks, the little power we've gained, the military government we have put in power, this will have to go to the front. Who will then look after the government? So, they want China's help—with her help they want to capture India. By themselves they can't even defend their own country, but with the help of China want to extend their territory, capture Kashmir. This is the carrot they are after!

Tariq Ali: Talking about Kashmir …

Bhashani: The Kashmiris, themselves, are trying to do what they can. They're trying. Some went to Vietnam for training. Had they gone 20 years ago they would have done a lot. However, when they realised there's no help from anywhere, they started a small clandestine organisation—only recently. China helps them. About 25 or 30 people went to China too for training … This thing has to be done. If the Naxalite make a little more headway in India. But the thing needed most is public sympathy. In India anti-China propaganda goes on all the time. Despite this propaganda there are more pro-China people in India than there were before. Perhaps they might increase on account of the Naxalites—so far it's a new movement. All those in this movement are pro-China. No one supports them—just as no one supports Al-Fatah, neither America nor Russia …

Tariq Ali: But the Naxalites' organisation isn't yet so good.

Bhashani: It only started three or four years ago. How much can they do—three or four years? The thing they did—the most important thing—was to organise a party. It was started by thirteen people who were expelled from the Communist Party. How much can thirteen people do in such a vast country? Now they've set up a committee on an All-India basis. They can't really do very much more on the basis of Marxism-Leninism—especially against CP, which is the official party. Then there's Jyoti Basu's Marxist party—which too is a pro-China party. It's quite an achievement to organise a party against both of these, and not only on a provincial basis but on an All-India basis. When will the guerrilla war start—that depends on China. The more she supplies, the more … but China won't supply arms until the training is over. She probably gives some money and a few small weapons. She won't let better type of weapons be wasted at this stage, unless the movement becomes strong. Naxalite hero, Al-Fatah there, both have contacts with China. The Chinese people will help as much as they can. So far people (here) help the Al-Fatah because they are Muslims. But when they'll see that a Vietnam type war has begun all the capitalist countries will wash their hands of them. But if these three become strong [i.e. China, Al-Fatah and Vietnam] the whole [present power structure] in Asia will collapse. No government can remain unaffected. But unfortunately it's not merely the imperialist they (Al-Fatah) have to guard themselves against—they have to protect themselves from Nasser, from Jordan, nationalist governments—all. Now they are fighting against America and Israel, tomorrow they'll be fighting against Nasser and other nationalist governments. That's why Pravda announced with such emphasis that we want an amicable settlement … No progressive will support this view. Are they (the Russians) supporting the oppressors or the oppressed? Israel hasn't yet received application (in UN?), though she might get through Russia. If that happens whom will Russia be supporting—the capitalists? Russia's programme is very bad.

Tariq Ali: There's a need for the Revolution there too, Maulana!

Bhashani: Yes, their policy is wrong; it's the same as that of America …

Bhashani: … That's what Bhutto says, too (i.e. he is a socialist); and Mujib. But socialism doesn't come about by saying. Ho Chi Minh says as well as does. There's a world of difference between Bhutto's saying and Ho Chi Minh's saying …

Tariq Ali: Is Mujib's chief support in the towns in East Pakistan, Maulana?

Bhashani: Neither in the towns nor in the villages. Whoever gets the money he's the base, who doesn't get isn't. People get passports, licenses, etc. through Mujib. Those who don't get some personal gain don't join him. He was a good organiser—Mujib.

Tariq Ali: How long did he work for you?

Bhashani: Eight years. But his outlook changed completely. Became so arrogant. Now he thinks he's the only leader in Pakistan. The person who gives up an ideology and runs after leadership, what good can he do? There's nothing in leadership—make ideology your leader.

Tariq Ali: Quite. But was Mujib a socialist at any time?

Bhashani: No. He was a progressive, certainly. But he yearns to become the prime minister or the president. That's the only goal he has.

Tariq Ali: Did you meet Nehru many times?

Bhashani: Yes, many. He was very fond of me. There was a deep relationship between us—what an industrious man he was!—But Kashmir destroyed him. If the Kashmir issue hadn't arisen and had the people around him not been bureaucrats and capitalists, Nehru would have occupied a very high place—Very hard-working man—and a pundit, too. The whole history of the world ...

Tariq Ali: And Abul Kalem Azad, Maulana?

Bhashani: He was a political leader. There was hardly another political mind like him in Asia. But Maulana changed his view during his life. He wasn't so keen on socialism. Leaders have to follow the progress of consciousness among the people. When I was in the Muslim League, I became aware that Hindus were the capitalists and Muslims were the labourers; they were educated, Muslims were illiterate. Only now have Muslims got some education ...

Tariq Ali: Now they are capitalists, too.

Bhashani: Yes, times change. If you had come to Bengal 15 years ago, you wouldn't have found anyone except peasants. No professor, no *darogha*, no magistrate, nothing—all ploughed the land. Whatever may or may not have improved in Pakistan, at least educated people have increased in the nation. Capitalists have also increased. But not workers, so much. If at the same time the number of workers had increased, consciousness would have grown ...

In 1903 I joined a terrorist movement—here in Bengal. Our aim was to kill a few government officers. At that time our enemy wasn't the capitalist, but the British officer. We thought of financing ourselves by robbing. But in those days there wasn't any public support. Had the public supported us we'd have been successful: People say why do you indulge in terrorism, why do you create trouble. If you won't put your demands in a constitutional way we won't support you.

Tariq Ali: Do peasants say that too?

Bhashani: Yes. But they don't mind if they are asked to seize land of big landlords and jagirdars. There's gain for them in that. The Naxalite have no other aim except this—to seize the land by force ...

The American *Times* called me the 'Prophet of Violence'! The other day another reporter came; ate here. A TV reporter came. Altogether seventy-eight reporters came. Everyone asked, Maulana, why do you indulge in such things? Why do you burn the houses? If you went on burning the landlords' and jagirdars' houses, kept murdering them, there'll be none left in a month's time! Why don't you carry out your work constitutionally—set up an organisation—issue a manifesto—start your work on Marxist lines—make use of the voting procedure. But this is terrible that you commit murder and arson.

So, I said, this is what an Islamic revolution is like! If I followed your advice, socialism won't come about even in the next fifty years! Who's going to wait that long. The Muslim likes to do what pays immediately. Fifty years is too long a time. I want to establish socialism within a year! Now, tell me, how can this be done except by burning the houses? You saw, didn't you? When the mill owners were under gherao, they at once yielded—'Halea, don't kill us, we'll give you whatever you want!' At a single stroke wages were increased by Rs. 25, 32, even 55. Had we gone about it according to the procedure—deputations, memoranda, Labour Act, appeals to Labour Commissioner, and all that crap—even in 50 years we wouldn't have secured as much! So, you see, this is what the Islamic Revolution would be like. In 13 years we conquered the whole world, now nobody gives us even a subscription. Not even 4 annas. We haven't got even a single newspaper. Can't even afford to pay the rent of our house. There's no whole-timer in our party; no typewriter, no cyclostyling machine, no clerk, no peon. I am the president, the peon, the clerk, everything. One has to do it. If we rob these capitalists of 10 lakhs, 50 lakhs, we won't have any lack of funds. What was the *Mal-e-Ghaneemat* (booty), if not this? When they saw that they didn't have any money, they put 10 per cent tax on all the booty obtained from the Kuffars and the Jews. Ninety per cent was divided among the mujahids, in order to induce them to fight again.

Tariq Ali: Even Lenin, when he organised the Bolshevik Party, he had to raid the banks.

Bhashani: This is necessary. Otherwise, how can you do your work. No one will give you even 2 annas. Take this Students League. In the days of the gherao they obtained Rs. 50 lakhs from Chittagong, Narayanganj, etc. Rs. 50 Lakhs! They used to go to every house. People used to say, 'For God's sake, protect me.' 'Give us 1 lakh rupees,' they would say. 'Yes, we'll give you 1 lakh, but protect us!' Saigol, Bawany, Adamjee, all these big capitalists, some gave Rs. 2 lakhs, some 3 lakhs, ... Rs. 50,000, Rs. 90,000, and so on.

Tariq Ali: The Jamaat-i-Islami made much propaganda against you and the NAP in America, London, Beirut, that you have got money from China, and that Maulana lives in a palatial house ... Yes, they wrote this!

Bhashani: As they say, if you speak a lie a hundred times, it'll come true! But how long will the Jamaat last on lies. They keep on propagating lies in the 'Ittehad'. For example that Maulana is going to buy a house for Rs. 3 lakh from the Shamso estate. What lies! The estate was acquired by the government. I had acquired a small portion, some few years earlier, on which I wanted to establish a college—there's a boarding house there. Even thirty or forty years ago I had planned that if I lived I would build a college to commemorate the memory of Maulana Mohammed Ali, who was a sincere and selfless leader. Eleven years ago I set up that college. It's now a degree college ...

Festival of the Oppressed

Ahmed Bashir

Sandal Bar was once a desert where the Jangli tribes of the Punjab lived a near wild life. Even when the British were in full control of the province, these tribes never accepted their rule and used to raid the rest houses, tehsils and police stations, and kidnap British officials. The British worked out a plan to populate these parts by creating zamindars, jagirdars, etc., as the only way to suppress the Janglis. There was, however, no water. So, within ten years of their rule the British built a canal and divided up the Neeli Bar area, where Sahiwal is situated now, among Sikh army officers, jagirdars and chiefs. These landlords suppressed the Janglis and secured the authority of the British.

Seeing that the experiment worked, the English turned to Lyalpur, Jhang and Shorekot and planned new canals. The Sikhs of the East Punjab came to know of the free distribution of the land, so they organised bands of followers and began roaming these parts in the West. Whichever piece of land any of these Sikhs desired, it was given to, provided that he proved his loyalty to the English and possessed a band of followers. Gradually, the whole area was given out. The Janglis, who were the original owners of the land, however, didn't receive even an inch.

After some time when they became reconciled to their fate, the Janglis willy-nilly offered themselves as farm labourers or for some other menial work. And they hold this position to this day. They were, however, not only destroyed economically: against them was mounted a powerful campaign which branded them as vagabonds, robbers and murderers. Despite all this, and despite their powerlessness, they never really reconciled themselves to the social system created by the British, whose backbone were the big landlords. They protested against the injustice they had to suffer by attacking those landlords and by carrying off their cattle, whenever they could. They became so expert at this that they could transport goods and cattle over several miles within a single night. This tradition is still alive among them, though nowadays local landlords keep the Janglis in order to use them against rival landlords or political leaders, or to ruin independent small farmers.

Toba Tek Singh is situated near Jhang and Lyallpur. The land here is very fertile. On one side of Toba Tek Singh are small landowners, on the other big landlords of Jhang and Lyallpur. The people who live here are strong and healthy, and comparatively well off. Seventy per cent of its population has had schooling up to primary level. And the political consciousness among the people here is such that it is the only district in the whole of Punjab where Ayub Khan won his election against Miss Fatima Jinnah by only two votes. The capitalist press in Lahore regards Toba Tek Singh as a thorn in its side and when it has occasion to refer to it, it never mentions it by name, but as the 'Leningrad'.

This area too was a desert; and since it was relatively far, it attracted settlers rather late. After the powerful Sikh band-leaders, land was also given here to the loyal Muslims of Sialkot and Hoshiarpur. Then the rush of the smaller loyalists started. The British didn't much trust the Muslims of West Punjab; nor was there any need to depend on them, since the above-mentioned experiment had proved successful.

Near the place where there is now the Toba Tek Singh Station, there used to be a pond (*toba*), where the travellers used to being their cattle to drink. But for their own use there was no water. Before the area became fully populated, a saintly old man by the name of Tek Singh built a cottage near the pond and devoted his life to supplying drinking water to the Sikh and Muslim travellers. Every morning he would fetch the water, for which he had to walk miles, and sit down with his jars waiting for any travellers that might come that way. Sometime afterwards, a baker established his business nearby, followed by a *banyia*; and so, gradually, people began to settle around the spot, and had land allotted to them.

Tek Singh saw many vagabonds and robbers establish themselves as landlords, but he spent his own life providing water for strangers, and one day, a long time after the wilderness had turned into a settlement, he died quietly in his cottage. No one knows where his body was burnt or where his ashes were buried. No one even knows whence he came, who his relations were, or whether he belonged to any tribe.

Politically, Toba Tek Singh has figured in many a context. Bhagat Singh belonged to these parts; it was in this area, too, that the Kisan Movement before Partition was based; Sohan Singh Josh was inhabitant of this town; and Manto wrote a story entitled 'Toba Tek Singh' in which the name was used as a symbol of life and revolt against tyranny. No one knows Tek Singh, but the *toba* is still there on whose edge he had built his cottage. The people of the town have now erected a fence around it.

The people of the Toba are very independent by nature. Wheat, sugar-cane and cotton grows here in abundance, but Ayub Khan was very angry with this district and never allowed any textile or sugar mill to be built here. So, the high-quality cane goes to waste; it is either utilised to make *gur* domestically, or used as fodder for the cattle. The cotton has to be sent to far off places to be sold, with the result that the transportation cost claims much of the profit. But the farmer here is hardworking, and the land is rich; so that the revenue from one tehsil here amounts to the revenue of the whole of the Rawalpindi division. The robust and bold temperament of the Punjabi people is largely to be found among the small farmers: there is abundant proof of it in Toba Tek Singh. There's little doubt that if the land were distributed justly in the Punjab, it will lead to a great flowering of human material.

The Conference

We were disappointed to see the numbers in Lyallpur. This is an industrial city, so we were expecting at least twenty to twenty-five thousand people. But there were hardly more than three thousand. The reason for this was given to us later: the train which was supposed to arrive at 1:30 p.m. came at 3:30 p.m. That morning there had also appeared the news in the papers that the government had banned the carrying of sticks or other weapons in Toba Tek Singh under Section 144. Taking advantage of this, the PDP and Jamaat-i-Islami workers spread the rumour that Section 144 has been imposed on Toba Tek Singh so that a meeting of more than five persons can't be held there; consequently, people were told, there would be no conference and the train had been cancelled. So, a lot of people, when they saw no sign of the train, left. The mill owner also played a trick: the Zeenat and Crescent Mills imposed double overtimes to prevent the workers from leaving. But despite this a number of workers' groups had gone to the Toba early that morning.

Sheikhupura, Sangla Hill, Gojra, wherever the train stopped, Maulana Bhashani made a short speech. Everywhere the workers of the Peoples Party were well organised and shouted, 'Bhutto, Bhashani Bhai Bhai'. It was here that we realised fully that the Peoples Party was very well organised and wanted a union with Bhashani's NAP. The Punjabi people are not yet aware of the subtle differences in the policies of these parties. To them, both seem to be travelling the same socialist road, both are against capitalism … so they deeply desire a united action by the two parties.

When the slogan of 'Bhutto, Bhashani Bhai Bhai' is raised, all respond to it with one voice. Truth is, this is merely an expression of the people's rage against capitalism and jagirdari; they express this rage whenever they find an opportunity for doing so. They are not afraid of socialism; in their religion there is room for it. To the watchdogs of capitalism this manifestation of the people's inner longing cannot give anything save alarm and anxiety.

There were many attempts to make the meetings at Toba Tek unsuccessful. In this region people are extremely fond of kabaddi. With the help of the local education authority no less than twenty-two tournaments were announced to take place that day with nearby villages. Chiniot, Lalian and at other places it was announced with great relish that the conference would be cancelled on account of the tournament. In the Toba area itself one Major Gama, whom Ayub had made a landowner, went round in his jeep in the various surrounding villages to 'inform' people that the conference had been cancelled. With him were also some maulvis armed with the fatwahs. And yet the groups of singing, dancing peasants wouldn't stop. Contingents after contingents converged upon the town, and every time they passed through a village they were accompanied by even larger numbers of men, women and children, who would rush out of their houses, out of their shops, out of their villages, to fathom the cause of this unusual madness.

Bhashani's Reception

The train arrived at Toba Tek Singh at 6:15 p.m. The fervour and affection with which the Maulana was received can't be described in words without sounding incredible. Outside the station was a multitude of people wearing red caps which, from the window of the train, looked like a surging sea of red flowers. The leaders of the contingent raised slogans, but no one cared; for everyone, carried away by his enthusiasm, was shouting slogans of his own. Their throats were sore with continuous yelling; their tongues, parched and tired, hung out; their eyes bulged with eagerness and emotional strain. Then there was the constant noise of the drums from innumerable points in that sea of people, where the peasants danced and sang. They all wanted to have a glimpse of their aged leader, who had come from so far to talk to them of their problems, their sorrows, and above all to guide them …

In Allah Rakha's garden there was a vast city of tents. It was announced that people should choose their tents. We were doubtful if there would be enough for all. But on entering the garden we found hundreds of new tents; there were also large tents for large groups. Restaurants and shops were decorated as if for a fair. There was abundance of food, at very low prices ...

Small contingents had been arriving one after another since the morning. Bahawalpur, Rahim Yar Khan, Bahawal Nagar ... there would hardly be a village in Punjab from where at least one or two young men hadn't come. Then the Hari Committee from Sindh; students from Baluchistan; numerous students societies from Punjab and NWFP; political parties; Khaksars; writers; poets ... impossible to count them all! It looked as if the whole of West Pakistan had flooded into Toba Tek Singh. It was about 3 o'clock in the morning that we went to sleep; until then the village groups were arriving in a continuous stream. Each party was accompanied by a drum and arrived in a burst of singing and dancing. The whole town was awake that night. The roads were crowded with people. The doors of the houses were open: anyone who wanted to spend the night in a house was welcome. Food was continuously being made; beds were laid; *hookas* were ready. There was no question of introduction. No need to express your gratitude. Every citizen was eager to participate in the event and to make sure no one left with a bad impression of the city. Despite the enormous crowds there was no fight—and what is most astonishing, nobody used a swear word even in the Punjabi songs that are normally packed with them!

Socialist Morality

There were women's contingents from some cities. At night, the girls went about the town by themselves, yet no one even as much as cast an objectionable glance at them. If they happened to pass through a crowd, they were given way; the drums stopped. Ours is not the age of socialist morality, but that of capitalist shamelessness. But at Toba Tek Singh we had a glimpse of that morality!

Many villagers could get red caps—it was almost impossible to provide so many. In any case it's not customary in the Punjab to wear caps. So innumerable people wore red *pugries*. Many of them had come on horseback, holding red banners ...

The Conference Begins

The conference began at 10 a.m. and finished at 5 p.m., though there were still many speakers who hadn't spoken. The stage design was very unusual. We in West Pakistan have no tradition for public meetings: only a table and a chair and, probably, a sofa, are laid on the stage for the leaders; the people sit respectfully in front and listen to their words of wisdom. In Bengal there is a long tradition connected with public meetings. The stage here was designed on those lines, and could accommodate some 500 people. Only *daris* were laid on the stage and everyone, great or small, sat squarely on the floor—among them was also Maulana Bhashani. There were flags all round. In front were laid tables for the reporters; behind them were the peasants.

The Condition of the Peasants

Chowdhury Fateh Mohammad is a well-known peasant worker in this area. He has a firm grasp of the agricultural problems of West Pakistan. He presented an analysis in which he pointed out that Pakistan's villages earn 78 per cent of the total foreign exchange and 56 per cent of the national income; but the zamindars who constitute 1¼ per cent of the population own 49 per cent of the total cultivable land in Pakistan. Mechanisation in agriculture has added to the numbers of farm labourers and landless peasants, which has even further limited the distribution of agricultural wealth. The big landlords live a life of luxury in the cities: they visit the villages twice a year during the harvest season to collect the wealth and then return to cities and to their irresponsible living. The condition of the peasant has been deteriorating every year and has come to such a pass that he can't even be sure of two meals a day.

He demanded that the government should abolish revenue on land up to 12 ½ acres, and assess the revenue on the lines of income tax; save the weavers by abolishing tax on village industries, like the handloom. He pointed out that the poor villager has to pay many 'taxes' as bribes, and in the end they are left with hardly anything for their children.

Chowdhury Fateh Mohammad demanded that trade with foreign countries should be nationalised, so that the mill owners and the importers do not get the opportunity of stealing the foreign exchange and depositing their money in foreign lands with the collaboration of the foreign companies. He also demanded that landless peasants should be given land and that the elections be held on the basis of classes.

While he was speaking, Maulana Bhashani came in and was greeted by slogans, flinging of caps into the air and cheers from the audience. The Maulana acknowledged the greetings, looked around, and said: these capitalists and monopolists have got into such a panic that they are throwing millions of rupees into the political struggle; they get mullahs to brand other Muslims as *kafirs*; divert attention from real problems by talking of the ideology of Pakistan and of Islam. They want to destroy this country. We shall expose them. The governments of the past twenty-three years have cheated us. They know no other way of developing the country's resources than borrowing loans from America. People, arise! Fight on the economic, social and cultural fronts! Help the revolutionary workers! Organise every village ...

After this, which wasn't his proper speech, the Maulana sat down, and was followed by Faiz Ahmed Faiz, who was leading the contingent of the writers and articles. Faiz read extracts from a poem, which had an electrifying effect on the conference.

The Presidential Address

Rao Mehroz Akhtar was presiding the session. He told the audience how the peasant movement had developed and said that the student and the worker's movement was also linked to the peasant movement. Begum Mian Iftikhar Uddin usually doesn't attend political meetings, but hadn't been able to resist this conference. She told the audience that the decision to usurp *Pakistan Times*, *Imroz*, and *Lail-o-Nahar* was imposed on the government of our country by America at a meeting in Tehran. She was followed by Masih-ur-Rehman of East Pakistan (he was arrested soon after the conference), who said that the demand for regional autonomy is heard on all sides these days. What will the people gain by it, he asked? The people of both wings are mutual brothers, because both are deprived of their rights. 'For your sweat, we shall give our blood!' The kind of assembly that is being proposed will not be able to formulate a constitution. 'I had not expected,' he said, 'that the Punjabi peasant was so alive ...' Then Haji Danish spoke: he told of the plight of the peasants in East Pakistan, where the children of the peasants are denied even that which is given to dogs in the homes of the rich people.

The Plight of the Haris

Then West Pakistan's Abid Hassan Manto, Kaneez Fatima, Bashir Bakhtiar and other delegates addressed the conference. They all unanimously demanded class representation in the coming elections. But Din Mohammad of the Sindh Hari Committee made an impassioned speech. Brothers, he said, the inhumanity you have spoken of is nothing in comparison with what one has to suffer in Sindh. In the heyday of Muslim League one had to obtain the government's permission even to buy a piece of cloth for a shroud. A poor man went to the District Magistrate [DM] with an application for a shroud. The application was returned to him with the remark that he should try another day because the DM was going out for dinner! Din Mohammad related many incidents to show how the people were being robbed by the CSP officers on the one hand and the pirs, fakirs and the moulvis, on the other ...

Maulana Bhashani addressed the afternoon session. He spoke of the Pakistan Movement. Pakistan, he said, wasn't made by either Ayub Khan or his officers; it was made by the people, made for themselves, and made in the name of God. It is therefore the people who are the real owners of the country. The capitalists say that I want to burn the mills and factories. That is a lie. If I'll burn the mills and factories, how am I going to establish socialism? We have to establish Islamic Socialism here; indeed, we have to spread Islamic Socialism everywhere in the world. Islam or Pakistan can never be in danger from socialism ... The peasants are suffering in both East Pakistan and West Pakistan. I swear that there are some peasants in East Pakistan who often do not see even a grain of rice for months. The labourers are not able to earn even as much as 4 annas a day. And now India is building the Farakka Barrage which will turn Sattargaon into a desert. The country is falling into ruin; the masses are frightened and confused ...

* * * *

The conference ended with a message from Mr Bhutto. It is quite obvious that as far as the people are concerned they treat the two parties as one. They cooperate with each other in organising meetings, processions, etc. ... The Kissan Conference was a historic event in the life of the Pakistani peasants as well as in the movement for social justice that is gathering force. Its success was in no small way due to the mutual cooperation of the workers of the two parties concerned.

Book Review: *Islam and Capitalism* by Maxime Rodinson

M. S. Sfia

Man is the object of the historical situation, but may also be its subject, according to his concept of it—that is according to his view of the fundamental and thus paramount importance of the eternal inquiry into the roles played by being and consciousness, the objective and the subjective, the actual structures and the ideas, respectively, in the future of mankind. The inquiry is perhaps as ancient as man's self-reflection, but was defined with a fresh sharpness at the time of the French Revolution by those regarded as ideologists (Concordet, Destutt de Tracy, etc.). However, it would be necessary to return to Marxism in order to pose this question in its modern form, a form greatly indebted to Hegel and which has remained essentially unsurpassed. More recently Sarte referred, in his 'Critique de la raison dialectique', to the importance and reality of this question, and to the fundamentally Marxist terms in which it continues to arise and assert itself.

This points to the interest of any research directed towards an elucidation of the problem, and in particular to the work by Rodinson.[1] According to the conclusions drawn from one case study, this work is indeed attempting to supply some rudiments of a reply to the above-mentioned general inquiry. What principal characteristics has the economic and social history of the Muslim world assumed, and what sort of role has Islam played there? What will lead us to the final answer to this first problem in place of ideology in general and religion in particular during the global development of societies? Such is the problem with which we faced.

Maxime Rodinson is a French orientalist, well-known for his works which combine a historian's erudition with a sociologist's broad scope; (c.f. in particular his 'Mohamad', published in 1961 by the 'Club du Livre Progressiste', in Paris—a work of capital importance; a new edition is being prepared by 'Editions du Seril'). Rodinson is a sociologist who

1. Maxime Rodinson, 'Islam et Capitalism', Paris, Editions du Serial, 1966, p. 304.

rejects the hyper-factualism from which, it is claimed, a certain objectivist positivism may be drawn, and holds the unshakeable conviction that, on the one hand, the empirical task of fact-collecting cannot render much without directive hypotheses, and that on the other hand such hypotheses are validly supplied by general Marxist theses. However, this kind of Marxism is just as anti-dogmatic as is possible, for, on the one hand, it lays no claims in scientific work either to the philosophical orientation of Marx and his posterity, or to their ideological inspiration, but only to the major methodological features and important sociological/historical theses which emanate from them, the validity of which is generally accepted. On the other hand, Marxism assumes the role of Ariadne's clow in the complexity of actuality, adapting itself to the facts and applying the most generally adopted scientific proceedings to them ... whether implicit or subconsciousness.

It is not long before we come to the point at which this clearly asserted orientation is far from detrimental to the scientific rigour and level of the research undertaken; there is an equal degree of competence and selectivity in the choice and treatment of the information, which is remarkable for its abundance and value. In effect, we are presented with a rich yield of facts concerning the economic and social development of the Muslim world. Although Rodinson resisted writing a manual of social and economic history of the Muslim world (p. 8), this work provides an imposing collection of information on the subject in a very useful and virtually irreplaceable synthesis. The work contains numerous pertinent comparisons of the facts of Jewish and Christian history, enabling us to relate one to the other in phenomena studied, and to review false or flimsy assertions which could lead to a narrow study of isolated cases. In short, we are dealing with a work which has precision as one of its central strengths, a quality which is all the more welcome as it relieves us of the approximations of fantasy and impression which arise too often in Islamology (some of these approximations are quoted and refuted in the book).

As for precision, we have firstly the example of a discussion of the concept of capitalism which, is similar works, is as frequently used as it is rarely defined. As the author demonstrates, in the wake of the Polish sociologist, Julian Hochfeld, many realities are qualified by capitalists in everyday language. There is a type of capitalist production, that is, a way in which the concern functions. Then there is a capitalist sector, that is, the totality of concerns with a capitalist mode of production. Finally, there is a capitalist socio-economic structure, that is a society in which this capitalist sector predominates. However, all this relates to modern capitalism, the capitalism of production. The latter 'was born of belated medieval European forms of commercial and financial capital' (p. 24), forms which are generally held (by Marx, Max Weber, Sombart, etc.) for the necessary though insufficient condition of the appearance of this capitalism of production or capitalist socio-economic formation. It is thus important to outline more clearly this area in which modern commercial and financial capitalism predominates in a pre-capitalist economic context; this is what Rodinson calls 'a capitalist sector'. Thus, the problem is to see if such a sector—an ancestor of modern capitalism—existed in the medieval Muslim world under conditions comparable to those which it assumed at the end of the European Middle Ages.

Before tackling this problem, the author sets out to show that the elements of economic doctrine contained in the Koran and Sunna (tradition, a very important factor as well as the Holy Book of Islam), did not in their totality condemn the principle of capitalist activity—on the contrary. In particular, the famous prohibition of *riba* (loan on interest) seems to him to have been too vague to have had a decisive influence, and, as for viewing it as an effective prohibition to be respected, was it not possible to revert to the aid of the *hiyals* (ruses or wile) which are nothing short of compromises reverted to by Europeans at the same time in order to avoid the Christian prohibition of loans on interest? Although it would appear that, contrary to various theses held in the West, Islam did not prevent the appearance of capitalist type of activity along with the objective progress, it is no more true that according to the vision so often held by certain Muslim apologists Islam was animated in its initial rise by a true ideal of social justice. If the latter is understood in the vague sense of mystico-humanitarian aspirations born of an uneasy conscience, then the apologetic affirmations of some Muslim theologians or thinkers would be reduced to banalities which are applicable to all religions; if, on the other hand, one attributes its modern significance to 'social justice', and takes into account its precise implications, especially regarding the statute of property and socio-economic and political equality, then one would deduce that Islam, being just another religion, could not motivate an ideal which could justifiably be called 'democratic', still less 'socialising' or 'socialist'.

This being so, it is now possible to pose the aforesaid problem—that of the existence or non-existence of this capitalist sector in the Muslim world of the Middle Ages. In other terms, we are now concerned with verification at the practical level of what has already been studied in theoretical terms at prescriptive level. Same procedure, same conclusions. Firstly, during the Middle Ages, like a vast empire greater than the largest 'common market', a far from negligible capitalist type of production and capitalist sector developed in the shadow of Islam; these flourished in a socio-economic situation which, in these conditions, at that time and to such an extent, could only accentuate great heterogeneity. Here Rodinson outlines all the diversity and complexity of this economic and social reality of the former Muslim world stating that it is just as abusive to see in this the 'feudalism' retained by 'historical materialism' as the 'Asiatic type of production' to beloved of certain Marxists. Furthermore, it is absurd to qualify as 'just' this society characterised by 'a poignant contrast between the most unparalleled luxury of wealthy concerns and circles, and the most abject misery in which the masses stagnated' (p. 88), as do the Muslim apologists, taking up their positions this time on the scale of real history and not the ideal, so often reinforced by their religion.

However, some would hold that the problem is not so much to see if the Muslim world contained at some given time the embryo of capitalism; as an ideology which is hostile to modern capitalism. Does the latter not require a certain kind of 'rationality' (according to the Weber formula) which one could discern in the European mentality but not in that of persona belonging to an Islamic civilisation (no more, however, than in that of the Chinese, Indians, etc.)? No, replies the author who, in an extremely interesting comparative chapter, clearly establishes the essentially 'rationalist' nature of Koranic ideology and Islamic culture and, on a firmly based argument, vigorously demolishes in particular the well-known stereotype of 'Muslim fatalism'.

After this, Chapter Five completes the picture in outlining 'the contemporary capitalism of Muslim countries, and Islam'. Questions raised here are mainly of Western impact and of the depth and nature of the religious influence on this recent economic development. This simply serves to stifly demonstration and to prolong the initial conclusions in the sense of an affirmation of '*the neutral nature of ideology with regards to the forces essential to social evolution*'. Not that Rodinson underestimates the role which ideas could play in some circumstances, nor that, as Marx said, the idea in turn is sometimes a material force, capable of becoming very active; on the contrary, he realises the absurdity of a spiritual world reflecting the material basis passively and fleetingly, and points out that the picture of man as a product of circumstances should not make us forget that 'the educator must be educated'. However, in his study of the economic and social history of the Islamic countries, he feels able to infer that this dialectic of infrastructure and superstructure has a place in a historical trajectory which, *on a long-term basis, and in accordance with the general tendency of a development curve*, indicates an orientation and rhythm conditioned in the final analysis by the true state of collectivities. The dynamic of social structures, he tells us briskly but not vaguely, obeys the logic of production situation which in its essence defines a 'total man', a simultaneous product and initiator of his own history. This totality, far from excluding the hierarchy of the social scale, governs them along with the primordial tasks of the society, and its concrete praxis—these are the theories concerning ideas and the individual which thwart the historical agent and arbitrarily grant privileges to some dimensions of his behaviour, contrary to the dialectic and totalising progress which Marxism should make when it escapes from those deformities which render it a vulgar economy.

What provisional conclusion may be drawn from all this as to the future of the Muslim world? That its development should be recognised precisely as a total phenomenon, a phenomenon in which, admitting of the irresistibility of a socialist option in one form or another, the spontaneous development of new structures could not outpace the mobilising ideology—Islam with all its weaknesses, ambiguities, and, in a word, its essential inadaptability to this purpose, could not accomplish this. Marxist ideology, in spite of its deviations, has proved itself the most accomplished mobilising progressive ideology in the modern world (p. 242). However, Rodinson does not elaborate further on these final reflections: he promises us another work entitled 'Islam and Socialism'.

'Islam and Capitalism', the content of which we have reviewed is an important contribution both to knowledge of a particular cultural sphere and the general struggle against certain kinds of idealism in the concept of history. Of course, in certain extracts we would have liked the author to have given us more positive clues to the role of Islam in the societies referred to: for example, at one point he puts forward the hypothesis that theological controversies could correspond to the class struggles or other forms of social conflict; the reader here awaits a case study to illustrate this interesting point, but remains unrewarded. So we are left hungry as regards a precise visualisation of the concrete functioning of these societies with the complex dialectic of their infrastructural and superstructural elements, etc. Similarly, as Rodinson is party to the idealist thesis which Max Weber defended in 'The Protestant Ethic and the Spirit of Capitalism', one would have preferred a more detailed discussion of the arguments of this German sociologist to the brief allusions in Rodinson's work. However, these are merely the 'desiderata' of a reader who whets the appetite for a work of this quality—superlatively interesting for all, and extremely useful, in particular, to intellectuals of Muslim culture.

(Translated from French by Mary Fasiluddin)

The Military Takeover in America

by an American Observer

The American invasion of Cambodia is one link in a chain of events which amounts to a military takeover in Washington, unprecedented in modern history. The decision to invade Cambodia originated with General Westmoreland who has long been an advocate of total war in Indo-China; of pursuing the 'enemy' to Hanoi and of performing 'surgery' on China's nuclear installations. His hero is the late General MacArthur, who wanted to carry the Korean war into China and use nuclear weapons but was sacked by President Truman for his dangerous ambitions. As if by coincidence, one of general MacArthur's most vociferous supporters for dropping the bomb on China was a fledgling senator called Richard Nixon. In 1954, Mr Nixon's and the generals' plan to drop the atomic bomb on Vietnam was so advanced that President Eisenhower was reported to have leaked the story in order to discredit it and prevent the Vice President and his military friends from igniting World War Three.

In the Kennedy years, the Pentagon began to build up its network of 'legislative liaison officers' whose job was, and still is, to seduce politicians with fat military contracts in return for votes on the floor of the House or the Senate. Under Kennedy, Johnson and Nixon these military 'managers' of Congress have done their job well.

Asia has been kept on the boil; China has been isolated from the world. Forty cents in every dollar of the national budget have gone to building more and more weapons and testing more nuclear bombs than ever before.

In the meantime, Pentagon's influence has accelerated. The Pentagon now accounts for half of all government officials and its contracts keep alive some 22,000 arms companies. Pentagon money feeds one American in five. And all the while the power circle has been shrinking. By 1968, forty-four billion dollars spent on arms went to just 110 companies. In the boardrooms of these companies: 2,200 generals and admirals.

The invasion of Cambodia was 'sold' to the President by General William Westmoreland as necessary to destroy the secret headquarters of the Viet Cong high command. It was not a difficult sell.

Afterword

Kamran Asdar Ali

In *Mangrove*, the first part of a recent series of films, Small Axe by the director Steve McQueen we witness a group of West Indian immigrants and their struggle for dignity and racial equity in the London of the late 1960s. The story depicts how the Caribbean immigrant population's harassment by the police led to an actual trial of activists in the early 1970s. The film is a snapshot of a particular moment in London's history when a diverse population of workers, students, intellectuals, professionals, and political exiles, mostly from ex-British colonies, converged in the city and made it into a vibrant and cosmopolitan space. The late 1960s was also a time when student and workers-led movements—the anti-war movement and the struggle for civil rights in the United States, student protests in France, and the Naxalite movement in India, to name a few—were occurring across the globe. Much like the characters depicted in the film *Mangrove*, who were influenced by the reigning progressive ideologies of the times, London-based Pakistani activists, Iqbal Khan and Aziz Kurtha, organised a group of like-minded Pakistani students and scholars to initiate a left-oriented publication, *Pakistan Left Review* (*PLR*), in 1968. The *PLR* was clearly a pioneering effort. Soon after it ceased publication in early 1970s, the progressive intellectuals, Eqbal Ahmad, Feroz Ahmed, and Aijaz Ahmad, collaborated with others to publish *Pakistan Forum* from North America, which later in the decade transformed into the *Pakistan Progressive*. There were other similar attempts in Europe and North America during the military rule of General Ziaul Haq in the 1980s.

Stephen Lyon and Nadir Cheema (the editors of this volume) located the entire run of the *PLR* and have now brought it forward to be published. They need to be commended for their immense service for preserving this specific part of Pakistan's progressive history. The five issues of the *PLR* become an invaluable archive that helps us understand the deliberations and debates raging within the Left at a pivotal juncture in Pakistan's history, the late 1960s. Lyon and Cheema also sensitise the readers to the cultural history of immigrant intellectual life in London and how generations of immigrants have made the place their own. In reading the various introductory essays, one is actually reminded of London's depiction in Samuel Selvon's 1950s novel, *Lonely Londoners*, about young

256

West Indian immigrants and their relationship with the city. Such a treatment of South Asian immigrant life in the 1960s awaits to be written. However, we get a hint of this life in Salima Hashmi's (who was part of the group) introductory essay for this volume. She discusses Iqbal Khan's collaboration with Aziz Kurtha and his 'powers of persuasion and commitment to the scope of *PLR*'s agenda'. She further gives us a glimpse of the time all of them shared in the London of the late 1960s, the protests against apartheid in South Africa, marches for Nuclear Disarmament, and large demonstrations to end the war in Vietnam. Hashmi and the volume editors remind us of how discussions and deliberations for the *PLR* were held at the University of London Union, at the home of Mohammad Afzal (an ex-Communist Party of Pakistan (CCP) member and Trade Unionist, who was living in London) and his wife, Joan Afzal, and occasionally at Tassaduq Ahmad's (an East Pakistani leftist journalist in exile who was Faiz Ahmed Faiz's friend), Ganges restaurant on Gerrard Street in Soho (the film, *Mangrove*, was also named after the restaurant where the Caribbean activists met). Hence by (re)introducing the magazine to a new generation, the editors help us to remember and appreciate how educational institutions, domestic spaces, and cultural venues (not to forget eateries) in London provided spaces for South Asian students, migrants, and political exiles to come together, react to events, plan future political strategies, organise marches, and much more.

These were of course days of student protests and talk of revolution and change in most parts of the world. It should hence be obvious that sensitive and committed young students and scholars from Pakistan were just as keen on being part of this changing world and wanted to play their part in struggling toward a more just and humane future for their own land. Iqbal Khan (who was studying philosophy) and Aziz Kurtha (working on his doctorate in Law) were joined in this endeavour by Salima Hashmi (then an advanced art student), by Tariq Ali (activist and student leader of the New Left and an emerging writer), by Rehman Sobhan (who was completing his graduate studies in economics) and others ... people who continued to play important and impressive roles in shaping the future of South Asia through their writings and their immersion in fields of politics, education, art, aesthetics, publishing, economics, policy planning, and by building institutions. The volume's introduction also reminds us of an earlier set of South Asian students who in the 1930s established the Progressive Writers' Association (PWA). The PWA was one of the most influential literary movements in the decade preceding the Partition of British India. It was initially formed by a group of Indian students like Mulk Raj Anand, Sajjad Zaheer, and Ahmed Ali who were living in England during the 1930s (at Nanking restaurant, not from Ganges). From its very inception, the PWA (very much like the later *PLR*) was influenced by socialist and anti-colonial tendencies although it was open to all those who broadly agreed with its manifesto—that called for a new literature which addressed progressive ideals and focused on the issue of poverty, deprivation, and servitude of the Indian masses—it soon became closely aligned with the Communist Party of India. Almost thirty years later, the story of the *PLR* shows how young Pakistani progressives in London may have followed a similar path in seeking to discuss and debate the country's future political trajectory. The *PLR*, with all the blemishes in its production quality (type written, cyclostyle printing), was rich in ideas, arguments, opinions, points of view, original writings, interviews, and its editorial policy evidenced a deep sensitivity to the question of diversity and ethnic plurality within Pakistan. Within this context, by reading through the different issues of magazine we realise how in the late 1960s a group of Pakistani students/activists brought together a range of left perspectives that were non-doctrinaire in their approach. For example, in their very first issue the editors published translated excerpts from Herbert Marcuse's (Frankfurt School) essay, 'Ethics and Revolution' in Urdu and Bangla (showing their commitment to cultural and linguistic inclusivity). Publishing Marcuse, who along with his colleagues (such as Max Horkheimer and Theodor Adorno) is credited as the founder of the New Left and a person who was critical in his writings of the Soviet Union, in an introductory issue made clear how the editors were willing to take political risks in order to open up the Left to new and provocative ideas.

* * * * *

Let me share a brief history of Pakistan since its Independence to offer a social context for what the *PLR* editors were responding to after a decade of military rule in Pakistan and the country's deteriorating social, political, and economic situation. As most of the readers are aware, Pakistan had a very nascent communist movement and its young Communist Party of Pakistan started work in an international climate in which the Pakistani state became enmeshed in Cold War politics soon after its Independence (1947). British and US intelligence agencies worked closely with the higher echelons of the Pakistani state to curtail the 'communist threat'. In the 1950s, this relationship intensified and Pakistan's political and military leadership took the country into

US-sponsored anti-communist treaties such as Southeast Asia Treaty Organization (SEATO) and Central Treaty Organization (CENTO), leading to severe repression of the Communist Party and its eventual banning in 1954.

Further, a political crisis had engulfed Pakistan since the early part of the 1950s which culminated in the dissolution of the first Constituent Assembly by the Governor General, Ghulam Mohammad, in October 1954. Between 1954 and 1958, Pakistan saw the changing of prime ministers at regular intervals. Mohammad Ali Bogra, Chaudhry Muhammad Ali, Huseyn Shaheed Suhrawardy, I. I. Chundrigar, and Firoz Khan Noon, all served short stints. The country ratified its first constitution in 1956 by an assembly that was indirectly elected (along with nominated members). As Pakistan became a republic in 1956 the ailing Governor General, Ghulam Mohammad, was replaced by Iskander Mirza as President, a person who had been waiting in the wings for his chance at the helm of affairs. Despite the constitution and the non-representativeness of the assembly, the promised and necessary elections were continuously postponed. With high food costs, a political system that was bordering on farcical, and the increasing dissatisfaction among the population, an election and a legitimately elected civilian government may have been the only way out of the social and political impasse. In contrast, on 8 October 1958, the President, Iskander Mirza, a proponent of 'controlled democracy' at the best of times, worked with the Army Chief, Ayub Khan, to suspend the constitution, to dismiss the provincial and central governments, to ban all political parties, and to postpone the elections indefinitely. In a counter-coup on 28 October, Ayub Khan took over supreme power and sent Mirza into exile. The incoming regime's anti-communist and anti-labour character was partly due to its authoritarian character, but also due to the Pakistan army's ongoing close alliance with the US, and subsequently Pakistan served on the front lines of the US anti-communist policy in the region.

The military takeover of the Pakistani state in 1958 intensified the repression against labour, political parties, and civil liberties. During General Ayub Khan's rule (1958–1969) bureaucrats and ex-army officers began directly running major industrial units. This was an era of unprecedented growth in the wealth and holdings of Pakistan's industrial houses. They moved into banking and insurance which supplied them with the funds for further expansion. Pakistan's growth was heralded by economists from the United States as a model for the rest of the Third World and as a premier example of 'free enterprise'. Gustav Papanek, the head of the Harvard Advisory Group to Pakistan, would affectionately call Pakistan's state-sponsored bourgeoisie 'robber barons' and argued that the rising social and economic inequality contributed to the economy's growth and would eventually lead to the improvement in the living conditions of the lower income groups.[1]

Between 1947 and 1958 the economy had been sluggish in its growth (GNP 3.2 per cent); the largest employment was in the agricultural sector which contributed about 50 per cent of the output. However, manufacturing in this period had a growth rate of 9.6 per cent. In contrast, during the entire Ayub era the GNP rates hovered around the 6 per cent mark and manufacturing still maintained a high 9.1 per cent growth. Even the agricultural sector grew at a rate of 4.1 per cent as huge subsidies were given to large landowners for mechanisation, with additional public investments in irrigation and drainage works.[2] By the mid-1960s the industrial sector accounted for almost 20 per cent of the GDP and about 18 per cent of the working population was involved in industrial labour. Pakistan was still primarily an agricultural economy with 40 per cent of the GDP and 61 per cent of the labour force tied to the agricultural sector. Yet the change was phenomenal in comparison with Pakistan of the 1950s. However, irrespective of Papanek's above mentioned 'rosy' predictions, all through the 1960s retrenchment and dismissals were common tools for disciplining factory workers. Concentration of wealth in Pakistan by the end of the 1960s was argued by experts to be with twenty-two families who controlled 87 per cent of the banking and insurance and 66 per cent of the industrial wealth of the country.[3] The heavy reliance on foreign capital for the industrialisation process faced a major setback when after the 1965 war with India, World Bank funds were cut off and then resumed at much lower levels. As the entire structure was built on a large inflow of foreign capital the growth began to sputter. Bad harvests in 1965 and 1966, and the demand of the East Pakistani middle classes for a more equitable share of the spoils of development, created a major political turmoil in

---

1. See Tariq Ali, *Can Pakistan Survive?* (London: Penguin Books, 1983), p. 69.
2. See Ishrat Husain, *Pakistan: The Economy of an Elitist State* (Karachi: Oxford University Press, 1999).
3. See Rashid Amjad, 'Industrial Concentration and Economic Power,' in *Pakistan: The Roots of Dictatorship*, eds., H. Gardezi and J. Rashid (London: Zed Press, 1983), pp. 228–69; and Shahid Javed Burki, *Pakistan Under Bhutto* (London: Macmillan Press, 1988). An interesting analysis of this period is also given in Tariq Ali, *Pakistan Military Rule or People's Power* (New York: W. Morrow, 1970).

the country.[4] Ayub Khan's much heralded 'decade of development' hence came to an abrupt end when in 1968–9 students, intellectuals, the urban poor, peasants, and the working classes participated in a massive civil disobedience movement. Spearheaded by the Pakistan Peoples Party (PPP) and National Awami Party (NAP) in the West and the Awami League in the Eastern province this movement was not only against the political bankruptcy of the Ayub regime but also a protest against the deteriorating economic conditions and the increasing inequality in the distribution of wealth. It is in the last year of Ayub Khan's regime, as opposition to his rule was intensifying in both wings of the country, when the *PLR* was first published. By following the articles in the various issues, the reader gets to revisit this particular time in Pakistan's (still consisting of two wings) political history through a series of writings on the economic situation and the prevalent political atmosphere. We also get a sense of this history through the published interviews of people like Zulfikar Ali Bhutto (the emergent leader of PPP) and Maulana Bhashani (an established voice in progressive politics in Pakistan and the leader of a faction of the NAP).

If we take an example from the one of the issues, and read Rehman Sohban's brilliant assessment of the economic reasons for the political crisis Pakistan faced in the late 1960s (an article that could be published in a top-ranked academic journal), we become aware of the underlying causes for the social disparity in East and West Pakistan. The article, 'The Economic Basis of the Current Crisis', along with a companion piece by Iqbal Khan, also provides a window into the debates within the Left on the autonomy question for East Pakistan. A debate that is extremely instructive to those interested in understanding the economic history of Pakistan just prior to 1971, the year when Bangladesh became independent as a sovereign state. As Ayub Khan's military regime was finally being forced to relinquish power in 1969 through a movement that had the overwhelming support of the working class, students, and radical left groups, Sohban, in his article in the *PLR*'s Spring 1969 issue, comments on the initial urban nature of the anti-Ayub unrest. He argues that this was due to the resentment against the suppression of civic freedoms and the barriers placed on political expression. Further,

---

4. See Hamza Alavi, 'Class and State,' in *Pakistan: The Roots of Dictatorship*, eds., H. Gardezi and J. Rashid (London: Zed Press, 1983), pp. 40–93; and Rashid Amjad, 'Industrial Concentration and Economic Power,' in eds., H. Gardezi and J. Rashid (London: Zed Press, 1983), pp. 228–69.

according to him, it was because of the social inequality prevalent in urban areas where the top 5 per cent of the population earned 26 per cent of the income and the bottom 50 per cent earned a mere 21 per cent in all of Pakistan. He argues that this income gap's social effect on the livelihoods of students, shop assistants, clerks, and low-level office workers (not to mention industrial workers) created conditions for them to protest against the Ayub regime. The regime, Sobhan argued, was also not supported by the majority of the population consisting of urban poor and peasants, as along with the erosion of liberties there was no material improvement in people's lives either. Both social equality/justice and civil liberties had been casualties during Ayub Khan's 'decade of progress'.

The article further discusses the call for economic and political autonomy by the Bengali middle class from the centralising and controlling state in West Pakistan. This sentiment was radicalised by the demands of the students linked to the peasants and industrial workers in East Pakistan who were in turn joined by the urban poor, most of whom were surviving on less than one rupee a day, while many were surviving on even less. Sobhan, in a sensitive passage, argues that to understand the anti-Ayub demonstrations in East Pakistan in the late 1960s we need to appreciate that it was not only the students and factory workers, but as on any such occasions the urban poor; the unemployed, the casual labourers, 'street urchins', pick pockets, beggars, vendors, and others who live in hovels and pavements and who are considered the most marginalised in any society participated in the protests.[5] Sobhan ends his paper by calling for a socialistic solution of distribution of wealth and resources and advocates that East Pakistan should gain partial autonomy from Pakistanis if the country was to remain united. He, however, warns that if the Pakistani state responded to the legitimate demands of its Bengali population through a more aggressive militarised action in order to control popular sentiments, it would only intensify the resistance and the students, its working class allies and peasants would join hands and turn East Pakistan into a battlefield for national liberation. He could not have been more predictive.

The important thing to note is that the following article, 'On the Question of East Pakistan', in this same issue, Iqbal Khan echoes Sobhan's political analysis and goes a step further by spelling out

5. To read a more recent analysis of the protests in 1969 that emphasises the participation of the urban poor, see Nusrat Sabina Chowdhury, 'Dhaka 1969,' *Economic and Political Weekly*, Vol. 56, Issue No. 44, 30 October 2021.

what was needed to be accomplished by the Pakistani state to keep the country united. This sequencing of the same argument by writers who represented different wings of the country (Rehman Sobhan from East Pakistan and Iqbal Khan from West) shows a commonality of purpose and provides us with an appreciation of how the editors created such synergies to stress important political arguments to its readership. In his paper, Iqbal Khan argues that for East Pakistan to accept a national government, the province should be given the numerical strength it deserved in the parliament due to its population size. He emphasises that national incomes should not be arbitrarily distributed among different regions, but should focus on specific needs and be proportional to the region's contribution to the national income. Perhaps, Khan states, East Pakistan should be given preferential treatment in all future distribution of resources and national investment due to the prior discrimination it had suffered since 1947. Like Sobhan, Iqbal Khan also stresses the point that this economic investment in East Pakistan cannot be left to the private sector, rather the state needed to nationalise the major industries and commercial activities and regulate the economy through a national plan of development, in a way calling to socialise the country's economy. However, the most important point raised by this article is that East Pakistanis are suspicious of how they are made to follow the diktats of the West Pakistani political and military elite due to their monopoly over the instruments of violence. Hence Iqbal Khan categorically mentions that East Pakistani fears can only be allayed if they are allowed to raise their own army and air force and are responsible for their own defence. These were indeed radical propositions, but very much in line with the emerging Bengali political sentiments on how the country could stay united.

In March of 1969, Ayub abdicated as a result of political disturbances and a new military regime came into power with the promise of social and political reform and of holding a national election based on adult franchise in 1970 (the first time in Pakistan's history). The Awami League, the party representing the majority of the Bengali population under Sheikh Mujibur Rahman's leadership, for the forthcoming elections put forward six points as a political strategy to negotiate with its West Pakistani counterparts in the 1960s. These six points, not that dissimilar to the above discussed points presented by Iqbal Khan in his article, asked for the supremacy of the legislature, for the federal government to retain control of only defence and foreign affairs, for two freely convertible currencies (to safeguard against flight of capital from East Pakistan), for the authority to collect revenue by the provincial governments (the federal government would get its share), for two separate foreign accounts and, finally, for the right of provinces to raise their own militia. There was also a call for moving the naval headquarters to East Pakistan. This was not a secessionist argument; rather, it was a response to the political maltreatment by the West Pakistan's elite political structure and a call for autonomy and equity. In the December 1970 elections, the Awami League emerged as the largest party, and it should have been invited to form the government and initiate the process of constitution-making. Sheikh Mujibur Rahman became the undisputed voice of the majority of the Bengali population. Instead, between January and March 1971 the then ruling military junta twice postponed the dates for convening the National Assembly (parliament). It also started an incessant drive to portray the six points, the major demand by the Awami League, as a conspiracy to break up the country. It is ironic that the regime had earlier permitted the Awami League to conduct its campaign on these very points for an entire year. Somehow they became a problem after the Awami League's victory in the fairest and most free elections ever held in the country. Then came the night of 26 March when the world witnessed one of the most brutal shows of violence unleashed by a standing army on its own citizens. The horror of that night, when many Bengali intellectuals, academics, students, political workers, and common people were killed, is another unwritten and unremembered part of Pakistan's history. This was followed by nine months of continued killings, rapes, and general mayhem, further alienating the East Bengali population from a solution that could have kept Pakistan together (the fear raised by Sobhan in his article).

In official circles, this violence was justified as necessary to maintain the nation's integrity. The path taken did not save the country from the ensuing death, destruction, and subsequent division, along with the humiliation of surrender by the Pakistan Army to its Indian counterpart in December 1971. Perhaps the only viable route to avert this catastrophe for all sides was to convene the elected National Assembly session and respect the will of the people by handing overpower to the majority party. The assembly could have voted for autonomy or secession, but it would have shown a democratic and peaceful way out of the impasse.

I have highlighted this particular aspect of the published material from the *PLR* partly because in 2021 Bangladesh commemorated the fiftieth anniversary of its independence. It helps us remember that important and eventful period, what in Pakistan is generally not even a part of the national consciousness ... rather it can be described as national collective amnesia. Hence I shared the above discussion with readers to re-emphasise the importance of these articles as repositories of Pakistan's (and Bangladesh's) collective past. The chapters compel us to recall and understand history as it was unfolding, providing evidence of the seriousness of the debate that was occurring at least among some of the progressive intellectuals on the question of East Pakistan within the broader spectrum of Pakistani political discourse (*Pakistan Forum* was also supportive of the demand for autonomy by East Pakistan). However, these insightful and predictive voices of people like Rehman Sobhan and Iqbal Khan (among many others) were ignored and unfortunately, to the detriment of the people of both wings of Pakistan, rejected by the ruling elite.

* * * * *

Let me return to the issue of plurality of voices and opinions that are present in the *PLR*. Followers of Pakistan's political history may remember that by the early 1960s various Left groups had also started to feel the impact of the Sino-Soviet split within international communism. There were other differences on the issue of the Indo-Pakistan War in 1965 in which some Leftists took an openly anti-India stance as China was supportive of Pakistan during the war. These and many other disagreements (some basically related to personalities and mere factionalism) led to the fracturing of the till then unified underground Communist Party (which was supportive of the National Awami Party, a left of Centre party formed in 1957) and it formally split in 1966 into pro-Soviet and pro-Chinese factions. These differences, personality clashes, and the rising tide of Maoist radicalism against the more established leadership within the NAP itself led to a break in that party by 1967–8. One group was favoured by the pro-Chinese Left and represented by Maulana Bhashani, and the other was linked to the pro-Soviet Left and was led by Mahmud Ali Kasuri and then by the nationalist Pashtun leader, Khan Abdul Wali Khan, the son of Ghaffar Khan. In the late 1960s, a breakaway faction of the NAP (led by Mohammad Ishaq in Punjab and Afzal Bangash in NWFP) formed the Mazdoor Kisan Party (The Worker Peasant Party).

It is interesting to note that in the very last *PLR* issue we find a reflection of this politics in the analytical pieces by Iqbal Khan and by Feroz Ahmed (a fellow progressive who was completing his PhD in sociology in North America). In his article, 'Has the Revolution Arrived in Pakistan?', published in Spring of 1970, Iqbal Khan severely criticises the radical Naxalite[6] tendencies within the NAP (pro-Peking, Bhashani group) that were advocating a spontaneous uprising of the masses in order to bring about a revolution. Khan argues that such a move would lead to chaos and anarchy and be severely suppressed. An upsurge not based on prior work of organising the masses and not willing to create a coalition of all like-minded progressive groups would not have the strength to resist the response by the state and its military (which was still in power in 1970). He goes on to strongly suggest that the NAP (Bhashani) should not boycott the forthcoming elections (to be held initially in October of 1970) or fall prey to some adventurist Naxalite idea of guerilla warfare. Rather, Iqbal Khan argues, at that particular juncture in Pakistan's political culture, the NAP (Bhashani) should participate in the forthcoming elections and also assist other Leftist parties to get elected so that they can keep the repressive and right-wing forces in check in the future National Assembly.

As much as Iqbal Khan was critical of the 'extremist' tendencies in the pro-Peking Left, Feroz Ahmed in his article in the same issue, 'Leftist Debate in West Pakistan', in contrast takes the NAP (pro-Soviet, Wali Khan) to task for not coming closer to the NAP (Bhashani) and the Peoples Party, the logical allies and Left of Centre parties, while creating anti-Ayub or anti-military alliances with parties that represented feudal interests or the religious right. It further criticises the class character of NAP (Wali) as being supported by landlords and feudal elements within the various regions of Pakistan (Pashtun, Baloch, Sindh) and are not sensitive to the plight of the peasants and the urban poor. There is also an anti-Soviet tilt in the argument and Feroz Ahmed argues how the Soviet Union was using this group to promote its anti-China policies in Pakistan. In the end the author condemns the NAP (Wali) to be playing a reckless game in Pakistani politics. As students of the period would remember, despite the friction within and between the leftist groups in Pakistan, it was clear that in the prevailing international atmosphere and the political realties within Pakistan, the Maoist groups with more radical anti-imperialist slogans (anti-Americanism and support for the people of Vietnam), their anti-India stand and call for active (and armed) struggle became more popular among the youth and the students. This

---

6. A revolutionary insurrection in West Bengal (India) that was started in 1967 by the Communist Party of India, Marxist-Leninist a break-away faction of the Communist Party of India, Marxist. It was led by Charu Majumdar and his eight documents argued for a protracted war against the state-led by the downtrodden peasantry. It was highly influenced by Maoist political ideology.

said, my reason to share this debate was to again emphasise the plurality of views that the *PLR* represented. It included a broad spectrum of Leftist points of view and encouraged countervailing and different assessments of Pakistani politics from a Left/Progressive perspective. As stated above, the first issue had a translation of Herbert Marcuse's work and the final issue had two articles that favoured two very different analysis of Left politics, but each one of them was accommodated and welcomed within the pages of the *PLR*. This in itself shows the democratic and inclusive ethos of the editors (and the *PLR* collective) as it gives a message of non-sectarian politics, of accepting a plurality of views in debates, and discussion without silencing and censoring opposing arguments. An important lesson indeed.

* * * * *

In her book, *Cruel Optimism*,[7] Laurent Berlant argues that, at least in the West, a sense of economic precarity has penetrated the lives of those who previously had aspirations of upward mobility. The neo-liberal turn has now made what some call the new planetary petite bourgeoisie (the small property owners, the ex-union workers, the professional managerial class), vulnerable to the vagaries of the current capitalistic system; there are no guarantees that the life one desires or imagines will ever come to fruition. This contemporary global moment has intensified long-term patterns of economic disenfranchisement, Berlant suggests, by the shrinkage of the welfare state, the privatisation of publicly held utilities, the increase in pension insecurities and the flexible regimes of capital that are based on contractual relationships between owners and workers rather than long-term job security. It has further led to the erosion of unions, which gave hope of upward mobility to the working class. Similarly, in Pakistan, the current economic model, and its reliance on foreign capital and loans from international financial institutions, somewhat follows Berlant's argument. Despite the difficult political times, the five *PLR* issues share a sense of promise, a sense of hope for the future of Pakistan. They offer analysis that is sincere, thoughtful, and in solidarity with those who are considered to be the downtrodden and the marginalised within a given society. There was a transformational hope in the proclamations and a learning from history, a memory of the past (albeit a Marxist vision of history) that informed the editors and writers

---

7. Laurent Berlant, *Cruel Optimism* (Durham, NC: Duke University Press, 2011).

to imagine a more socially just and egalitarian future. The end of the 1960s led to the creation of Bangladesh (1971), the defeat of the broader Left, and the imposition of military rule in Pakistan again in 1977. In Pakistan today there is a lack of job security, an increase in contract labour in the industrial sector along with high rates of unemployment in the formal sector, flexible manufacturing regimes and the dominance of informal/service sector work, creating new challenges for those involved in organising industrial workers. In the rural areas, unfavourable and changing land tenancy laws, the failure to distribute agricultural land and the impact of climate change have led to continuous migration patterns to the cities or, for those who are lucky, to the Gulf Arab States. Further, inflationary pressures such as high food prices, lack of growth in the industrial sector, and an anaemic private investment rate are bound to create further social conflict. It should not be a surprise to us, like Berlant argues, risk, uncertainty, and precarity have also become constitutive social experiences for many in Pakistan. Today, the ability to formulate a decipherable politics has also vanished and old tools to transform the world have become suspect, partially due to the events of the late 1980s and the collapse of global socialist experiments. Yet the need to address the urgent social concerns of generating employment, providing a living wage, attending to housing requirements, and refocusing on health and education systems that create opportunities for a better future for all citizens remains as valid as it was when the *PLR* was being published. In these terms, the struggle of underpaid public employees or the increasingly inaudible voices (and unorganised) of the urban poor in the Pakistan's public sphere today are not different from those experienced by the poor and the disenfranchised in the early 1960s. In addition, the lack of unionisation, the increase in contractual work and the incessant ethnic violence that keeps the working poor constantly divided call for a serious rethinking of political strategies for the future. Each generation of political activists surely create their own template to face the challenges of their own epoch. Although one can treat the *PLR* as an archival document, it could also be engaged with as a tradition that can teach activists of today how to struggle toward a more just and equitable future.

Appendix : Spring 1969

Who's Who in CIA?

Dr Maddar

Friends Not Masters!

A small book called, 'Who's Who in C.I.A?' was published in Germany in 1968 by Dr Maddar. It contains, apart from a description of the extent and scope of the American espionage system, a list of the names and short biographical sketches of some 3000 C.I.A Agents known to have been operating in 120 countries. The list of agents having operated in Pakistan is among the longest. The editors of the *P.L.R.* with the permission of the publishers of 'Who's Who' present below extracts from the list of agents known to have 'operated' in Pakistan. Readers, from the big cities at least, will no doubt recognise the names of a few friends if not masters!

Abbreviation: OpA = Operating Area.

ABELL, JANE S.
b: 29.5.1929; L: Hindi. OpA: Karachi, Bombay, New Delhi (1st Secretary), Washington.

AHRENS, MARTIN B.
b: 7.8.1927; in India. OpA; Karachi, Taiz, New Delhi (Adviser).

AKINS, RICHARD T.
b: 3.11.1916. OpA: Murree, Rawalpindi, Ankara (Attaché).

BLEE, DAVID HENRY.
b: 20.11.1916; L: Hindi. OpA: Karachi, Pretoria, New Delhi (1st Secretary).

BONER, WILLIAM C.
b: 12.10.1927. OpA: Karachi, New Delhi, Cairo (Attaché), Washington.

BROWN, ALLAN W.
b: 3.6.1929; L: Turkish. OpA: Karachi, Dacca, Ankara (Political Officer).

BROWN, WILLIAM R.
b: 17.10.1926 L: Arabic. OpA: Cairo, Jakarta, Beirut, Taiz, Lahore, Karachi. (Adviser).

BUSH, ROBERT N.
b: 8.6.1915. OpA: Saigon, Karachi (Security Officer).

CAMPBELL, WALTER L.
b: 2.8.1914. OpA: Ankara, Calcutta, New Delhi. Journeys to India and Pakistan; 1946–55.

CAPRIO, GENE F.
b: 21.2.1911. L: Italian. OpA: Rome, Taipei, Bucharest, Dacca (Consul), Washington.

CHASE, GORDON.
b: 29.10.1932. L: German. ÓpA: Karachi, London (2nd Secretary), Washington.

CIZAUSKAS, ALBERT CHARLES.
b: 1.3.1920. L: German. OpA: Karachi, Batavia, Jakarta, Surabaya, Milan, Bonn, (1st Secretary), Washington.

CLEMENTS, LEON J.
b: 7.5.1916. OpA: Rio de Janeiro, Dacca (Security Officer).

CONDON, HERBERT T.
b: 14.2.1913. OpA: Karachi (Attaché), Washington.

DASPIT, ALEXANDER BARROW
b: 14.1.1909. OpA: Karachi, Athens, Guatemala, Paris (Attaché).

DEAN, DORA
b: 24.2.1911. OpA: Tokyo, Yokohama, Kobe, Karachi, Bangkok, Cairo (USIA Officer).

DELIGIANIS, GEORGE
b: 19.8.1931. OpA: Baghdad, Cairo, Vientiane, Marrakech, Washington, Dacca (USIA Officer).

DEMBO, MORRIS
b: 19.8.1931. L: Hindi, Urdu. OpA: Bombay, Pretoria, Karachi, Nairobi, New Delhi (1st Secretary).

DENNIS, EARL MONROE
b: 15.6.1922. OpA: Prague, Zurich, Khorramshahr, Karachi, Rawalpindi (Adviser), Washington.

DESPRES, EMILE
b: 21.9.1909. OpA: Paris, Belgrade, Karachi (Director of the Institute of Economic Development).

DIBBLE, GORDON K.
b: 14.4.1923. OpA: Ankara, Lahore, Dacca (Consul), Washington.

DONALD, DR. GORDON JR.
b: 4.9.1917. L: Hindi. OpA: Lahore, Jakarta (1st Secretary).

ECHOLS, MARTHA GANS
b: 29.5.1922. OpA: Munich, West Berlin, Bonn, Karachi, Saigon, Lome (Adviser)

EDWARDS, CHARLES W.
b: 21.11.1906. OpA: Tripolis, Dacca, Magadisc, Nairobi, Lagos (Adviser).

EVERTS, STOCKWELL
b: 29.7.1923. L: Hindi, Urdu. OpA: Dacca, Karachi, Murree, Rawalpindi (2nd Secretary) Washington.

FALK, KURT M.
b: 12.2.1916. OpA: Seoul, Saigon, Karachi, Isfahan, Teheran, Taiz (Attaché).

FAY, JOHN F.
b: 17.11.1921. OpA: Kathmandu, Dacca, Washington, Istanbul (Consular Officer).

FISK, ERNEST HARLAN
b: 28.1.1906. OpA: Geneva, Canton, New Delhi, Lahore, Kathmandu (Consul General), Washington.

FOOSE, RICHARD T.
b: 19.5.1920. L: Spanish. OpA: Frankfurt/Main, Reykjavik, Goteborg, Lahore, Mexico City (Consul), Washington.

GIVENS, DR. MEREDITH B.
b: 11.1.1899. OpA: Frankfurt/Main, Manila, Karachi, Washington.

GOULD, BURTON M.
b: 7.9.1926. OpA: Karachi, Lagos, Washington, Addis Ababa (Adviser).

GRAVES, THOMAS V.
b: 23.8.1914. OpA: Ankara, Lahore, Karachi, Pretoria, Beirut (Attaché).

HAGEMANN, JOHN K.
b: 11.12.1911. OpA: Copenhagen, Karachi, Teheran (Trade Attaché).

HAHER, DONALD F.
b: 16.7.1923. OpA: Kabul, Karachi, Lahore (Consul), Washington.

HAIGHT, HUGH T.
b: 9.9.1928. OpA: Calcutta, Dacca, Cairo (Attaché), Washington.

HATAWAY, JAMES D. JR.
b: 24.7.1928. L: German, Hindi. OpA: Salzburg, Dacca, Berne, Karachi, Rawalpindi (Political Officer).

HERMANN, JOYCE R.
b: 12.8.1919. L: Arabic. OpA: Lahore, Warsaw, Bombay, Beirut, Jerusalem (Consul).

HESS, CLYDE G.
b: 22.2.1923. OpA: Baghdad, Khartoum, New Delhi, Karachi, Saigon (Information Officer).

HOEKSEMA, DR. RENZE L.
b: 13.9.1919. OpA: Lahore, Teheran (Attaché).

HORAN, DONALD C.
b: 22.3.1923. L: Urdu. OpA: Madras, Kabul, Georgetown, Washington, Peshawar (Press Officer).

HULEN, ELMER CULBERTSON
b: 15.2.1919. L: Korean. OpA: Dhahran, Athens, Busan, Seoul, Windsor, Halifax, Karachi, Rawalpindi (1st Secretary).

HUTCHINSON, HERBERT M.
b: 2.7.1925. L: French, Hindi. OpA: Frankfurt/Main, Freiburg, Kabul, Naples, Lahore (Consul), Washington.

IRVIN, DR. FREDERIC BRINKER
b: 13.10.1913. L: French, German. OpA: India, West Berlin, Bonn, Rawalpindi (Cultural Officer).

JACKSON, LONBM RICHARD
b: 31.10.1931. L: French. OpA: Peshawar, Geneva, Berne, Washington, Saigon (AID Officer).

JANUS, ROBERT B.
b: 25.9.1917. OpA: Jakarta. Saigon, Dacca (Security Officer).

KAMPRAD, WALTER T.
b: 1.4.1918, L: German. OpA: West Berlin, Baghdad, Lahore, New Delhi (2nd Secretary) Washington.

KASHE, RICHAED HARRY
b: 25.6.1921. OpA: Karachi, New Delhi, Cairo. (Attaché), Washington.

KELSEY, WARREN ARTHUR
b: 12.6.1923. L: Russian OpA: Moscow, Lahore (Consul), Washington.

KIERMAN, FRANK A. JR.
b: 19.4.1914. OpA: Nanking, Hong Kong, Karachi, Nairobi (Consul), Washington.

KOBAYASHI, TADAO
b: 8.10.1926. L: Spanish OpA: Karachi, Medellin (Consul), Washington.

KREISBERG, PAUL H.
b: 13.4.1929. L: Mandarin. OpA: Bombay, Taicbung, Hong Kong, Karachi (1st Secretary), Washington.

LANE, EDWARD H.
b: 1.12.1922. OpA: Amman, Lahore (Adviser), Washington.

LAX, MORRIS H.
b: 1.6.1923. L: French. OpA: Karachi, Bombay, Paris (2nd Secretary).

LLOYD, RUPERT ALISTYNE
b: 21.12.1907. L: French. OpA: Monrovia, Budapest, Karachi, Abidjan, Paris, Lyons (Consul).

LONG, RICHARD GRAHAM
b: 30.12.1927. L: French. OpA: Lahore, Nice, Algiers, Paris (2nd Secretary).

LUCIUS, HALLOCK R.
b: 19.3.1929. L: French, German. OpA: Karachi, Stuttgart (Vice-Consul), Washington.

MASTERS, EDWARD EUGENE
b: 21.6.1924. L: Hindi. OpA: Frankfurt/Main, Karachi, Madras, Jakarta (Consul).

MATSUI, VICTOR MASAO
b: 2.6.1923. OpA: Phnom Penh (Exposed as organiser of putsch), Karachi (Expelled for subversive activity, 1966).

MCCARTNY, JOHN. R.
b: 27.3.1923. L: Arabic, French. OpA: Paris, Lyons, Bonn, West Berlin, Beirut, Damascus, Karachi (Press Officer).

MCELROY, JESSE D.
b: 4.3.1915. OpA: Manila, Busan, Hong Kong, Dacca, Jakarta, Bonn (Administration Officer).

MICHAUD, MICHAEL A. G.
b: 22.8.1938. OpA: Dacca (Vice-Consul), Washington.

MILLER, DR. WILLIAM BAYARD
b: 4.4.1923. L: German, Spanish. OpA: Karachi, Hamburg, Quito, Bogota, Panama (1st Secretary).

MILLIGAN, L. EUGINE
b: 23.1.1919. OpA: Hong Kong, Canton, Karachi, Cairo (Political Officer), Washington.

MONSER, PHILIP R.
b: 18.6.1928. OpA: Hong Kong, Karachi, Buenos Aires (Attaché).

MOODY, SIGURD V.
b: 1.4.1916. OpA: Karachi, Ankara (Social Attaché).

MOSCOTTI, DR. ALBERT DENNIS
b: 14.9.1920. OpA: Bangkok, Karachi, Madras, Washington, Kuala Lumpur (Social Attaché).

MURRAY, WILLIAM J.
b: 16.1.1922. OpA: Karachi, San Pedro Sula, Havana, Monterrey, Bogota (Attaché), Washington.

NAAS, CHARLES W.
b: 24.1.1925. OpA: Karachi, Calcutta, Kathmandu, Ankara (2nd Secretary), Washington.

PYLE, LELAND A.
b: 24.8.1907. OpA: Dacca, Sao Paolo, Santos (Consul).

QUINLAN, CLIFORD J.
b: 20.10.1922. L: Arabic, German. OpA: Frankfurt/Main, West Berlin, Karachi, Kaduna, Beirut, Sanaa, Cairo (1st Secretary).

RALL, AKTHUR FREDERICK
b: 7.6.1915. OpA: Managua, Havana, Bogota, Salisbury, Lome, Dacca (Consul).

REDFORD, RALPH HUBBARD
b: 30.5.1916. OpA: Karachi, Kabul, Angoon, Jakarta, Taipei, Kathmandu, Istanbul (Consul), Washington.

RFED, SUMNER COLE
b: 17.11.1917. L: French. OpA: Paris, Karachi, Bonn (2nd Secretary), Washington.

RICKAND, DONALD C.
b: 2.3.1928 in Burma. L: Burmese. OpA: Karachi, Durban, Rangoon (Attaché).

ROMANKIRV, METRC
b: 17.8.1923. OpA: Rawalpindi (Political Officer).

PLR Issue Autumn, 1968

Facsimile of first three pages

P.701/646

Pakistan Left Review

পাকিস্তান লেফ্‌ট রিভিউ

پاکستان لیفٹ ریویو

PAKISTAN LEFT REVIEW

AUTUMN NUMBER

CONTENTS

A VIEW FROM THE LEFT   /   (Editorial)

AN EXCLUSIVE INTERVIEW WITH Z.A. BHUTTO   /   Aziz Kurtha

AN OPEN LETTER TO BHUTTO   /   Tariq Ali

BOOK REVIEWS   /   Anwar Khan

ETHICS AND REVOLUTION   /   Herbert Marcuse

(URDU AND BENGALI TRANSLATIONS OF EXTRACTS)

A NEW POEM   /   Faiz

Price 3/- each   Annual subscription 15/-
                                   (including post)

Pakistan Left Review is intended to be a quarterly journal. Its continuation
depends on your financial support. Please do all you can to widen its circulation.
Annual subscriptions and donations should be sent to Pakistan Left Review, Pakistan
Society, University of London Union, Malet Street, London, W.C.1.

Please note:

Our next issue (which will contain more pages) will have two important
articles - one on education and another on the present economics of
East and West Pakistan - which must be read by every Pakistani. It
will also include a translation of extracts from Frantz Fanon's book
THE WRETCHED OF THE EARTH.

Published by: Pakistan Left Review, Pakistan Society,
             University of London Union, Malet Street,
             London, W.C.1.   The views expressed by the
                                                       contributors in this journal
Printed by: North London Offset Services Ltd.,   are solely the responsi-
             51 High Holborn, London, W.   bility of the writers and in
                                                       no way implicate the printer
                                                       or the publisher.

VIEW FROM THE LEFT

This journal is a means of protest. It is being launched out of great concern for our fellow-countrymen in Pakistan and a deep anxiety about the way the destiny of our country is being shaped. In this, our first issue, and subsequent issues, there will be much criticism of Pakistan, its society, its institutions, and even of its people. It is necessary to make it clear at the very outset that the aim of such criticism will not be to ridicule our own people, to show our superiority over them (a charge often justifiably made against those educated in the West) nor will it be to undermine the faith of our people in their country. On the contrary, our criticism will be motivated by the desire to see in Pakistan an end to the humi-liations and injustices that are inflicted daily upon our people, an end to poverty and ignorance, and an end also to the greed, the vulgarity and the unreason which are perpetuated in the names of economic progress and religion by a handful of exploiters, upstarts and mullahs.

Of course, if you look at official surveys and statistics, listen to the politicians, or read those foreign journalists and authors who have a vested interest in the existing state of affairs in Pakistan, there would seem to be hardly any cause for concern. Has Pakistan not made very good progress in industrialization? Has it not achieved an annual growth rate which is probably the highest among the underdeveloped countries? Indeed, the success of economic planning in Pakistan seems to have been such that the Chief Economist of the Planning Commission could confidently predict that the increase in the number of jobs in the coming year will be "a little higher than the population rise" - a goal, in his own words, "made possible by the tremendous development in every department, in every nook and corner of Pakistan". Similar success stories are told about the health services, Education, and foreign affairs. In short, as the President has said

"In spite of the handicaps with which Pakistan began its life, the throes of birth and teething troubles, and the fact that this little infant was born in the teeth of bitter opposition from powerful sources, this country has by the grace of Allah gone from strength to strength".

But, if the picture of Pakistan depicted by such claims and statistics is true, how can one explain the fact that, judging by the per capita annual income, Pakistan still remains, even after twenty years, one of the poorest countries in the world? Nor do figures for per capita income paint an unduly pessimistic picture; for the inequalities of income distribution are so great in Pakistan that about 66% of the country's insurance funds and 70% of its industrial effort is in the hands of twenty families!

And how can one also explain the fact (if the success story of Pakistan is correct) that even after twenty years cholera, small-pox, plague and a host of other diseases are as endemic in the country as ever; that a vast number of people remain all their lives either semi-starved or ill-nourished; that the health facilities

275

Note of permission by Aziz Kurtha

22 September 2017

I was the editor of Pakistan Left Review (PLR) published between 1968-69 in London. PLR held copyrights of all the material published in the five issues of the journal. I give exclusive copyrights to Nadir Cheema to reproduce all or any part of material appeared in PLRs and to make it accessible to scholars and researchers engaged in examining that period of Pakistan's history.

My co-editor was Tariq Ali

Yours sincerely

Aziz Kurtha

1 West Park Road
Kew Gardens
Richmond TW9 4DB
United Kingdom

I am a witness and I was one of the PLR team of organisers and a contributor —

Salman Hashmi

Photos of the editors of the *PLR*

Aziz Kurtha

Iqbal Khan

A note to get *PLR* Subscription

Index

A

Abedin, Zainul, 23, 201
Adamjee Jute Mills, 97, 239
adult franchise, 82, 109–10, 121, 220, 263
Agartala Conspiracy Case, 111, 125
Ahmad, Tassaduq, 7–8, 20, 257
Ahmed, Feroz, 2, 4, 9, 17, 256, 265–6
Ahmed, Novera, 24, 203
Alavi, Hamza, 2, 194
Al-Fatah, 206
Ali, Anita Ghulam, 126
Ali, Chowdhury Muhammad, 223, 231, 259
Ali, Tariq, 2, 4–6, 12, 17–19, 59–60, 231–9, 257
America, 149, 193, 233–4, 235–6, 239, 246
American: 'aid' programmes, 149; antagonism, 50; farm machinery, 220; imperialism, 5, 59; invasion of Cambodia, 254; military assistance, 194; military strategy, 196; private investment, 195
American-backed Afghan regime, 5
American-led resistance, 13
Anand, Mulk Raj, 8, 258
Arp, 199
Ashe, Geoffrey, 61
Awami League, 32, 93–4, 98, 110, 216, 261, 264
Azad Pakistan Party, 216

B

Bakhtiar, Bashir, 247
Balochistan, 7, 9, 12
Bangash, Afzal, 265
Bangladesh, 9–12, 17, 24, 26–7, 30–5, 261, 264–5, 268
Bashir, Murtaza, 24, 203

Basic Democracies (BDs), 9, 52–3, 59, 82, 89–90, 113, 121
Basic Principles Committee, 106
Bengali (language), 8, 17, 110; language movement of 1952, 33
Bengali(s), 17, 31–3, 63, 233, 264; bourgeoise, 94; cultural rights, 33; entrepreneurs, 94; indigent, 95; middle class, 92–4, 98, 262; Muslims, 94; political sentiments, 263; population, 262–4
Berlant, Laurent, 267–8
Bhashani, Maulana, 6, 112, 125–6, 208–10, 214, 218, 222–3, 226–7, 231–9, 242–3, 245–7, 261, 265–6
Bhutto, Benazir, 7
Bhutto, Zulfikar Ali, 6, 9, 12, 21–2, 45–9, 50–60, 100–2, 124–6, 148–9, 150, 222–3, 226–7, 232, 236, 242–3, 247, 261
Black Lives Matter, 1
Bloomsbury, 8–9, 19
Bogra, Mohammad Ali, 259
Bourgeoise, 84–6, 91, 93–5, 124
Braque, 199
Brines, Russel, 62–3
Brohi, A. K., 106

C

Cabinet Mission, 29
Cambodia, 206, 254–5
Cambridge University, 6, 10–11, 16
Capitalism, 47, 51–2, 87, 94–5, 150, 216, 219–20, 243, 249–52
Capitalist, 2, 42, 56, 59, 84–5, 95, 98–9, 106, 116, 120, 135, 171, 185, 187, 190, 208, 211, 218–19, 221–2, 225, 231–2, 235–9, 241, 244, 246–7, 249–51, 267